TOM APPERLEY
GAMING RHYTHMS: PLAY AND COUNTERPLAY FROM THE SITUATED TO THE GLOBAL

Theory on Demand #6

Gaming Rhythms:
Play and Counterplay from the Situated to the Global

Author: Thomas Apperley

Design: Katja van Stiphout
DTP: Margreet Riphagen
Printer: 'Print on Demand'
Publisher: Institute of Network Cultures, Amsterdam 2010
ISBN: 978-90-816021-1-2

Contact
Institute of Network Cultures
phone: +3120 5951863
fax: +3120 5951840
email: info@networkcultures.org
web: http://www.networkcultures.org

This publication is available through various print on demand services.
For more information, and a freely downloadable pdf:
http://networkcultures.org/theoryondemand.

For Raina J. León

CONTENTS

Acknowledgements

There are many people to thank for helping me over the years that it took me to write this book. It could never have happened without the generous people who supported me in both my professional and private life. Thanks to my family in New Zealand: Jane Apperley, Mark Apperley, Bella Hannah, Felix Hannah, Kate Hannah, Lane Hannah, Zoe Hannah, Samir Lee, Wendy Lee, and especially my grandmother Enfys McKenzie. My friends in Venezuela also deserve a special mention. I could not have done the most important part of this project without your support. Muchas gracias: Susana Mendez, Hector Hannibal Rattia, Pavel Rojas, and Javier Saavedra. To my colleagues, thank you for your friendship, guidance and wisdom—Justin Clemens, Sean Cubitt, Michael Dieter, Nicole Heber, Darshana Jayemanne, Kyle Kontour, Umi Manickam-Khattab, Christian McCrea, Bjorn Nansen, Nathaniel Tkacz, and Christopher S. Walsh—this book would not exist without your helpful advice and encouragement. Thanks also to my students at the University of Melbourne, University of New England, and Victoria University, particularly: Phillip Anderson, Sindre Buchanan, Jun Shen Chia, Djorde Dikic, Adrien Husson, Rachel Law, Diego Leon, Dale Leorke, Andy McPherson, Archana Prasanna Kumar, Jia Wei Ng, Elizabeth Redman and Kathryn Sullivan. More than anyone, they have been the collective victims of my interest in digital games. Thanks also to Geert Lovink and Margreet Riphagen at the Institute of Network Cultures in Amsterdam for generously allowing me this opportunity. Finally, thank you to Scott McQuire for his helpful, inspiring, and kind mentorship.

This research was made financially possible through an Australian Postgraduate Award, and travel and fieldwork grants from the Faculty of Arts at the University of Melbourne.

INTRODUCTION

The word 'digital games' evokes an immense repertoire of possibilities. It is difficult to provide an exhaustive list of the hardware, the software, the people who play them and the spaces where they are played. Beyond this, there is a vast amount of materials that are ancillary to actual play—in the form of after action reports, FAQs, guides, walkthroughs, and wikis (to name a few). Digital games are ubiquitous, promoted as a technology for the whole family by wholesome stars like America Ferrara, Nicole Kidman, and Beyoncé Knowles. Negative accounts also abound; every time there is a school massacre journalists race to pin the crime on one game or another. The mainstream press and media industries have a rather two-dimensional approach to digital games: horror stories about addiction, isolation, obesity, and violence; or excitement over the latest innovation Blu-ray, iPod apps, Project Natal, and such. An audience does exist who are willing to understand gaming in a more 'culturally' sophisticated way, demonstrated by examples such as the Canadian cult television series *JPod*—based on the novel by Douglas Copeland—and the cult 'stoner' film *Grandma's Boy* produced by Adam Sandler, which both parody the banality of labor in the digital games industry. Although usually digital games are not dealt with sophisticatedly, for example *Reign Over Me* uses the digital game *Shadow of the Colossus* as a metaphor for isolation felt by the main protagonist. Prone to locking himself away for marathon gaming sessions in order to block out the grief over losing his family, we know that when at the end of the film Charlie Fineman (Adam Sandler) starts playing the game with others that he finally is recovering. But despite the growing preeminence of digital games in the media—and in culture more generally—there remains a sense of unease. Beneath the hype about the latest game technology are concerns: what are digital games are doing to us (or even worse to the children)? A concern that this book will argue should be supplemented by: what are people doing to—and with—digital games?

This book is about digital games, the people who play digital games, and how they play them. This poses a large problem: even when discussing one game, each instance of play is different. Combine this with the thousands of digital games, and the millions of players, and it is apparent that the number of individual instances of game play is unfathomably large. What these instantiations do have in common is that they are enacted locally. There are many variables involved in establishing the local—which is always a contested and shifting site—experience of digital game play: drink, food, friends, hardware, light, mobile phones, music, and software. The mundane reality of classes, commitments, deadlines, homework, internet bills, sleep, and work, must also be negotiated. This book aims to demonstrate the significance of nexus of the everyday and the local instantiation of game play as starting point for concept building in the study of digital games. Through case studies of two internet cafés, in Melbourne, Australia and Caracas, Venezuela, this project demonstrates how useful and generalizable concepts can be developed from understanding digital games as they are played. The specific localized experience of play can be connected to a global experience of digital game play, which ameliorates, exacerbates, and rescales the unease about the dynamic between games and players.

The concept of rhythm—via Henri Lefebvre's *Rhythmanalysis: Time, Space and Everyday Life*—provides the tool for examining the negotiations between rhythms in the local instantiation of digital game play, and for scaling the rhythms at the local level through tracing their connections to global rhythms.[1] The multiple manifestations of digital game software provide a flexible, poly-rhythmic repertoire of possible games (and experiences within games), that intersect with the everyday rhythms of the location. In the context of everyday life the local rhythms intersect with and enact the global through a process of adaptation, configuration and harmonization on the part of the players.

Positioning digital game play in everyday life is significant. Play is not a rupture, and digital games should not be understood as fantastic, virtual experiences but as embedded and situated in the material and mundane everyday. This is illustrated by the normalcy of digital games in contem-porary computerized, networked life: they are used to advocate, educate, proselytize, and train. More importantly, they are regarded as a pathway into intangible forms of knowledge—collective, creative, procedural, systemic—that are essential for post-industrial labor. The rhythms of digital games are not just playful, they insinuate themselves into the necessities and compulsions of everyday life. Yet they provide an unprecedented platform for creative improvisation. The ambigu-ity of this tension between creativity and training in play reflects the wider concern: Do games 'do' things to us, or us to them?

But the pathway from play and entertainment to more serious, constructive pursuits is character-ized by blockages as much as it is by smooth segues. Established pathways from play to work are exemplified by recruitment of 'mod' designers to the digital game industry. Other segues are examined in this book: the creative industries, serious games, and digital game art. For some these segues mean inclusion in the creative, knowledge economy, but for many others, marginal-ized by gender, race, nationality, language or economic status, that opportunity is not guaranteed, because the pathway from play to work is characterized by blockages just as much as it is by segues. Blockages are arrhythmia, barriers, interruptions, divides which prevent the smooth transfer of skills and competencies that are established through game play—and engagements with wider gaming culture—from being utilized in labor. The blockages interrogated include social and cultural blockages like censorship and economic blockages caused by lack of access to the necessary technologies.

The tensions and ambiguity in digital play between creative practice and training, and segues and blockages cannot—and should not—be constructively resolved. Rather, this book argues that the notion of 'counterplay' encapsulates how the play of digital games draws on these contradic-tory currents.[2] Counterplay suggests a leveler, a global connection that can be traced through common rhythms in the practices of play that resonate in the local. As a practice, counterplay suggests that whatever games may do to us, this issue is inseparable from what we do to them. It is easy to focus on the futility or banality, of digital game play, to suggest that their digital environ-ments are characterized by choices and configurations that are largely meaningless, or at best devoid of politics. Counterplay provides a counterpoint to this view.

This book consists of eight chapters. The first two deal with introducing the notion of the dig-ital game ecology and suggesting how the concept can be used to draw connections between the global and the local, and the general and specific. Chapters three, four, and five provide an ethnographic—'thick'—description and analysis of situated digital game play, drawing on case studies of internet cafés in Melbourne, Australia and Caracas, Venezuela. The final three chapters address the tension and ambiguity between training and practice, and blockage and segue that is encapsulated by counterplay.

Chapter one uses Matthew Fuller's notion of 'media ecology' to focus on describing the digital game ecology.[3] This ecology is the vast dynamic repertoire of cultures, experiences, games, practices, relationships, and technologies that are drawn upon to produce local instantiations of play. The chapter traces the key tensions in the digital game ecology with particular emphasis on the recurring theme of control. In digital games, at the extremes of this paradigm, the interactive choices—the configurations of the game made by the player—are largely illusory; beneath this façade of freedom are highly structured forms of control and modulation.

Chapter two proposes an approach to digital game research that places the body at the center of a nexus that mobilizes both virtual and material resources to produce various gaming situations. The chapter develops rhythmanalysis as a method of tracing the connections between the body of the gamer and the digital game ecology, and suggests a more nuanced approach to the issue of control in digital games by examining creative adaptations and dressage.

Chapters three, four and five are focused on exploring digital games and digital game play as it was actualized in two locations: Cydus, in downtown Melbourne, Australia and Cybercafé Avila, located in inner suburban Caracas, Venezuela. Chapter three describes the highly situated contexts in which these instantiations of gaming take place. Chapter four marks the key disjunctions, and explores the connection and similarities, between the two locations by examining rhythms in both gaming situations. Chapter five illustrates how the rhythms of games establish both specifically local and global rhythms, through a discussion of *Grand Theft Auto: Vice City* and *GunBound: World Champion*.

Chapter six, focuses on segues between digital game play and forms of labor, by examining the creative industries, serious games and digital game art. Each category suggests a vision of play that positions it as a segue to work without adequately addressing the various blockages and barriers that individuals might experience. However, these segues also suggest that digital games as a medium are inherently and intrinsically an artistic, creative, meaningful and serious form of expression. The notion of counterplay is used to mark these qualities, and situate them in relation to currents of control.

Chapter seven, explores the global significance of these blockages, suggesting that while there are major government and industry attempts to control and regulate digital games, that counterplay provides players scope to sustain a global digital game ecology. This highlights the regional and uneven global composition of digital game players, and underscores the political and economic stakes of digital games.

The final chapter examines the significance of counterplay, arguing that digital games, while exhibiting many characteristics of the modulation of control society also provide a platform for adaptation, creativity, and practice. The concept articulates the contradictory and ambiguous role of digital game play in the contemporary era, while pointing to moments where it makes forms of politics possible in the everyday.

Notes
1 Lefebvre, H. (2004). *Rhythmanalysis: Time, Space and Everday Life.* London: Continuum.
2 de Peuter, G. and Dyer-Witheford, N. (2005). 'A Playful Multitude? Mobilising and Counter-mobilising Immaterial Game Labour'. *In The Fibreculture Journal* 5.
3 Fuller, M. (2005). *Media Ecologies: Materialist Energies in Art and Technoculture.* Cambridge: MIT Press.

CHAPTER ONE
DIGITAL GAME ECOLOGIES

…the emergent media of the video game has to be grasped as a whole, a systemic devel opment of the complexity and flexibility of media technologies and cultural forms in the digital era—McKenzie Wark.[1]

…I'll try to make some sense of what I call the gaming situation by trying to pinpoint or at least locate the most crucial and elementary qualities that set it apart from dramatic and nar rative situations—Markku Eskelinen.[2]

These quotes demonstrate a great difference in scale, reflecting widely different approaches to the demarcation of the 'digital game' as an object of study. At stake in this variance is conceptualizing digital games as either 'closed' or 'open' systems. The large scale, macroscopic, and open approach conceptualizes digital games in continuity with existing media in aesthetic, cultural, industrial, and technological practices. While the microscopic approach is focused on establishing the 'gameness' of the gaming situation by emphasizing the discontinuities between digital games and other media forms. The latter position was strongly enunciated in game studies' nascent moment, and has been nominally coined 'ludology'. Digital games should be situated in relation to both these positions; acknowledging their unique characteristics, but still conceptualizing them in relation to global communication media and technologies. Mapping these relations, provides a perspective on digital games, that puts them in an ecological dynamic with cultures and technologies while also marking the unique attributes of digital games.

Digital games are often distinguished from other entertainment media through the notion of interactivity. In *Cybertext: Perspectives on Ergodic Literature*, Espen Aarseth, in order to refine the term 'interactive' introduces the concept of the 'cybertext' to describe the intricate feedback system that exists in certain types of texts, including but not limited to digital games, that are characterized by a 'mechanical organization' and an 'integrated' reader.[3] He describes the role of the human actor in the process of configuring or organizing the cybertext as 'ergodic', a term that emphasizes the: 'non-trivial effort [that] is required to allow the reader to traverse the text'.[4] Using this refined notion of interactivity to approach a purely mechanical traversal of the text marks a widely different approach to the notion of 'interactivity' to that commonly taken in contemporary media and cultural studies, which establish interactive meaning production between audiences and producers of media texts.[5] Interactivity in relation to discussions of digital games typically refers to this physical, cognitive process of producing the digital game, rather than the reflexive process of negotiating a meaning.

This shift in focus from cooperative—and subversive—meaning production to mechanized traversal in digital games is a key concern in game studies. The issue emerges in Ted Friedman's discussion of *Sid Meier's Civilization II*.[6] He interprets the centrality of the mechanical operation of the game to the experience of play as creating a situation where the ideological structures behind the game must be accepted in order to win, or effectively play the game.[7] However, Bogost argues that digital game players' migrate easily between the two systems of interactivity—the ergodic traversal and the orthodox negotiation of audience interactivity—to engage both their configurative and critical faculties in the production of meaning.[8] The movement and feedback, between these simultaneous modes of engagement is a crucial element in understanding the digital game experience. This movement underscores the continuities and discontinuities between digital games and other media, and the need for a contextual, dynamic, ecological, and situated understanding of digital games.

The continuities between digital games and other media are demonstrated by the concept of media 'convergence'. Convergence is characterized by: 'the flow of content across multiple media platforms, the cooperation between multiple media industries, and the migratory behavior of media audiences who will go almost anywhere in search of kinds of entertainment experiences they want'.[9] Kinder argues that digital games have an important role in the media industries development of convergent products.[10] Flew stipulates that the technological shift to the digital has had an importance impact on the culture of media, from both industry and audience perspectives.[11] Henry Jenkins suggests that a major impact of convergence is the power that it gives the audience, which widens the scope that they collectively have to negotiate with media producers.[12]

The cultural dominance of convergence suggests a new significance for digital games in the wider context of popular culture. In this context digital games are a vital part of what Kinder dubs the 'media supersystem': branded media content that exists on multiple platforms.[13] The predominance of the media supersystem has led to the emergence of many prominent media products that originated from digital games—like the successful *Tomb Raider* film franchise—and conversely the movement of many brands into digital games, most notably FIFA.[14] Also related to this emerging cultural significance is an aesthetic influence that, while typically associated with spectacular cinema, can be found in even the most banal cultural productions.[15] In terms of the aesthetic of 'gameness', the title sequence of the ABC Network's *Home Improvement,* is a prosaic example. Consequently, despite their interactive mode of audience consumption, Darley, argues that digital games are in an aesthetic continuum of 'surface play' with other contemporary visual digital forms.[16] The relationship between digital games and other media demonstrates significant feedback and reciprocity: traditional media forms are reinvigorated by remediating aesthetics from digital games, while digital games draw upon the aesthetics and themes of other media.

To maintain fluidity between discussing the specificity of digital games, and their more general contextual relations to in relation to media, technologies and global cultures this chapter introduces the notion of 'media ecology'.[17] This is developed through an application of Henri Lefebvre's notion of rhythmanalysis to explain the flexibility, openness, unevenness, and variances of digital games.[18] The tension between training and practice in digital game play also requires contextualization in relation to these two approaches.

Mapping the Digital Game Ecology

Context is extremely important for understanding the consumption of digital games. Digital game play takes place in widely varied environments and situations: Somali-New Zealanders playing counter-terrorists in *Counter-Strike*, in an internet café in Hamilton, New Zealand; Korean international students playing *Ragnarok Online*, together side-by-side in Melbourne, Australia; and Venezuelan youths practicing English in *Habbo*. The notion of digital game ecology is introduced in order to move between these varieties of practices of play, and locate and connect them in a wider cultural context. This section describes the notion of media ecology, introduces the general characteristics and tensions of the digital game ecology, and introduces the issue of uneven access in the digital game ecology.

Media Ecologies

Describing media as ecology emphasizes the uncertainty and open potentially that emerges from the combination or integration of numerous phenomena. This potentiality of the media ecology is 'open' in the sense that – while focusing on the relationships and interdependence between people, objects, technologies, environments – it addresses complex non-linear notions of feedback, and cause and effect. It suggests that all media are connected and imbricated with other media, technologies, activities as well as wider social relations. Matthew Fuller in *Media Ecologies: Materialist Energies in Art and Technoculture*, states that the media ecology: 'indicate[s] the massive and dynamic interrelation of processes and objects, beings and things, patterns and matter'.[19] Media Ecology provides a way of approaching the study of digital games that accounts for the way that they are situated in other technologies—computers, mobile phones, networks, televisions—and activities (leisure, work). Fuller suggests that examining how these various constituents operate in imbricated, mutually dynamic, reciprocal relations may unfold '"hidden" dimensions of combination and invention' in the relationships.[20]

The concept provides a degree of flexibility to make fluid movements from the general—that is the demarcation of the particular relations as ecology—to the specific analysis of individual objects, beings, and patterns, and the relations between them, within that ecology. Media ecology thus indicates the necessity of an oscillating movement between the specificity of the local and wider global perspectives. Digital games extend out of the individual mechanical operations of the games, software, and players' into wider cultural assemblages that elicit a mutual and reciprocal transfiguration of contexts. The notion of media ecology invokes a general 'connectedness' of digital games in messy and complicated assemblages, that avoids the artificiality of conceptualizing them as closed systems: tidily discreet, virtual, hermeneutic objects. Fuller's account of media ecology suggests a method of accounting for the 'dynamic and non-linear combinations' of relations between different media forms and industries as a field or system, of which digital games are a part.[21] Furthermore, media ecology emphasizes that systems are not defined by their constituent parts;[22] thus systems are not fully mapped and realized, they are dynamic, emergent, and open. These factors, suggest that an account of digital games that emphasizes their regional or local variances will be particularly useful in demonstrating how specific activities in situated locations, what Fuller describes as 'a particular conjunction of elements',[23] combinations and re-combinations of games, networks, objects, people, and things exceed a general account of "gaming" as an activity, by revealing cultures of use that deploy creative, innovative and inventive practices despite strong structural restraints.

The significance of the connections within and between games and other media and technologies is substantial. But it is the manner in which digital games are embedded in, and connected to, other activities that suggests alongside the well-established critiques that are concerned with

their structuring of meanings and actions, there is considerable scope for creativity and innovation in digital game play that also needs to be understood. In *The Three Ecologies* Felix Guattari
uses the notion of the 'ecosophy' to describe the interrelated and irreducibly interconnected
ecologies of the mind, the social, and the environment.[24] This highlights the openness of the
ecologies, which are always shifting to new frames of reference, often carrying over into spheres
outside that which was originally designated. But, particularly important for the conceptualization
of the digital game ecology is Guattari's notion of the ecology of the mind; which suggests the
important role of the mass media in shaping individuals' subjectivity.[25] The ecology of mind, like
any other ecology, requires diversity to survive, and Guatarri lambastes the mass media for establishing particularly homogenizing frames of reference for people to imagine their lives, or ways of
being. This theme—the homogenizing role that the media plays in shaping subjectivity—has been
an enduring trope in the study of the media and also digital games.[26] By examining digital games
in an ecology, in the complex entanglements of players' everyday lives, new possibilities for play,
and being, are made visible.

The 'digital game ecology' is a re-interpretation of Fuller's media ecology, it broadly describes the
technological, industrial and global contexts in which digital games and digital game technology
are developed, marketed, and consumed. To cover this issue fully is impossible; this book focuses
on discussing the general issues that have been central to scholarly debate that frames the
digital game ecology.

Interactive Circuits

The intersecting, and interactive, circuits of technology, culture, and marketing, outlined by
Stephen Kline, Nick Dyer-Witheford and Greig de Peuter in *Digital|Play: The Interaction of Tech-
nology, Culture, and Marketing*, provide a useful starting point for describing the digital game
ecology. In this key work of game studies scholarship, they describe the digital game player
as being simultaneously: 'discursively positioned as a protagonist within a fictional scenario'; 'a
"user" of computers and consoles that are increasingly linked to a networked telecommunications environment'; and in a high-stakes negotiation between consumer and producer, where the
latter group deploys 'surveillance, prediction, solicitation, and elaborate feedback relations' as
strategies to attract consumers.[27] This configuration highlights the subtle, complex and dynamic
inter-relations of the digital game ecology. The three circuits each produce a critical tension,
respectively: homogeneity of content, inequality of access, and a contradiction between play and
commodification.

Homogeneity is framed as an opposition between 'violence and variety'.[28] They, and many other
scholars, suggest that the subject positions available in most commercially released digital games
reflect a bias that stems from their historic emergence in the Cold War environment as military
simulators and training tools.[29] This is most often discussed in terms of the US-oriented military
perspective that can be found in many digital games, for example *America's Army*, *Delta Force:
Black Hawk Down* and *SOCOM: US Navy Seals*.[30] Beyond the blatant military perspective of
many games, scholars also suggest that digital games have a default masculine subject position
that women and girls players must successfully negotiate to enjoy the game.[31] However, several
other prominent games and genres are far removed from this 'militarized masculinity', for example, Jenkins specifically points to the success of *The Sims* franchise in offering a less gender

biased experience of game play.[32] *The Sims* is one of a few games that also offer the possibility of explicitly 'queer' or non-heteronormative subjectivities.[33] In addition to issues of gender and sexuality, scholars have also noted also the clearly European-American bias in subject positions available in a wide variety of digital games.[34] Even when the representation of race or ethnicity is not an issue, the narratives and actions of digital games are often framed in relation to a US-oriented geo-political context. These homogenizing factors have a great deal to do with the industries perception of the audience, and obviously are reflection of what they believe will be successful in the marketplace.

While there are significant trends that suggest there is room for diversity in digital games, it is important to bear in mind that the industry and technology of gaming do have a strong connection to the US military. This relationship is not a secret. In November 2008, the Associated Press—picking up a story from *Stars and Stripes*—widely reported that the US Army was committing to spending fifty million dollars to develop combat-training digital games over the next five years. The Army did not plan to develop their own games but rather 'watch trends in commercial digital games', in order find the appropriate software that they would then use to 'mod' the desired training applications.[35] Recent scholarship has dealt with the use of digital games as training simulations by the US army.[36] While this is a perfect example of how digital games are used as a form of training, understand the disciplinary function should be contextualized in relation to the creative ways that they are incorporated into everyday life. Digital games are ambivalent, having both a capacity of training and practice, which is largely determined by the context—factors outside of the particular games—in which they are played.

The second contradiction between 'enclosure and access', emphasizes how the orthodox production cycle of commercial digital games increasingly mobilizes the audience in the production process.[37] The investigation of this breakdown between work and play, and the proprietary and legal issues that it raises has become something of a refrain in game studies scholarship.[38] Kline et al. make the innovative step of connecting this breakdown between consumer and producer with the ongoing conflict between the software industry and pirates, arguing that: 'piracy is the shadow aspect of the interactive play industry's own labor practices'.[39] Furthermore, they connect this issue to the uneven global labor practices that locate the software industry in the 'North' while the digital game consoles are generally manufactured under license in the *maquiladoras* of the 'South'.[40] This division reflects a major movement in networked global society to relocate manufacturing offshore to developing countries with cheap labor while the goods remained owned by and produced for developed countries.[41] Kline et al. suggest that a substantial proportion of the global digital game piracy industry involves the black market software economy in countries of the 'South', implying this is a 'tactical' response to global inequalities.[42] This reveals important variances in the global digital game ecology around the issues of access to software through piracy. These variances are further exacerbated by the material need for expensive *hardware* to play digital games, and for many contemporary commercial games, a high-speed internet connection.[43] While the notion of digital game ecology highlights this unevenness, it also moves beyond the dichotomy of have, or have not, to explore and examine a variety of different, but unequal practices, and consider what is at stake in differing forms of inclusion.

The final tension outlined by Kline et al. is between digital games' status as a commodity and the freedoms and flexibility associated with play. For them, digital games are located in a 'promotional web' of unprecedented depth and scope.[44] This tension stems from the 'interactive' marketing practices of the industry, which the authors argue blurs the line between advertising and surveillance. At stake is the commodification of play. This concern dovetails with that expressed by Kinder, who argues that digital games suggest a new form of empowerment for children defined by consumption.[45] Marshall reiterates the usurpation and structuring of play through its imbrication in the system of capital. For Marshall the media supersystem is: 'a complete system of interaction for the audience with all forms of investment and engagement made possible and realizable'.[46] The closed system of engagement envisioned by Marshall is the antithesis of the openness, creativity and dynamism of the media ecology approach. However, his position is to an extent supported by the assessment of Kline et al.; who report that the emphasis on information gathering in the marketing process has a negative impact on creative production. They argue that the digital game industry has become focused on developing licensing, branding, and synergistic marketing, rather than innovative and unique products.[47] Commodification greatly complicates plays' status and role in society. When play becomes commodified, it becomes reliant on the logic of commerce, rather than the pleasures typically associated with play; and the imbrication of play and commerce means that any subjectivities produced through play, are not solely playful, experimental, or creative, but linked to—and subsumed in—a system of consumption. The digital game ecology is challenges the notion that the media supersystem is closed and tightening because the notion situates digital game play in relation to the locations, movements, objects, people, and times that comprise everyday life.

These three circuits of homogeneity, access, and commodficiation provide a general and 'global' account of the digital game ecology. This book investigates local manifestations of these circuits and tensions through specific case studies that demonstrate material and situated practices of play. The aim of these case studies is to situate this global account in relation to the everyday life of digital game players. This is where this project diverts from Kline and his colleagues': it positions the abstract circuits of technology, culture and marketing in the lived experience of players' through material accounts of play. These global circuits are enacted on a daily basis in thousands of contexts throughout the world, imbricating—and establishing segues between—the general and global, and the local and specific.

Global Industry?
The notion that digital games constitute a global industry suggests a particular smoothness in the description of the manifestations and praxis of that industry. Aphra Kerr argues that the regional variances that exist within the industry are primarily a consequence of the considerable localization that products go through.[48] Thus, while the digital games industry has a global reach and a transnational outlook, the specific qualities of particular regions and countries still have an important role in shaping the digital game ecology. However, local variances in digital game distribution and consumption that can be explained culturally, cannot account for the concentration of the industries' production and manufacturing in certain regions. The large majority of games are produced in the areas that also dominate their consumption, the global 'North', particularly the USA and Japan.[49] Other areas with industries that produce to global markets are South Korea, China, Canada and Europe. Australia, New Zealand, and some other smaller economies also have small industries that produce games with global distribution, but most other countries—if they have a

games industry at all—produce only for the local or regional market. Despite the existence of small localized industries, the centers of digital game financing and publishing are concentrated in global cities like Tokyo, Los Angles and London.[50]

The digital game industry and players have a particularly close relationship, thus the unevenness in the distribution of the industry globally has a major impact on the experiences of players. This suggests that—once considered globally—players of digital games are divided by differing forms of inclusion that are strongly based on the closeness of their relationship to the digital game industry.

The structures and practices of the digital games software industry are also an important factor in determining the status of digital game play globally. Their inflexible operation plays a key role in establishing the existing inequalities of access. The following issues are closely related: the ongoing anti-piracy actions by the industry; and the uneven access to digital games caused by the digital game industries approach to the localized distribution, support, and pricing. Because piracy often is used as a way of mitigating the unevenness, the anti-piracy actions of the industry enforce these inequalities. Anti-piracy policing of digital game software is global in scale, Kline et al. point out that the Industrial Designers Association of America have accused over fifty countries, mainly in the developing world, of either aiding piracy, or being negligent in its policing.[51] Access to the structure of the digital games industry also varies according to location, different games will be distributed (possibly at different prices), and products may or may not be supported. For example, Xbox LIVE in June 2010 was available in the following countries: in Asia (Hong Kong, India, Japan, Singapore, South Korea, and Taiwan); in Europe (Austria, Belgium, Denmark, Finland, France, Germany, Ireland, Italy, the Netherlands, Norway, Portugal, Spain, Sweden, Switzerland, and the United Kingdom); in North America (Canada, Mexico, and the U.S.A); and in Oceania (Australia and New Zealand). Xbox users outside of these regions are unable to access game features that require Xbox LIVE, particularly online multiplayer features and downloadable content. Although Microsoft has promised to expand the service by the end of 2010, to include countries in Africa (South Africa), and South America (Brazil, Chile, and Columbia), as well as expand its European service to cover the Czech Republic, Greece, Hungary, Poland and Russia.[52]

However, in some cases the digital game industry will put a great deal of effort into making products palatable to specific local markets, by publishing special 'localized' versions of a game designed for that market. The typical industry localization processes involves editing out content to fit a countries censorship specification, or re-scripting games produced in local languages for other audiences,[53] for example the removal of the controversial 'hot coffee' mod from *Grand Theft Auto: San Andreas* which allowed its re-release in Australia after the original version had been taken from the shelves.[54] In other cases a similar process is used to make a game release for a niche market appear palatable to a wider audience, for example the translation of the Japanese Nintendo DS rhythm-game *Osu! Tatakei! Ouendan* to *Elite Beat Agents* by iNiS for the US market. This did not simply involve linguistic translation, but also a carefully considered recasting of the protagonists from male cheerleaders to a parody of CIA/FBI 'spooks', changing the songs used from J-pop to recognizable US pop hits, and introducing many US-themed 'teenaged' storylines. The global digital game industry is able to cope with local variances in the digital game audience that can be accommodated by conforming to local laws, social norms, and languages, particularly when it comes to the USA and other major markets, due to the profitability of this accommodation.[55] If the changes are not perceived as profitable then they will not be made, and often the games will simply not be distributed in those regions. *Osu! Tatakei! Ouendan* was brought to the industries attention, because of the large number sales being made through US imports. Subsequently iNiS decided to remake the game specifically for the US market.[56] These variations indicate that the global market is not usefully conceptualized and an abstract category, but is rather comprised of numerous specific local instantiations.

The consumption and production of digital games, in a global context shaped by local factors; is uneven, both between and within nations. But inequality does not necessarily mean that digital games cannot be considered global, as the digital game ecology is shaped through myriad and plural local situations that collectively enact the global. Warschauer notes that globalization is a two-way process that involves both the flow of media from dominantly Western international centers, and a process of 'relocalization' by periphery cultures.[57] The regional and local variances in the digital game ecology do not mean that this medium does not establish global connections. Unequal access does not prevent the emergence of—within an ecology characterized by uneven access—a number of connected, communicative and interactive game spaces that constitutes a global space that both opens new, and reconfigures old connections between people, places, objects and ideas.

The case studies of digital games cultures of use that are presented in this book focus on the specificity and embeddedness of the locations, as well as their broader interactions with global games industry and culture. In *Territory, Authority, Rights: Global Assemblages*, Saskia Sassen states: 'It is the combination of the embeddedness of the global along with its specificity that gives meaning to the notion of overlap and interaction among the multiple spatialities and temporalities of the national and the global'.[58] Each case study is an empirical examination of what Sassen describes as 'cultures of use'.[59] Following this concern, this project does not simply outline the technical features of digital game play in these locations, nor to examine the 'impact' of the activities on the players, rather these embedded instantiations of digital game play in are examined in 'terms of specific cultures and practices through and within which users articulate their experience'.[60] In order to examine the embedded aspect of digital game play, the role of digital games in the everyday lives of their players' is significant; as each specific instantiation of digital game play takes place in relation to the global digital game ecology, but is enacted through a specific culture of use that is also situated in the everyday lives of the players'. The everyday thus is an important tool for understanding how the various practices and cultures of gaming develop in relation to the specificity of the local situation.

Gaming and Everyday Life

The significance of digital game play, particularly of the tension between training and practice, is contextualized through the players' experience of the everyday. In *Critique of Everyday Life: Volume 2* Lefebvre states: 'everyday life is profoundly related to all activities, and encompasses them with all their differences and their conflicts; it is their meeting place, their bond, their common ground'.[61] By situating digital games in everyday life, the digital game ecology encompasses the practices and processes of play, and the locations in which they are enacted. This shifts away from understanding digital games as an immersive experience and examines them within and a part of the labour, tasks and pleasures that constitute everyday life. The notion of the everyday plays an import role in highlighting the specificity of the experience of digital game play, which avoids the abstraction of studies based solely on industry, marketing, or textual analysis. Furthermore, the notion that the everyday has a rhythm,[62] provides a tool that traces themes across the entire digital game ecology.

Rhythmanalysis

The notion that everyday life is made up from cycles, repetition and recurrences is an enduring theme in the work of Lefebvre. In *Everyday Life in the Modern World*, originally published in 1968, he states: 'Everyday life is made of recurrences: gestures of labour and leisure, mechanical movements both human and properly mechanic, hours, days, weeks, months, years, linear and cyclical repetitions…'.[63] Key to the process and experience of everyday life is the negotiation between the cyclical rhythms of nature and the linear, mechanical rhythms imposed by contemporary society. Lefebvre expanded this theme considerably in his later work using the notion of rhythmanalysis. This marked a shift in his work's focus from space, to the intersections of time, space, and human activity. He states: 'Everywhere where there is interaction between a place, a time and an expenditure of energy there is *rhythm*'.[64] In this framework each moment was composed of intertwined rhythms, the natural rhythms of the body are 'bundled' together with the rhythms of the social, rational and mechanical. Rhythmanalysis is a useful framework for understanding digital games for two reasons: first, it provides a way of conceptualising the intersection of everyday life and the digital game ecology; and second, it suggests that in games and the wider digital game ecology there is scope for the players to innovate, whilst still understanding the complicated relationship between training and practice.

Rhythmanalysis provides a conceptual tool that is able to cope with approaching the analysis of the intersection between everyday life and the digital game ecology on a number of different scales. Or at least it provides a useful segue between the specific situated analysis of doing a 'close reading' of a particular game and the inevitable generalizations that are a part of the 'big picture' of digital game play. By linking macro- and micro- analysis, rhythmanalysis involves switching between magnitudes, shifting in scope 'from particles to galaxies'.[65] This opens the possibility of tracing rhythms across different scales, from local to global, or the specific 'situatedness' of a particular location, to the vast generality of the digital game ecology and demonstrating their blockages, disjunctions, divergences, imbrications, and segues. This flexibility evokes Fuller's description of the media ecology where patterns rather than objects become the subject of analysis.[66] The rhythm is also a pattern or rather it contains multiple patterns within a 'polyrhythmic' ensemble that is enacted through the interactions of time, space, and the everyday.

Rhythmanalysis, demands that the complexity of the situation be unfolded. Each situation is comprised of multiple components that are combined and enmeshed in particular ways. Lefebvre describes the practice of rhythmanalysis, the study of rhythms, as opening and unwrapping an intertwined bundle.[67] The bundle is 'composed of various rhythms, each part, each organ or function having its own in a perpetual interaction which constitute an ensemble or whole'.[68] This ensemble of various rhythms is dubbed 'polyrhythmical', as it consists of various rhythms of varying 'speed, frequency [and] consistency'.[69] While rhythms are characterised by reprises and returns, by linear and cyclical repetitions, Lefebvre maintains that there is no 'indefinite identical repetition', as the everyday is an inexhaustible reservoir of the new, the unpredictable, and the different.[70] The polyrhythmic ensemble is never completed or closed; rather it is conceived as an 'open totality'.[71] Rhythmanalysis recognizes structure, in the form of repetition, and difference, in the form of context, this is what makes it a useful tool for conceptualizing the creative role of the player as the producer and negotiator of difference in the ensemble. This opening of the bundle to trace the connections and disjunctions within and between the polyrhythm that comprises it, suggests a similar agenda to Fuller's media ecology; that even if made up of similar components, each situation is unique; comprised as by rhythms and relations, as much as it is by tangible, material objects.

What rhythmanalysis brings to the digital game ecology is the body, or bodies, something that is conspicuously absent from the themes drawn from the work of Kline and his co-authors. Lefebvre argues that for the rhythmanalytical project the body is a constant reference.[72] Using rhythmanalysis to analyse the digital game ecology highlights the body as a crucial nexus. Bodies are where everyday life interfaces with the game screen; it is through the body that the gaming technology is experienced, and the body is the site where these diverse fields are contextualized and interact. The importance of the body as a site where the rhythms of the digital game ecology and everyday come together, to harmonise, to clash, to feedback into each other, and to resonate, will be expanded in the following chapter. This configuration of rhythms is suggested in Andrew Murphie's discussion of differing registers of duration. He states:

> we are talking about complex, mutually enveloping durations in which the player – and, in a sense, the game itself, the computer, the PS2, the network – is caught up. This also suggests that embodiment in games is not simply a matter of a given body playing a given game, let alone a "player and a game" in neat separation. It is a matter of a body and a game immersed in the production of shifting durations – registered, for example, in a different heartbeat (or perhaps increased consumption of pizza and beer).[73]

The body produces its own rhythm, while the games rhythm varies, together the rhythms enact a 'duration', a moment of congruence where the games rhythm and the rhythm of the everyday take on a common refrain, which can be interrupted with any variance or difference in either rhythm.

The everyday is not a hermeneutically defined sphere. The main advantage of using rhythmanalysis and the everyday as conceptual tools for understanding game play is in the manner in which they demand rigorous connections be drawn between digital game play and other objects, locations, people, and activities. Wander points out that everyday life is a global concept; the everyday life led by the modern nations of the 'first' world is inexorably linked to the conditions of the so-called 'third' world.[74] Lefebvre's work is characterized by a concern about the relationship between centres and peripheries, and how the latter avoid and challenge the homogenizing of the centre. This morning's coffee, taking the tram to work, playing a game of *Red Dead Redemption* on the PS3 in the evening, each is a part of everyday life, and of its analysis. The study of everyday life is not a glorification of mundane activities, but a drive to understand them, and their connections to wider human affairs, rather than dismissing it as trivial and eliminating the quotidian from the scholarly agenda.

Resonances

While particular games, and game genres, have certain rhythms, it can be equally argued that the digital game ecology as a whole has a rhythm of its own. However, this rhythm is neither homogenous nor homogenizing. Digital games are composed of widely diverse, although prone to particular dominant, rhythms. Despite of these dominant rhythms, digital games may be insinuated into the wide variety of—bodies, spaces, times—the rhythms that make up everyday life. This is because of the flexibility of the polyrhythm and the creative input of the player. The polyrhythmic digital game ecology is open to heterogeneous, myriad, and plural local cultures of use. This contradiction between homogeneity and diversity need not be resolved. The tension can be mapped, and conceptualised fruitfully by recalling Lefebvre's discussion of metropolitan centres and peripheries. He is able to leave this contradiction unresolved, by describing the tension in the following way: 'there is a tendency towards a globalizing domination of centres... ...which attacks the multi-dimensionality of peripheries, which in turn perpetually threatens unity'.[75] In terms of this opposition, Kerr's description of the global industry, the digital game ecology acknowledges the plural and multi-dimensional peripheries: individual 'cultures of use' which are in turn shaped by the global, homogenizing concerns of the digital game industry. But because the digital game ecology is polyrhythmic, it can be viewed as a whole, and that local variances may be explained in terms of the congruence between specific rhythms within the polyrhythmic digital game ecology, and the rhythms of everyday life. The digital game ecology is enacted through a multitude of specific instantiations of congruence between its polyrhythm and the specific everyday rhythms of the local

Allow me to offer an example to demonstrate this framework. Nintendo's critically acclaimed *Animal Crossing* digital game series demonstrates how polyrhythm enables digital games to insinuate into multiple contexts and situations in the players' everyday life. First released in Japan for the Nintendo GameCube as *Animal Forest*,[76] it was renamed *Animal Crossing* for its US (and subsequent global) release. The renaming was the only significant change that occurred during its adaptation to a wider market. The basic game play remained identical: a real-time virtual life set in a small rural village of compulsive letter-writers, dominated by seasonal variations, and with abundant fruit, fish, insects, fossils and artefacts to discover and collect. However, the shift to the North American—global, English speaking, as opposed to national, Japanese speaking—market is significant. Many other games developed in local markets are never adapted for the global audience, the PlayStation2 game *Steamboy* was only released in Japan, despite the anime film on which the game was based having U.S. release as a studio-produced dub featuring prominent Hollywood actors. The major shift in the rhythm of the game occurred with the 2005 release of *Animal Crossing: Wild World* on the Nintendo DS. The shift to a portable handheld console vastly multiplies the potential that the peculiar rhythm of the game has for intersecting with everyday life. The game was characterised by short bursts of play, while weeds were pulled and fruit, flowers and shells were gathered, followed by lulls in play, periods of waiting and aporia.[77] The *Animal Crossing* series had no clear goals, just sets of objects to collect and spaces to explore, so while it required a number of different modes of engagement to the various tasks of play, there was no linear necessity to progress. Navarro in his *Gamespot* review of *Animal Crossing: Wild World* states: that it, 'ultimately surpasses the last game, simply because of how much better suited its style of gameplay is for a handheld system like the DS'.[78] The shift to portable, flexible play meant that now it could be played in the transitionary spaces, and fragments of time, which are characterised by boredom (the classroom, the doctor's waiting room, the tram) greatly increasing its potential to match the rhythms of everyday life.[79]

Beyond the material technology of games, the virtual experience also plays an important role in establishing resonances between the virtual (and global) world of the digital game and the real (and localized) culture of use. The resonance may be established through the veracity of the games' simulation, or by way of a congruence of the experience portrayed in the game, and the lived experience of the player. Each of the following authors argues that some aspect of the game must be sufficiently 'real' to resonate in everyday life. The players' must be able to recognize something from their own life in the digital game, although this does not mean their understanding of the game will be literal.[80]

•   King and Krzywinska argue that the players' pleasure in gameplay may be enhanced if it is located in a recognizable context.[81] The context can be provided through genre, branding, or ideological significance.[82] Context may be provided through esoteric notions like 'good' and 'evil', or the game having a particular socio-cultural or geo-political context. The role that context plays in the digital game ecology is demonstrated by the example of *Hearts of Iron* which is banned in the People's Republic of China for 'distorting history and damaging China's sovereignty and territorial integrity'.[83] Apparently because of the game's portrayal of Tibet, and other regions of China as independent nations.

•   Bogost outlines the notion of the 'simulation gap', which he describes as: 'the gap between the rule-based representation of a source system and a user's subjectivity'.[84] While digital games do necessarily require abstraction in their systems, if the simulation gap is too large the game will not be contextualized for its fidelity, but rather for its fantastic, entertainment value.[85] While the existence of a simulation gap is necessary in order for a piece of software to be contextualized as a game, the significance of the gap varies greatly. This register of resonance is particularly useful for recognising the contextualization of simulation games, and has a great deal of significance when it comes to games that represent contested processes. Turkle's criticism of *SimCity* is exemplary, she points out that the absence of race in this simulation of urban development removed a key critique from the game's representation of the process of urban decay.[86]

•   Wark takes an almost antithetical position. He states: 'Games are not representations of this world. They are more like allegories of a world made over as gamespace. They encode the abstract principles upon which decisions about the realness of this or that world are decided'.[87] Everyday life is an imperfect vision of gamespace rather than vice-versa. While digital games lack complexity, everyday life lacks the consistency, fairness and coherence of digital games. Subsequently, Wark suggests that digital games may act as a critique of the 'unreality' of everyday life.

•   Galloway argues that for a digital game to be realistic, visual verisimilitude is exceeded by a need for social realism. This form of 'realism' suggests the need for a strong resonance between the theme and activities in the game and the everyday lives of the players. He states that a 'special congruence' is required: 'between the social reality depicted in the game and the social reality known and lived by the player'.[88] This goes beyond the notion of context described by King and

Krzywinska, to what Galloway describes as a 'fidelity of context'.[89]

This variety of fashions in which the digital games resonate in everyday life not only highlights the polyrhythm of the ecology, but it also emphasizes the significance of embedded localized experiences and contexts to the ecology. This is important when considering local variances in consumption. While the Xbox version of *Tom Clancy's Rainbow Six 3*, features Venezuela in the storyline, its narrative—featuring terrorist threats to US oil supplies—is rooted in a US-centric geo-political context that is incongruent with the experience of most Venezuelans. The various cities presented in *Driv3r* suggest a resonance with the primarily US audience. Starting with the famil-iar, Miami, the locations become increasing exotic as the player gets closer to cracking the crime ring of international car-smugglers. Nice and Istanbul are not included to capitalize on interest for the game in France and Turkey, but rather to provide the backdrop for the virtual tourism of US gamers. However, despite the universal acclaim of the fidelity of the simulation it is unlikely that *Ricky Ponting Cricket 2005* has much resonance in everyday life outside of Australia.[90]

Digital games are rooted in the everyday, as an activity, technology, and 'virtual' experience. The global digital game ecology is situated in everyday life through the notion of rhythmanalysis. Eve-ryday life has its own localized rhythms, as does the digital game ecology. Where these rhythms are congruent gaming bodies are produced. The polyrhythmic digital game ecology is able to account for plural, myriad and multiple localized practices of play. This rhythm encapsulates the tension between the homogenized global and heterogeneous local practices, suggesting that digital game play may produce widely different experiences of a global space.

Rhythms of Control

Digital game play is fraught with a tension between training and practice. Is the player free to act in digital game, to make something of, or with the game that is "theirs"? Or are players merely playing with numerous repetitive variations of an algorithm where every possibility is already en-coded? When scholarship on digital games deals with this tension, the element of control often overlays and restricts the freedoms associated with play. The fact that a conflict exists at all sug-gests to some scholars that the multiplicity of possible subjectivities is irredeemably closed and captured. Ted Friedman argues that new forms of 'cybernetic subjectivity' are produced through digital game play.[91] This implies an uneven power dynamic between player and game. The fol-lowing section examines the emergence of the notion of cybernetic subjectivity, and how it was used to argue that digital games imposed their ideological perspective on players. The notion of cybernetic subjectivity is the cornerstone of the argument that digital games exert 'control' over the player; exemplified by Galloway's discussion of 'Algorithmic Culture' which uses Deleuze's notion of 'the control society' to explain the role and significance of digital games in the contem-porary epoch.[92]

Cybernetic Subjectivity

The concept of cybernetic subjectivity has been a reoccurring theme in the study of digital games. Freidman argues that rather than identifying with potential subject positions offered by the game, players come to identify with the computer itself.[93] Therefore the process of play involves 'learn-ing to think like a computer', and 'internaliz[ing] the logic of the program'.[94] Rhythmanalysis provides a useful contextualization of Friedman's perspective: the players are insinuated into the rhythm of the game through the process of play; they must 'fit' into the rhythm of the game, not vice versa. Freidman describes the process as follows:

> To win you can't just do whatever you want. You have to figure out what will work within the rules of the game. You must learn to predict the consequences of each move, and anticipate the computer's response. Eventually your decisions become intuitive, as smooth and rapid-fire as the computer's own machinations.[95]

This ongoing attuning process of learning to anticipate and respond to the computer's actions begins a rhythm of action and reaction that involves the internalization of the computer's rhythm by the player, or as Friedman would have it a 'merging of consciousness', precipitated by 'thinking like the computer'.[96]

The blurring of the boundary between digital game and player is taken by some scholars to argue that beyond imposing its rhythm on the player, the player is also forced to accept the ideological underpinnings of the game as absolute.[97] The peculiar rhythm of playing The *Sims*, of alternating between periods of design, with those of watching the 'sims' themselves interact with and within the designed environment and between stacking up lists of actions, and watching them unfold, is accompanied in this logic by an acceptance that career success can only stem from an intense micro-management of leisure time and the cultivation of friendships.

Friedman's argument is based on a reading of a particular game, *Civilization II*. Lahti has pointed out that this focus has the effect of homogenizing the pleasures, subjectivities, and experiences of digital game play.[98] In particular, Friedman's analysis focuses on the thought processes involved in playing the game, rather than the corporeality of the player's body. Lahti turns to the development of the three-dimensional view-point for the graphic interface of first person shooters as fulfilling a historic trend towards turning digital games into a corporeal experience, by turning the screen into a simulation of the players' own vision.[99] Lahti is technically correct, the body is never absent from play, even if it is absent from Friedman's analysis, as all games involve the physical act of the ergodic traversal, that utilizes the body' movement and vision.

Conversely, James Newman points out that Friedman's model is nevertheless applicable to all digital games. Newman, citing Friedman's work, argues that the linkage between player and the virtual world of the game should be considered 'as an experiential whole that synthesis, action, location, scenario, and not merely as a bond between subject and object within a world'.[100] The strategy genre of digital games—to which *Civilization II* belongs—emphasizes a particular mental process that is found in all digital games.[101] This process occurs at the corporeal level, a rhythmic, kinesthetic, ergodic configuration; hands on keyboard/controller, eyes on screen. However, a simultaneous mental process of interpretation occurs which relies less on a physical response to the rhythm of game, which is manifested through the corporeal configurative process, but is not necessarily dictated by it. There is a space between the physical configuration and interpretation of the game. The movement between these two imbricated processes provides a space for exploring and negotiating the resonances between the digital game ecology and the everyday life of the player that is flexible enough for creative, improvised, spontaneous, and stylistic adaptations of rhythms.

The territory of open and flexible interpretations of traditional media texts has been covered extensively in Cultural Studies. With Stuart Hall's work on encoding/decoding as a constant reference point a general consensus has evolved which suggests that the audience is able to individually and collectively negotiate meanings from text.[102] Jenkins, following Michel de Certeau, has called this process 'textual poaching'.[103] This freeing or opening of the text to myriad inter-pretations is encapsulated by Michel de Certeau as a systemic shift in the physical configuration of texts. He states:

> To read without uttering the words aloud or at least mumbling them is a "modern" experience, unknown for millennia. In earlier times, the reader interiorized the text; he made his voice the body of the other; he was its actor. Today, the text no longer imposes its own rhythm on the subject, it no longer manifests itself through the reader's voice.[104]

The interpretation of De Certeau's work has been influential in contemporary scholarship on fandom. De Certeau's argument that the shift from public to private reading—reading aloud to reading silently—creates potential space for the reader outside of the rhythm imposed by the text, suggests that by reading silently the modern reader escapes the exterior rhythm of the text and opens the text up to polysemy or polyrhythm. The above passage is notable because it gives a great deal of significance to *the process of the configuration of the text* as a key element that establishes the conceptual framework of the texts interpretation. It is apparent from the signifi-cance given to Friedman's work in contemporary digital game scholarship that the notion that digital games re-impose exterior rhythms, on their players' is given serious consideration.[105]

In a more general sense, the problem that this approach suggests stems from a perceived imbal-ance between the producers and consumers of the text. The consumers are forced to interact within a virtual world where all forms of action in that world are designed. This will be complicated in the following section, but even so Manovich's point that interactivity imbricates and channels people into the designer's patterns of thought is relevant.[106] Potentially the conceptual horizon, and life-world, of the player is limited by what the designers, and publishers, have conceived of as affordances. Manovich suggests that this is a case of being interpellated into the thinking pat-terns of another. Underlying this perspective on interpellation through design is a concern with that digital game play is a controlled experience with highly structured, low stakes interactions.

Allegories for the Control Society
The notion of cybernetic subjectivity, highlights the ambiguous power dynamic between player and game, and suggests that it may be the player who is disciplined by the rhythms of the game, rather than vice versa. Kinder and Marshall, perceive digital games as playing a role of molding players' into systems of interaction that are totally contained and channeled, yet project a my-thos of freedom. More recently Greig de Peuter and Nick Dyer-Witheford, have described digital games and the digital games industry as the paradigmatic media of Hardt and Negri's *Empire*.[107] They argue that the practices of the digital games industry and the content of games both repre-sent the logic of 'Empire'. This logic is total and represents the domination of the globe by aligned and imbricated military and economic forces. Global communication networks play an important

role in this domination, Hardt and Negri state:

> Communication not only expresses but also organizes the movement of globalization. It or
> ganizes the movement by multiplying and structuring interconnections through networks. It
> expresses the movement and controls the sense and direction of the imaginary that runs
> through these communicative connections; in other words *the imaginary is guided and chan
> neled within the communicative machine.*[108]

Marshall, and to a lesser extent Kinder, are gesturing towards guiding, controlled channeling, molding and modulation, that suggests to them the capture of the creative potential of play. However, de Peuter and Dyer-Witheford, are—through Hardt and Negri—able to enunciate a more nuanced position that balances the power of 'Empire' with the diversity of 'Multitude', which they see exemplified in various 'dissident applications of digital play' in alternative modes of digital game publishing, consumption, and distribution.

While the digital game ecology has a rhythm that allows for variation and nuance, this flexibility remains highly contextual. Galloway argues that the flexibility of the ideological positions that are allowed through the openness of digital games is effectively mitigated by their containment within the programmed algorithm.[109] It is in this sense, Galloway argues, that digital games become allegories for the 'control society' outlined by Gilles Deleuze in the essay 'Postscript on Control Societies'.[110] For Galloway any notion of ideological critique is subsumed in the digital game's reliance on the principles of informatics. Digital games represent information as manageable and quantifiable variables, and while the player has some flexibility in handling the variables of the game, this flexibility reflects the cultural shift to the society of control.

The control society, or society of control, emerges from Deleuze's later work, as a comment on Foucault's concept of the disciplinary society.[111] Primarily, the control society is introduced to mark what Deleuze perceives as a predominant cultural shift from organization around sites of confinement to more flexible forms of 'continuous control and instant communication'.[112] He writes:

> Confinements are molds, different moldings, while controls are a modulation, like a self-
> transmuting molding continually changing from one moment to the next, or like a sieve whose
> mesh varies from one point to another.[113]

This shift from molds to modulation is explicitly rooted in the new centrality of the role that computers and information technology have in taken society since Foucault's development of the concept of the disciplinary society.[114] A key metaphor that Deleuze uses to establish the difference between disciplinary and control societies is that of the highway. In *Two Regimes of Madness* he writes:

> Control is not discipline. You do not confine people with a highway. But by making highways,
> you multiply the means of control. I am not saying this is the only aim of highways, but that
> people can travel indefinitely and "freely" without being confined while being perfectly con
> trolled.[115]

This is the key to Galloway's particular reading of digital games; the flexibility of the interactive features of the digital game multiplies the means of control. All options, actions and possibilities are contained 'in quantifiable, dynamic relationships' in the digital code of the game's algorithm.[116] Even to make an intervention into the game outside of actual play, in the form of a 'mod' for example, also falls into this category. Because by being rendered into data; they become part of the algorithm, and thus according to Galloway annexed by its logic. 'Modding' in his argument, as much as play, is an unconfined, but controlled activity, symptomatic of the society of control.

Also useful for appreciating Galloway's approach to digital games is his notion of protocol. In *Protocol: How Control Exists After Decentralization*, he introduces protocol as a form of regula-tion that operates on the level of coding.[117] Protocols establish controlled channels within com-puter networks, taking on a role in Deleuze's society of control, similar to the original description of highways.[118] They facilitate the controlled flow, management, and modulation of information. Protocological control in Galloway's work is synonymous with Deleuze's society of control in the specific context of computer and networking technology. Protocol refers to the apparatus through which control is exerted over these networks. It represents a new paradigm of power that Gallo-way argues is outside the regulation of the individual nation-state, which exists and exerts control over the decentralized and de-hierarchalized network of contemporary computing.

From Protocol to Algorithm

In the shift from examining the internet, to digital games, Galloway's referent to the control soci-ety shifts from 'protocol' to 'algorithmic culture'. This move takes place in the context of specific genres of digital games, the real time strategy game (RTS), and the simulation game. It is in these game genres that Galloway suggests that the aesthetic or immersive experience is secondary. He states: 'Instead of experiencing the algorithm, one enacts the algorithm'.[119] This focus of the game play has shifted from actions within the algorithm, to acting upon the algorithm. Wark, in a similar vein, states: 'the artful surfaces of the game are just a way for the gamer to intuit their way through the steps of the algorithm'.[120] Algorithms in these cases, like protocol, are a way of referring to the technical apparatus of control society. Protocol is for Galloway: 'an algorithm, a proscription of a structure'.[121] Thus, the move indicates play is now taking place at a new level in relation to the structure of the algorithm or protocol. Rather than providing the structure for play, in these games genres at least, the algorithm has become the object of play.

For Galloway, this shift foregrounds the significance of digital games as a medium, and over-shadows any other 'narrative' or 'textual' potential of digital games, as the interpretation of the game becomes the interpretation of its algorithm, rather than its 'meaning'.[122] Like Friedman he conceives the play of such games as: 'learning, internalizing, and becoming intimate with a massive, multipart, global algorithm'.[123] Protocol is rendered visible by these genres, they are the allegory for the control society, and as such they present what he describes as unmediated 'con-temporary political realities'.[124] Consequently, Galloway locates a problem: as an understanding of the algorithm of the game emerges, the ideological underpinnings of the game are evacu-ated of meaning.[125] As everything is rendered into information, then playing with the algorithm becomes play with informatic code, and for Galloway this coding of ideologies into mathematical models negates any other form of critique. This logic bears some resemblance to Fredric Jame-son's lamentation of the lack of a critical space for reflection in a world totally subsumed in the demands of capital.[126] Galloway focuses on the way information is emptied of meaning through technological contexts, while Jameson's own work focuses on commodities, contemporary art and literature. They share a similar concern, which in the contemporary period is referred to vari-ously—as late capitalism, postmodernity, or the control society—traditional tactics of critique have become meaningless.

The problem arises from the nature of the control society, which has shifted from control ex-ecuted through discipline in particular sites, to a more widespread and dispersed form of capture. Henri Lefebvre describes this emergent epoch as having a: 'form of government where everyday life is totally organized'.[127] His concern is to understand this shift in organization from the level of the factory—that of production—to the level of everyday life. The spontaneous self-regulation of capitalism through competition is being replaced through the organization of everyday life. He believes that with the aid of corporate developed digital technologies society has become 'cybernetized', 'programmed', and 'functionalized'.[128] However, as everyday life becomes the site of capture by capital in the control society, it also becomes the site where the absoluteness of the control society is challenged.

Everyday life is inescapable. Lefebvre acknowledges that because it is largely lived without re-flection, it is difficult to work with. The scholar is a part of it, as they are a part of the bundled body that is the subject of rhythmanalysis. Scott Lash notes that critique in the information age is un-able to transcend information, and must instead supply its critique from within as a supplement to the original. He states: 'informationcritique must be inside of information'.[129] He does not lament this, rather he points to new paradigm that informatics precipitates, which suggests both new formations of power—Galloway's concern—and new potentials for creativity, innovation, and prac-tice.130 The new formations of power in the control society, exemplified by digital games, must be examined and understood in the context of the adaptive, creative, and innovative practices that take place in the course of play. While digital games play a unique role as both an organizer of, and escape from, the everyday through play digital games provide players with experiences that reinvigorate and re-conceptualize the everyday.

Conclusion

The digital game ecology accounts for the open possibilities of digital game rhythms, and the way that experiences of the play are enmeshed and aggregated with other technologies, objects and people. The interactive circuits proposed by Kline et al. demonstrate that the digital game ecol-ogy has a number of common attributes, but that they are not evenly distributed or received in a common manner globally. Each instantiation of play within the digital game ecology represents a particular local enactment of the global, what Sassen describes as 'cultures of use'. However, each individual culture of use is not solely a part of the digital game ecology, but is also situated in the everyday lives of the players.

Rhythmanalysis is introduced to provide an approach that includes the notion of the everyday in the digital game ecology. Rhythmanalysis also has a particular interest in bodies, and how rhythms are enacted and experienced through them, as well as having a similar interest in the open possibilities of aggregations and assemblages. Rhythmanalysis explains how the digital game ecology, despite various homogenizing forces, is a polyrhythm, the diversity of the which is demonstrated by the huge number of potential encounters with gaming in everyday life, and by the variety of ways that resonance between the game and the world may occur.

The tension between control and creativity that characterizes digital game play can be traced back to the notion of 'cybernetic subjectivity'. This notion suggests that the gamer is subject to the rhythms of the game; that the player is not executing agency, but following a pattern or algorithm, that play is training, not practice. This perspective provides a useful backdrop to the work of Galloway, particularly the intersections that he has drawn between digital games and the control society, which posits play as having no meaning beyond its allegorical reliance on informatic code.

Notes

1 Wark, M. (1994). 'The Video Game as an Emergent Media Form'. *Media International Australia* 71: 21-30.

2 Eskelinen, M. (2001). 'The Gaming Situation'. In *Game Studies: the International Journal of Computer Game Research* 1.1.

3 Aarseth, E. (1997). *Cybertext: Perspectives on Ergodic Literature*. Baltimore: John Hopkins University Press: p. 1.

4 Aarseth, *Cybertext*: p. 1.

5 Stuart Hall's (1980) description of encoding/decoding is the most significant and influential work on this notion in the field of media and communications.

6 Friedman, T. (1999). 'Civilization and its Discontents: Simulation, Subjectivity, and Space'. In G. M. Smith (ed.). *On a Silver Platter: CD-ROMs and the Promise of a New Technology*. New York: New York University Press: pp. 132-150.

7 See also: Apperley (2007b); Caldwell (1998; 2000); Douglas (2002); and Friedman (1995).

8 Bogost, I. (2006). *Unit Operations: An Approach to Videogame Criticism*. Cambridge: MIT Press: p. 14. See also: Myers, D. (2003). *The Nature of Computer Games: Play as Semiosis*. New York: Peter Lang. p. 78.

9 Jenkins, H. (2006). *Convergence Culture: Where Old and New Media Collide*. New York: New York University Press: p. 2.

10 Kinder, M. (1991). *Playing with Power In Television and Videogames: From Teenage Mutant Ninja Turtles to Muppet Babies*. Berkeley: University of California Press.

11 Flew, T. (2008). *New Media: An Introduction*, [3rd Edition]. Oxford: Oxford University Press: p. 36.

12 Jenkins, *Convergence Culture*.

13 Kinder, *Playing with Power*: p. 122.

14 Lash, S. and Lury, C. (2007). *Global Culture Industry: The Mediation of Things*. Cambridge: Polity.

15 The key work in digital game scholarship that deals with this notion is *ScreenPlay: Cinema/ Videogames/Interfaces*, edited by Geoff King and Tanya Krzywinska (2002).

16 Darley, A. (2000). *Visual Digital Culture: Surface Play and Spectacle in New Media Genres*. London: Routledge: p. 165. A more detailed discussion of this issue may also be found in: Bolter and Grusin (1999) and Ndalianis (2004).

17 Fuller, M. (2005). *Media Ecologies: Materialist Energies in Art and Technoculture*. Cambridge: MIT Press.

18 Lefebvre, H. (2004). *Rhythmanalysis: Space, Time and Everyday Life*. London: Continuum.

19 Fuller, *Media Ecologies*: p. 2.

20 Fuller, *Media Ecologies*: p. 8.

21 Fuller, *Media Ecologies*: p. 173.

22 Fuller, *Media Ecologies*: p. 173.

23 Fuller, *Media Ecologies*: p. 168.

24 Guattari, F. (2000). *The Three Ecologies*. London: Athlone Press: p. 28.

25 Guattari, *The Three Ecologies*: pp. 33-35. See also Pindar and Sutton's (2000: 6) translators' introduction.

26 For example Sue Morris's discussion of the 'game apparatus': Morris, S. (2002). 'First-person Shooters – A Game Apparatus'. In G. King and T. Krzywinska (eds.). *ScreenPlay: Cinema/videogames/interfaces*. London: Wallflower: pp. 92-94.

27 Kline, S., Dyer-Witheford, N., and de Peuter, G. (2003). *Digital\Play: The Intersection of Culture, Technology, and Marketing*. Montreal and Kingston: McGill-Queen's University Press: pp. 53-57.

28 Kline, et al. *Digital\Play*: pp. 55.

29 Kline et al. *Digital\Play*: p. 106. See also: Crogan (2004a) pp. 14-15; and Stallabrass (1996).

30 See: Galloway (2006) pp. 78-83; King and Krzywinksa (2006) pp. 59-75.

31 See: Carr (2002) pp.174-175; Cassell and Jenkins (1998); Cunningham (2000); Ray (2003); and Yates and Littleton (2001).

32 Jenkins, H. (2003). 'From Barbie to Mortal Kombat: Further Reflections'. In J. T. Caldwell and A. Everett (eds.). *New Media: Theories and Practices of Digitextuality*. New York: Routledge: pp. 249-253.

33 See: Consalvo, (2003a); and Consalvo and Dutton (2006).

34 See: Barrett (2006); Brand et al. (2006); Chan (2005); DiSalvo et al. (2008); Everett (2005): p. 312; Leonard (2006a; 2006b); Nakumara (2001); Ow (2000); Redmond (2006): pp. 110-112; Squire (2008); Sze-Fai Shiu (2006): pp. 109-110; Taylor (2006a): pp. 115-116.

35 'Army to Spend $50 Million on Video Games' (2008). kimatv.com.

36 See: Ghamari-Tabrizi (2004); Halter (2006); and King (2008).

37 Kline et al. *Digital\Play*: p. 201.

38 The following work discusses the issue in relation to digital games: Banks (2003); Banks and Humphreys (2008); Castronova (2003; 2005); de Peuter and Dyer-Witheford (2005); Flew and Humphreys (2008); Grimes (2007); Humphreys, 2003, 2005, 2007; Humphreys et al., 2005; Klang, 2004; Kücklich (2005); Lastokwa (2006); Moore (2005); Morris (2004); Pearce (2002; 2006); Postigo (2003); Ruggill et al. (2004); Smith (2007); Taylor (2002; 2006a); and Yee (2006).

39 Kline et al. *Digital\Play*: p. 215.

40 See: Herz (1997): pp. 113-117; Kerr (2006): p. 77; Kline et al. (2003): pp. 205-209; Lugo et al. (2002); and Takahashi (2002): p. 197.

41 For an extensive discussion, see: Castells, M. (1995). *The Rise of the Networked Society*, [Second Edition]. Oxford: Blackwell: pp. 77-162.

42 Kline et al. Digital|Play: pp. 214-217.

43 Jansz, J. and Martens, L. (2005). 'Gaming at a LAN Event: The Social Context of Playing Videogames'. *New Media and Society* 7.3: pp. 333-355.

44 Kline et al. *Digital\Play*: p. 57.

45 Kinder, *Playing with Power*: pp. 2-6.

46 Marshall, P. D. (2004). *New Media Cultures*. London: Arnold: p. 23.

47 Kline et al. *Digital\Play*: pp. 225-227. Elkington (2009) discusses this issue in relation to the critical failure of game-to-film adaptations. Caldwell (2003) deals with the issue of the hype and lack of innovation in new media entertainment genres in a more general manner.

48 Kerr, A. (2006). *The Business and Culture of Digital Games: Gamework/Gameplay*. London: Sage: p. 154.

49 Kerr The Business and Culture of Digital Games: p. 155. See also: Lange, A. (2002). Report from the PAL Zone: European Games Culture. In L. King (ed.). *Game On: The History and Culture of Videogames*. London: Lawrence King Publishing Ltd: p. 47.

50 Kerr *The Business and Culture of Digital Games*: p. 155.

51 Kline et al. *Digital\Play*: p. 215.

52 http://www.xbox.com/en-us/live/countries.htm

53 Consalvo, M. (2006). 'Console Video Games and Global Corporations: Creating a Hybrid Culture'. *New Media and Society* 8.1: p. 128.

54 Kerr *The Business and Culture of Digital Games*: p. 18.

55 Consalvo 'Console Video Games and Global Corporations': pp. 129-130.

56 Kohler, C. (2006). 'Cheer Squad: Why iNiS Want to Make You Happier'. 1Up.com.

57 Warschauer, M. (2000). 'Language, identity and the Internet'. In B. Kolko, L. Nakamura and G. Rodman (eds.). *Race in Cyberspace*. New York: Routledge: p. 156.

58 Sassen, S, (2006). *Territory, Authority, Rights: Global Assemblages*. Princeton: Princeton University Press: p. 390.

59 Sassen *Territory, Authority, Rights*: pp. 347-348.

60 Sassen *Territory, Authority, Rights*: p. 347.

61 Lefebvre, H. (1991). *Critique of Everyday Life: Volume 2*. London: Verso: p. 97.

62 Lefebvre, H. and Régulier, C. (1996). Rhythmanalysis of Mediterranean Cities. In E. Kofman and E. Lebas (eds.) Writings on Cities. Oxford: Blackwell.

63 Lefebvre, H. (1984). *Everyday Life in the Modern World*. New Brunswick: Transaction Books: p. 18.

64 Lefebvre, H. (2004). *Rhythmanalysis: Space, Time and Everyday Life*. London: Continuum: p. 15. Original emphasis.

65 Lefebvre and Régulier '*Rhythmanalysis of Mediterranean Cities*': p. 228.

66 Fuller, *Media Ecologies*: p. 4.

67 Lefebvre, *Rhythmanalysis*: p. 9.

68 Lefebvre and Régulier 'Rhythmanalysis of Mediterranean Cities': p. 230.

69 Lefebvre, *Rhythmanalysis*: p. 10.

70 Lefebvre, *Rhythmanalysis*: p. 6.

71 Lefebvre and Régulier 'Rhythmanalysis of Mediterranean Cities': p. 230.

72 Lefebvre, *Rhythmanalysis*: p. 67.

73 Murphie, A. (2004). 'Vertiginous Mediations: Sketches for a Dynamic Pluralism in the Study of Computer Games'. *Media International Australia* 110: pp. 83-84.

74 See pages xviii-xix of Philip Wander's 'Introduction' to Lefebvre, H. *Everyday Life in the Modern World: Volume 2*. New Brunswick: Transaction Books.

75 Lefebvre and Régulier 'Rhythmanalysis of Mediterranean Cities': p. 239.

76 An English translation of the original Japanese title.

77 Aporia is used here in the same manner as Aarseth (1999), to evoke the sense of boredom

and frustration that accompanies the near-completion of a level.

78 Navarro, A. (2005). 'Animal Crossing: Review'. *Gamespot.*

79 Apperley, T. (2007a). 'Games Without Borders: Globalization, Gaming and Mobility in Venezuela'. In G. Goggin and L. Hjorth (eds.). *Mobile Media 2007: Proceeding of an International Conference on Social and Cultural Aspects of Mobile Phones, Convergent Media, and Wireless Technologies* (pp. 171-178) Sydney: University of Sydney Press.

80 Chesher, C. (2004). 'Neither a Gaze Nor a Glance, but a Glaze: Relating to Console Game Screens'. *Scan: A Journal of Media Arts Culture* 1.1.

81 King, G. and Krzywinksa, T. (2006). *Tomb Raiders & Space Invaders: Videogames Forms and Contexts.* London: I. B. Tauris: p. 75.

82 King and Krzywinksa, *Tomb Raiders & Space Invaders*: p. 59.

83 'Swedish Videogame Banned for Damaging China's Sovereignty' (2004). *China Daily.*

84 Bogost, I. (2006). *Unit Operations: An Approach to Videogame Criticism.* Cambridge: MIT Press: p. 107.

85 Apperley, T. (2006). Genre and Game studies: Towards a Critical Approach to Video Game Genres. *Simulation & Gaming: An Interdisciplinary Journal of Theory, Practice and Research* 37.1: pp. 6-23.

86 Turkle, S. (1995). *Life on the Screen: Identity in the Age of the Internet.* New York: Simon & Schuster: pp. 72-73.

87 Wark, M. (2007). *Gamer Theory.* Cambridge: Harvard University Press.

88 Galloway, A. (2006). *Gaming: Essays on Algorithmic Culture.* Minneapolis: University of Minnesota Press: p. 83.

89 Galloway, *Gaming*: p. 84.

90 Swordfish Studios only published the game with that title in Australia and New Zealand, globally it was published as *Brian Lara International Cricket 2005.*

91 Friedman, T. (1995). Making Sense of Software: Computer Games and Interactive Textuality. In S. Jones (ed.). *Cybersociety: Computer Mediated Communication and Community.* London: Sage: p. 83.

92 Galloway, *Gaming.*

93 Friedman, 'Civilization and its Discontents': p. 135.

94 Friedman, 'Civilization and its Discontents': pp. 135-136.

95 Friedman, 'Civilization and its Discontents', p, 136.

96 Friedman, 'Civilization and its Discontents': pp. 136-137.

97 Caldwell, N. (2000). 'Settler stories: Representational Ideologies in Computer Strategy Gaming'. In *M/C Journal: A Journal of Media and Culture* 3.5.

98 Lahti, M. (2003). 'As We Become Machines: Corporealized Pleasures in Video Games'. In M. J. P. Wolf and B. Perron (eds.). *The Video Game Theory Reader.* New York: Routledge: p. 159.

99 Lahti, 'As We Become Machines': p. 161.

100 Newman, J. (2002). 'The Myth of the Ergodic Videogame: Some Thoughts on Player-character Relationships in Videogames'. *Game Studies: the International Journal of Computer Game Research* 2.1.

101 Apperley, 'Genre and Game Studies': p. 15.

102 Hall, S. (1980). *Culture, Media, Language: Working Papers in Cultural Studies*, 1972-1979. London: Hutchinson.

103 Jenkins, H. (1992). *Textual Poachers: Television Fans and Participatory Cultures.* London:

Routledge.

104 de Certeau, M. (1984). *The Practice of Everyday Life*. Berkeley: University of California Press: p. 104.

105 Freidman's (1999) work is discussed in some length in the following: Burrill (2008); Galloway (2006); Giddings (2007); Kerr et al. (2006); King and Kryzwinska (2006); Murphie (2004); and Newman (2002).

106 Manovich, L. (2000). *The Language of New Media*. Cambridge: MIT Press: pp. 60-61.

107 de Peuter, G. and Dyer-Witheford, N. (2005). 'A Playful Multitude? Mobilising and Counter-mobilising Immaterial Game Labour'. In *The Fibreculture Journal 5*.

108 Hardt, M. and Negri, A. (2000). Empire. Cambridge: Harvard University Press: pp. 32-33. Emphasis added.

109 Galloway, *Gaming*.

110 Deleuze, G. (1995). *Negotiations 1972-1990*. New York: Columbia University Press.

111 Foucault, M. (1995). *Discipline and Punish: The Birth of the Prison*. New York: Vintage Books.

112 Deleuze, *Negotiations*: p. 174.

113 Deleuze, *Negotiations*: pp. 177-178.

114 Deleuze, *Negotiations*: p. 180.

115 Deleuze, G (2006). *Two Regimes of Madness: Texts and Interviews 1975-1995*. Los Angeles: Semiotexte: p. 322. Working with a similar metaphor in Everyday Life in the Modern World (emphasis added, 1984: 100) Henri Lefebvre states: 'from a viewpoint of programmed everyday life, nothing can beat a motor-car'.

116 Galloway, *Gaming*: p. 100.

117 Galloway, A. (2004). *Protocol: How Control Exists After Decentralization*. Cambridge: MIT Press: p. 7.

118 Galloway, *Protocol*: pp. 241-244.

119 Galloway, *Gaming*: p. 19.

120 Wark, M. (2007). *Gamer Theory*. Cambridge: Harvard University Press.

121 Galloway, *Protocol*: p. 30.

122 Galloway, *Gaming*: p. 91.

123 Galloway, *Gaming*: p. 90.

124 Galloway, *Gaming*: p. 92.

125 Galloway, *Gaming*: p. 102.

126 Jameson, F. (1991). *Postmodernism or, the Cultural Logic of Late Capitalism*. Durham: Duke University Press.

127 Lefebvre, *Everyday Life in the Modern World*: p. 159.

128 Lefebvre, *Everyday Life in the Modern World*: pp. 64-65.

129 Lash, S. (2002). *Critique of Information*. London: Sage: p. 10.

130 An issue that Galloway deals with in his co-authored book: *The Exploit: A Theory of Networks* (Galloway and Thacker, 2007).

CHAPTER TWO
BODIES, COMPUTERS, AND OTHER AGGREGATIONS

> ...people may experience a seizure when exposed to certain visual images, including flashing lights or patterns that may appear in videogames...
>
> These seizures may have a variety of symptoms, including lightheadedness, altered vision, eye or face twitching, jerking or shaking of arms or legs, disorientation, confusion, or momen tary loss of awareness. Seizures may also cause loss of consciousness or convulsions that can lead to injury from falling down or striking nearby objects.

This warning, taken from the pamphlet accompanying the Xbox version of *Grand Theft Auto: Vice City*, suggests there may be very real, physical, pathological consequences to game play. While in this particular context the warning acts as a caveat—a legal disclaimer—the notion of the body becoming damaged or strained through excessive digital game play has also been deployed as a badge of pride, a material trace of the commitment and difficulty that is required to master a game. In Martin Amis's description of *Pac-Man* he notes: 'I have seen bloodstains on the *Pac-Man* joystick... ...I know a young actress with a case of PacMan Hand so severe that her index finger looked like a section of blood pudding—yet still she played, and played through her tears of pain'.[1] This description is a far cry from the notions of digital games as immersive virtual worlds, and the player as a virtual actor in those worlds. Amis is highly aware of the way that digital games engage the body as well as the mind of the player: 'the vivid melodrama of these games doesn't just involve and absorb the player: it makes him sweat and pant. With his lips thinning and his eyes bulging, he seems to take it all very personally'.[2] Even when play is finished, games haunt the players' sleeping hours as persistent after-images. One of Amis's interview subjects—a keen player of *Space Invaders*—reports: 'I used to lie awake hearing bleep bleep bleep chug all night, and seeing them dropping on me with my eyes shut'.[3] These physical reactions that affect the body during—and after—the act of play, are excess to the inputs required by the game. The material residue imprinted on the body through play—in the form of blisters, aches and strained retinas—are indicative that the body is an important node in game networks. These examples of extreme play demonstrate that the body is always implicated in digital game play.

This chapter develops the notion of 'situated gaming' in order to consider the implications of the including the body in analysis of digital game play. This body includes the materials, objects, people and things that are aggregated to produce the gaming situation—the material cultures of use of digital game play—that are crucial in shaping the gaming experience. This is important because these aggregations provide the everyday context in which the virtual is embedded and enacted; they demonstrate the various material constraints and—importantly—affordances that players must negotiate to produce play. The centrality of the body in the notion of situated gam- ing underscores that in the context of digital game play there is an underlying ambiguity between training and practice. This ambiguity is explicated by examining Lefebvre's notions of compulsion, adaptation, and dressage, which suggest that while digital games have scope for adaptation, they are also a key form of training or dressage in the contemporary epoch.

Situated Gaming

The situated approach to gaming follows from key research on audiences in the fields of digital games and digital media. King and Kryzwinska while exploring the issue of digital game genres, postulated four categories that had important and defining impact on the gaming experience.[4] While this taxonomy has important consequences for many aspects of the study of digital games; one category, 'mode', suggests a particularly crucial point; that factors exterior to the digital game itself could impact on its generic classification. King and Kryzwinksa argue that games played in certain situations or contexts may have more in common with each other than might be appreciated through a purely visual or interactive analysis. This point, that context has a key role in defining the play experience, is demonstrated by Morris, who points out that *Half-Life* is a completely different game, and play experience, when played as a single player game, than it is when played with others over a LAN (local-area-network) connection.[5]

Different contexts of play create completely different experiences. The term situated gaming is used to evoke the specificity of context that defines particular gaming situations. Situated gaming refers to the numerous specific and particular local cultures of use that make up the global digital game ecology. It invokes a 'situated ecology', a peculiarly local and situated niche or instantiation within the digital game ecology. The situated ecology is a specific ecotone where the digital game ecology and the local rhythms of everyday life intersect. The term 'situated' is used by Yates and Littleton in their essay 'Understanding Computer Game Cultures: A Situated Approach'. Using data gained from interviews with players, through contrasting the male-players' and female-players' perspectives, Yates and Littleton concluded that: 'we view gaming as taking place in "cultural niches" which arise in the complex interaction between games, gamers and gaming culture'.[6] Their statement reflects an ecological approach to conceptualizing the complexity of digital game play. The digital game ecology supports numerous niches of digital game play created by the variety of intersections of everyday life and the digital game ecology. But the notion of situated gaming does not solely refer to the social context of gaming, although it is important. Taylor provides a wider definition, she states: 'Play is situated between and reliant not simply on abstract ideas but also on social networks, attitudes, or events in one's non/game life, technological abilities or limitations, structural affordances or limits, local cultures, and personal understandings of leisure'.[7] Digital game play is located at the nexus of numerous concerns that impact on and shape individuals experiences of game play. The notion of situated gaming acknowledges the specificity of the various cultural niches, which characterize the digital game ecology, that emerge from the complex interactions of cultures, games, people, and technologies.

Situated gaming is an approach to examining digital games that is based upon two core principles: the materiality of the embodied experience of gaming, 'the gaming body', which is influenced by conditions stemming from the local cultures and contexts of play; and that the game experience is played out as a negotiation between the 'global' immateriality of the virtual worlds of the digital game ecology and the myriad material situated ecologies that are manifestations of the 'local'. The concept frames the gaming body as a node in the communicative network where the global medium of digital games encounters numerous local contexts. While, in terms of global production digital games follow a particular hierarchal dynamic, the ergodic process of play is in the framework of situated gaming, open to wider 'cultural inputs' that are both characterized by the local and by global influences.[8] This situated approach to gaming acknowledges the imbrication of the local and the global, and explores it in its embedded context.

Situated gaming also evokes two general themes that place this study against a broader political backdrop than the specificity of the concerns outlined above. First, situated gaming marks a fundamental tension between freedom and constraint in the consumption and play of digital games. Jean-Paul Satre in *Situations* uses the notion of 'the situation' to refer to the a priori constraints that exist that establish a rather narrow scope on freedom of the individual.[9] Digital games form a part of the 'mediascapes' of the contemporary epoch, and are thus a component of the global imagination of ways of being in the world, thus they have a peculiar impact on the lifeworlds of digital game players. Beyond participating in the framing of the conceptual horizons of individuals, actions within games themselves are characterized by a tension between training and practice, and the 'potential' freedoms found in game-play are almost always contextualized in relation to the rules, that are their structuring constraints. The practices of play, and counterplay, feed into the currents of training and practice that can be found within this often minimal margin.

Second, by locating the study of digital games in the field of everyday life, situated gaming is concerned with the quotidian, the possibility of the reinvention of everyday life. This suggests a link to the Situationist International, an artistic-social movement that was formally instituted from 1957, which was at its most prominence in France during the 1960s, particularly during the events of May 1968. Their manifesto demanded praxis intent on unleashing free and spontaneous creativity that they believed would lead to a revolution within everyday life. The Situationist International were linked both to Henri Lefebvre the key scholar of the quotidian and to Johan Huizinga, a cultural historian of play. Jappe's detailed analysis of Guy Debord's life and work, notes that this key figure of the Situationist International was influenced by Johan Huizinga's approach to play in *Homo Ludens: A Study of the Play Element in Culture*.[10] This issue is discussed further by Rodriguez, who notes the connection as a way of underscoring the significance of Huizinga's ideas in popular culture.[11] This book deals with the emergence of creative practices within the sphere of the digital game ecology and how they politicize and transform the everyday. Thus, the agenda of situated gaming is two-fold: to acknowledge and explore the tensions between training and practice in the gaming body; and to demonstrate a margin of flexibility that the situated ecology allows for that dynamic to be re-envisioned. Examining how particular cultures of use emerge at the nexus of the digital game ecology and the everyday life of the players, highlights the numerous ways that digital games are used to critique, re-imagine, and reinvent everyday life.

The Gaming Body
Recent artistic projects have explored the issue of materiality and digital games by examining the relationship between play and pain. *PainStation* by Tilman Reiff and Volker Morawe, involves a reconfiguration of a two-player version of the game *PONG*; based on the premise that the game is played with each player placing their hand on a panel that emits a small painful shock if they miss the ball. However, if either of the players' removes their hand from the panel the game is over. Thus, enduring pain becomes as important to success in the game as skilful play. Laso, in his discussion of *PainStation*, notes that even if pain is brought to the forefront of play, the majority of players still enjoy the experience.[12] The artists' second project adds a nuance to the connection

between pain and digital game play; another of the artists' projects *Legshocker*, is an addition the PlayStation2 game *FIFA 2002*, that each of the opposing players inserts their leg into. This device inflicts pain on the player when one of their team members was fouled; this meant rather than having to endure pain like in *PainStation*, players could inflict pain upon their opponents. Laso argues that this feature, the possibility of players inflicting pain on each other, increases the excitement of play by underscoring the connection between the virtual and the real.[13] By foregrounding the role of the body in the digital game experience Reiff and Morawes' art projects explore the manner in which the virtual gamespace is enacted, and embedded in the material world.

The key difference between the two projects is in their approach to pain: *PainStation* is primarily masochistic; while *Legshocker* also has a sadistic component. The element of sadism in digital games is traced by other scholars, who shift the frame of discussion from the sadism of digital game content, to explore the underlying dynamic of digital game play as a sadistic process.[14] *PainStation*, more clearly evokes the peculiar relation between players and pain. A relation that suggests masochism, rather than sadism; an aspect of digital game play which certainly is evident in Amis's early reports of digital game cultures. The pain is part of the shared experience of play, as wounds and injuries are compared, and seen as a symbol of dedication to a 'higher' pursuit. Amis's description of *Pac-Man* hand, mirrors the Nintendo thumb associated with *Super Mario Bros.*, the Nintendo palm linked with *Mario Party*,[15] and also the contemporary phenomenon of the Wii elbow.[16] But this self-inflicted pain is a part of the means of digital game play, not the ends of it, inasmuch as players ignore the pain to continue playing, rather than finding a particular pleasure in it.

The imprint of play on the body demonstrates the materiality of play. While previous emphasis has been placed on the virtual body's movement and actions within virtual worlds, digital game play also involves the body at the screen. A body that may be ignored during the course of play, as the linear time of gaming subsumes the cyclical demands of the body, causing pain, sleep, food, and bodily functions to be sidelined or even ignored entirely. The notion of situated gaming takes the body at the screen to be the centre of all digital game assemblages. This is not simply to reframe dialogues about digital game play in terms of bodies, but rather in terms of the spaces that the bodies occupy, and how the assemblages of software, hardware, bodies and spaces feedback into each other to create highly contextual situations of digital game play.

The body of the gamer has certain rhythms; recurrent needs to eat, drink, sleep, breathe and defecate, and more transient needs to socialize and move. Imbricated in this are the rhythms of play, the movement of the eyes across the screen, and hands on the keyboard or joystick. Other rhythms are enacted by and through the game, but these machine rhythms will be discussed below. This section focuses on the cyclical rhythms of the body, and how these rhythms structure the material experience of digital game play. This element of play is important to appreciating the significance that situated gaming places on the location in contextualizing the process of digital game play.

The body of the digital game player has numerous ancillary material requirements. The gaming body is not a body in the literal sense, but can be understood as collective or assemblage that is produced to meet the needs—and desires—of the body of the gamer. Lefebvre describes the body in rhythmanalysis as a 'bundle' or 'garland', which is composed not only of different objects, but also of rhythms, that are composed of time, places, and energy.[17] The bundle that is the gaming body is a polyrhythm, as it contains many diverse intertwined rhythms. Rhythms that are rooted in the mundane everyday, the need to: use a toilet, communicate with others, eat food, drink, work, and sleep. Also overlooked are more general material concerns: access to platform/hardware, adequate lighting, headphones and other sound equipment, a place to sit, power, software, spaces in which gamers will not be disturbed or disturb others; practical matters that are prerequisites for play, that shape—and importantly, also constrain—the experience. The bundle of gaming body is a network composed of the elements required to produce play with the literal body of the gamer as its central node.

How the cyclical needs of the body of the gamer underpin the gaming body is illustrated by the *South Park* episode 'Make Love Not Warcraft'. Cartman's Mom is drafted into the gaming body, providing support in the form of food supplies by delivering 'hot pockets'.[18] The episode underscores the grotesque element of the gaming body when during a crucial point in the protagonists' online battle; Cartman suffers from at attack of diarrhea. Using the intercom he summons his mother, who runs into the basement with a bedpan. Cartman still playing, leans forward and lowers his pants to violently expel the excreta, his mother catches most of it in the bedpan, the rest of it splatters on her arms and the floor. The explicit nature of this scene—which irrespective of questions of 'good taste'—explores the bodily limits to which gameplay must conform; is important as it places an emphasis on the grotesque element of the gaming body. The grotesque body, the body that transgresses and explores its limits, is linked to the notion of carnival. Bakhtin reads the grotesque body as a critique of the division between culture and nature, as a reassertion of the inclusion of humans in the natural world as opposed to the masters of it. He states: 'the grotesque body is not separated from the rest of the world. It is not a closed, completed unit; it is unfinished, outgrows itself, transgresses its own limits'.[19] The grotesque body—recontextualized into the discussion of digital games—also reiterates the openness of the gaming body. The ecological approach to examination of digital games conceptualizes the gaming body as open and connected to the wider world, rather than locked in an inward-looking circuit of cybernetic feedback. To study games in their situated context is to understand the gaming body as an assemblage that must be traced outside of its central couplet (player-game or operator-machine). The element of the grotesque suggests rather than the central couplet of the gaming body is not closed within a 'magic circle', rather it is open with reciprocal relations and influences to the 'outside' world.

The inter-relation of these various factors to produce the gaming body is a testimony to the activity's frailty. The emergent, unpredictable and ever-present demands of the everyday may intrude on and disrupt the process of play if the gaming body does not have the necessary contingency to meet them with rapid expediency. The gaming body places a peculiar demand on a space: curtains drawn in the daytime; a proliferation of fridges and food; seats and chairs are moved to bring the body at an ideal distance from the screen.[20] But, the organization of everyday life in order to produce the gaming body also underscores the mundane elements of digital gaming; which is often positioned as a break, rupture with, or even escape from, the bleakness of the everyday. Flynn argues that gaming consoles transform televisions from domesticated objects into virtual portals that are openings to: 'cybernetic fantasies of speed, danger, and freedom', which challenge the dominant understanding of the home as a domestic space.[21] Positioning digital game play solely as a rupture in the everyday—the mundane, the domestic—both overlooks the myriad ways in which the gaming body is both insinuated, and reliant upon the everyday. Lefebvre states:

> Today leisure is first of all and for (nearly) all a temporary break with everyday life. We are undergoing a painful and premature revision of our old 'values'; leisure is no longer a festival, the reward of labour, and it is not yet a freely chosen activity pursued for itself, it is a gener alised display: television, cinema, tourism.[22]

Conceptualizing digital game play as a type of rupture thus divorces it from the quotidian; the renewal of the festival that suggests everyday life could be different. A notion of digital game play without a commitment to the everyday implies that the activity falls entirely into the modulated leisure of the control society. The notion of the gaming body returns the study of digital games to the materiality of that experience, to the mundane reality within which play takes place, and the ways that play transforms the everyday. While digital game play may occur as a tactic of evasion from the pressures of everyday life, it remains a part of everyday life because the desire to evade everyday life permeates its existence.

The gaming body has a particular rhythm that intersects with the rhythms of digital games. This is an intersection of what Lefebvre calls linear and cyclical rhythms, which he describes as follows:

> The cyclical originates in the cosmic, in nature: days, nights, seasons, the waves and tides of the sea, monthly cycles, etc. The linear would come rather from social practice, therefore from human activity: the monotony of actions and of movements, imposed structures.[23]

The dominant rhythms of digital game are often linear, while the gaming body tends to be influenced by cyclical rhythms. The relationships within and between linear and cyclical rhythms are complex; the interactions often slip into unstable states, or 'arrhythmia', where one rhythm starts to dominate, or interfere with, the other. For the games' rhythm, and the rhythm of the body to resonate in each other, the rhythms must enter into a metastable condition that Lefebvre describes as 'eurhythmia'.[24] Eurhythmia is a state where multiple rhythms are integrated, and enmeshed in a larger rhythm. In the case of digital games, eurhythmia occurs when rhythm of the individual game and the rhythm of the situated ecology are compatible and complementary. Arrhythmia occurs when these rhythms do not so neatly intersect, or cannot otherwise be considered an organic whole, so that one comes to "drown out" or dominate the other. This can occur for numerous reasons. The cyclic rhythms of the body may come to dominate, as a particular instantiation of play is brought to a close because of a broken toilet, or a want of coca-cola. Or, in other cases, the linear rhythms of games may not "fit" the demands of the situated ecology—particularly issues like slow loading times, internet lag, or large gaps between saves—which leads to arrhythmia. However, it is not the case that arrhythmia is "bad", while eurhythmia is "good", because many cultures of use demonstrate forms of innovation and practice that emerge through dealing with or overcoming arrhythmia. The kinds of exclusion caused by arrhythmia are discussed in chapter seven.

The linear rhythm of digital games comes not solely from the mechanics and structures of the digital worlds, but also from the social structures that develop around their play. In Melbourne during the spring of 2006 while conducting research at Cydus, I came across a peculiar scene:

a group of restaurant workers arrived at the café early on Sunday morning right after work. The four men entered loudly, warmly greeting the café's employees, and organizing optimal seating. As they logged in to *World of Warcraft*, they began to discuss their agenda for the day's play. These four players planned to meet with a larger group in order to perform a collaborative mission or 'raid'.[25] While they were waiting for the rendezvous time they reflected upon their working situation at a 24-hour café, and also discussed their game avatars' 'talents'.[26] This discussion focused around one player's avatar, and while two of the other players provided contradictory advice, the fourth player took orders for coffee and headed to the close-by Victoria Market to get coffee. From the matter-of-fact conversation between the members of the group, it was apparent that the coffee was to alleviate the fatigue of working all night. While he was gone, the US-based administrator for the raid closed the roster, and when the fourth player arrived back to the café he was refused permission to take part in the raid because he had not entered his name in the roster by the stipulated rendezvous time. Consequently, he irately watched his colleagues play for several hours before returning to their shared accommodation to rest. The coordination of the raid had been complicated by the game server being located in the USA, along with most of the other people that were to go on the raid. The deadline of 11am Saturday in Los Angeles became 6am on Sunday in Melbourne. The disruption the body's rhythm, to the extent that additional sustenance is required, is not a new phenomenon; however, in this example it contributes significantly to arrhythmia. The gaming body's need for stimulants excluded it from play, because the linear rhythm of the game and the game community required that the cyclical rhythm of the body be subsumed.

At least Cydus had a bathroom, a place to extrude and expel waste. Located in the back, the facilities were rather poorly maintained (no soap or towels at the washbasin) and extremely dirty. I saw on more than one occasion people steeling themselves to go in there, taking a moment between play and defecation to mentally prepare themselves. Once I noticed a young woman leaving the bathroom visibly upset, drying her hands on her boyfriend's jacket before returning to the game of *Ragnarok Online*, that they were both playing. He was waiting for her to return, their avatars were side-by-side inside the virtual world of Ragnarok; while she was in the toilet, he was chatting with other players online and when she returned they quickly resumed their activities; looking for monsters to kill to get treasure and experience. The linear rhythms of games need to be flexible enough to enable players to leave the game world from time to time. But not all demands stem directly from the maintenance of the cyclic demands of the body; they may also come from the linear rhythms imposed by the social or cultural demands that dominate the location of play. While they are outside of the digital game itself they also posit interventions, and interruptions, to play which players must negotiate.

For the play of a particular game to take place, there must be a congruence, or eurhythmia, between the digital game's rhythm and the everyday rhythm in the location of play. This is demonstrated in the shift between online and offline interactions during the course of play in the environment of the internet café. In the twelve-computer internet café on Avenida Avila, in San Bernardino, Caracas some players alternated between digital game play and socialization; the shifts were immediately evident from their demeanor and the ways that they positioned their bodies. Silent concentration, focused at the computer screen, alternated with a more conversational and relaxed—but no less playful—attitude that involved looking away from the screen to make eye contact with others, looking at other screens, and even leaving the computer momentarily. This behavior included people who were not engaged in play, who were either using the computer for other reasons, who had come to the café to buy candy or cold beverages, or had entered the café deliberately to catch up with friends. This strong social milieu formed an additional layering of linear rhythms on the site. The impact of these rhythms was evident in both the types of games that were played, and in the style of play.

In the case of 'Cyber Café Avila', two common patterns emerged: digital games that had rhythms that repeated cycles of intense play followed by less interactive—either narrative or set-up—periods, for example *Grand Theft Auto: Vice City* or *GunBound: World Champion*; and digital games that were characterized by short bursts of rapid but intensely engaging play, which could be easily incorporated into a variety of other activities, like *Counter-Strike*.[27] The social context of the location also impacted on the style of play, in particular in relation to sound, where games with strong sound cues, like *Age of Empires II: The Conquerors*, were played without headphones—or with the headphones around the neck, but not actually sitting on the ears—so that the players could be included in the general offline sociality occurring in the site. This element of sociality multiplies the individuals included in the bundle of the gaming body. It also marks the flexible delineation of the site itself, as people would congregate outside both Cydus in Melbourne, and Cyber Café Avila in Caracas. In Venezuela, the congregations were primarily social and would often draw in passers-by momentarily; outside Cydus it varied, sometimes a collection of individuals smoking or checking their mobiles, other times a more clearly established group talking together. The gaming body, and the site of play, form core of a bundle of rhythms that may be construed widely by tracing the rhythms on a variety of registers and scales.

The gaming body is formed from entwined—and sometimes contradictory—cyclical and linear rhythms. Each of these rhythms brings new bodies to the aggregated bundle that makes up the gaming body. The analysis of digital game rhythms challenges the concept of digital games as a hermeneutic system, or a closing cybernetic feedback loop that engages only a player and an algorithm. Cyclical rhythms suggest that the physical needs of the gaming body, and the ways that meeting these needs are organized are an important part of the gaming experience. However, the linear rhythms of digital game play, and the sociality of play, indicate that both the machinic rhythm of play itself, and the wider rhythms of everyday life also have significant impacts on the experience of gaming.

Ambiguous Rhythms: Training and Practice

Digital games produce linear rhythms that entwine and mesh with other linear and cyclic rhythms to produce the gaming body. This dynamic is complex and fraught with subtle negotiations of power. These negotiations highlight the ambiguity that emerges in the situated ecology between 'training' and 'practice'. These particular terms in order to connect this discussion of digital games to wider concerns with technology and labor raised by Marx,[28] which are taken up by Benjamin.[29] Training, suggests a relationship to technology where the worker follows the rhythm of the machine. Marx states: 'It is not the worker who employs the conditions of his work, but rather the reverse, the conditions of work employ the worker'.[30] The worker—or in the case of the digital game the player—is trained by the digital game by fitting their actions into the machinc rhythm.

Practice, provides a contrast to training, it refers to the development, accumulation, and deployment of skills by the worker. Practices make use of machines, while training allows people to be of use to machines. As Benjamin notes: 'The unskilled worker is the one most deeply degraded by machine training. His work has been sealed off from experience: *practice counts for nothing* in the factory'.[31] This chapter uses Lefebvre's the concepts of compulsion, adaptation, and dressage to examine the ambiguity between practice and training.

Compulsion is the part of life that is neither work nor leisure, but even so is dominated by concerns that are not necessarily the individuals own.[32] Compulsions break down, and potentially collapse, the previously clearly defined boundaries between work and play. The notion of compulsion marks the shift from bureaucratic management of particular sites, to a general management of everyday life. In this manner, Lefebvre's notion of compulsion shares a similar concern with Deleuze's notion of the control society, as it suggests an extension of the means of control—or discipline—beyond a particular site or institution. Lefebvre, writing in the post-WWII period, marks the computer as the key technology of this shift. The contemporary role of computers in management of finance, transport, security, leisure and trade—all facets of contemporary being—accentuates the place, and times, that compulsion takes in everyday life.[33]

Adaptation is the creative aspect of everyday life, the process by which people turn 'nature and necessities' into 'creations and assets'.[34] Because of this concern with the creative input of the individual, adaptation shares much with the notion of practice. Although like de Certeau's '*la perruque*', adaptation suggests a flexible variety of activities that do not necessarily involve creative production in the strictest sense.[35] Adaptation has a great deal of significance for Lefebvre, who describes it as the process of actualizing the human being into their natural being.[36] To be denied an opportunity to turn necessities into creation, thus suggests a similar dehumanization as that ascribed by Benjamin and Marx to the worker in the mechanized factory. Adaptation is a crucial process for both negotiating the everyday, and maintaining the possibility of its renewal.

Dressage has much in common with the notion of training. Dressage is the training of the body—of gesture, gait, stature and composure—based on repetition.[37] In this respect, it describes similar processes as Foucault's notion of discipline.[38] Foucault argues that spatial and temporal organization of individual bodies are two of the key factors that mark the emergence of the disciplinary society.[39] Dressage is a notion that accounts for the move away from individual sites of discipline to a control society where the individual's body is not only engaged in disciplinary training during their engagement with institutions, but in their everyday life also.[40] However, dressage also suggests an ambiguity in relation to a strict disciplinary notion of training, as in Lefebvre's account it may also involve the initiative and actions of individuals.[41] Dressage suggests scope for adaptation; that training potentially may blur into practice.

The ambiguous role of adaptation in digital games suggests that while they support myriad forms of practice, that they also constitute a form of training because of the important status that activities strongly associated with game play—like collaboration, interactivity, participation, and productive consumption—have in contemporary society. Each of these concepts—adaptation, compulsion, dressage—are examined in the following section, focusing on the tension and ambiguity that arises between training and practice.

Compulsions

Digital game play is 'compulsive' for a variety of reasons; however, compulsion is not equivocal with addiction. Game addiction is a controversial notion that has acquired some attention in the past decade; in particular regarding the deaths in Wisconsin, USA of Shawn Woolley, an *EverQuest* player whose mother alleges committed suicide due to a tragedy that befell his character in the online game;[42] and Lee Seung Seop, who died after a fifty hour non-stop session of *StarCraft* and *World of Warcraft* at a internet café in Taegu, South Korea.[43] These examples illustrate situations where the gaming body breaks down into disparate rhythms, a state of arrhythmia caused by the cyclical rhythms of the body being subsumed in the linear rhythms of the digital game. Unhealthy and delinquent behavior have been associated with digital game play for a number of years. Loftus and Loftus' psychological study from 1983 discusses the link between obsessive digital game play, truancy, and petty crime. They concluded that while for some digital games brought out aberrant behavior, the vast majority of players used them responsibly.[44] Claims that digital games are addictive continue to emerge, for example the Smith and Jones Consultancy in Amsterdam, the Netherlands claims to be treating 'dozens' of game addicts as outpatients.[45] However, these pathological states, whether or not they are symptoms of addiction, are not examples of compulsions in Lefebvre's sense. Compulsion is distinct from 'addiction' as it is a typical part of the everyday, rather than a pathological state that interrupts its routine.

Computers and computer technology play a significant role in the system of compulsions that govern the contemporary epoch. Both Deleuze and Lefebvre have marked the computer as pivotal in extending the systems of control outside the individual institution to the organization of everyday life through a flexible system of control that without imposing strict boundaries on behavior establishes manageable patterns, channels, or flows that expand and shrink—a process that Deleuze describes as modulation—in relation to the particular pressures that are put upon them. Typical interactions with computers fall into a range of fields: work and of course, leisure (in which computers become increasingly important). Computers have also become integral to the increasingly growing period of compulsive time, which is neither work nor leisure: going to the bank, paying bills, making a phone call, buying clothes. All are processed and monitored through and with computers. Information technology is increasingly all-pervasive and is becoming ubiquitous in all facets of everyday life. This technology defines contemporary culture, variously described as the 'Networked', 'Information' 'Knowledge', or 'Hypercomplex' society.[46] While these concepts emphasis the significance of computer technology in contemporary culture by recognizing the strong relation between the two, they also allude to the power dynamic between individuals and machines that digital games reference allegorically.

Underlying the discussion of this power dynamic is the question: In the gaming body, are the linear rhythms of the digital game the dominant rhythm? The gaming body is polyrhythmic, composed of multiple rhythms of which the linear rhythm of the digital game forms just a part. However, the rhythm of the game is significant in relation to the notion of compulsion because the game is played as a process and interplay of reciprocal actions between player(s) and the computer(s), establishing an internal system of compulsions within the game, which must be accepted in order to play, and in many cases mastered in order to win. For Galloway the key to understanding digital game play is action. He emphasizes that: 'without the active participation of players and machines, digital games exist only as static computer code'.[47] In his analysis of digital games actions are divided into two categories, those made by the operator (player), and those made by the machine (computer).[48] In this configuration the driving force behind the actions in the game are the operator actions, machine actions are primarily to provide ambience, narrative, or enforce rules. The machine provides a space and structure for the actions but acts little itself. Galloway describes the cessation of operator actions as causing games to settle into meta-stable equilib-riums.[49]

This description works best with certain games that exemplify an ambient process—Galloway suggests *Shenmue*, *Ico*, and *Myst* —other gaming bodies fall apart into arrhythmia if the operator ceases to act. *Space Invaders* is an excellent example of the players' compulsion to act, as inac-tion on their part will lead to the games cessation, either due to rapid loss of 'lives' through alien missiles, or because the aliens advance to the bottom of the screen. Numerous contemporary games ascribe to this style of engagement, throwing the player in medias res and compelling them to act or be destroyed. Other games will cease play after a certain period of time regardless of the actions, or inactions, of the player. In the Kudos World Series mode of *Project Gotham Racing 2*, one of the challenges of the Coupe Series is a Timed Run through the Dawes Point Loop track in Sydney, Australia. On the bronze level of difficulty this means that the player must complete two circuits of the track in two minutes and five seconds, within this targeted time the player races against the clock, and a ghost car that shows their analogous position at that time during their previous fastest attempt. When the clock runs out, the Xbox takes control of the car and the race is over, in this case the computer enacts its own duration.

Most contemporary digital games include features such as save and pause that allow the player some distance from the immediacy of the compulsion to play, by offering them a chance to leave the game—more or less fleetingly—without losing any progress that they might have made. However, with the increasingly networked nature of digital games, and digital game cultures, it is difficult to offer such options in multiplayer, real-time situations. The increasing importance of networked gaming—both multi-sited and in particular locations—highlights the importance of moving beyond descriptions of player-machine interactions by examining the situated ecology of gaming to establish specific accounts of digital game play. Compulsions are further enhanced in this situation, by the increasing administrative role that player-developed networks play in online gaming that has produced an offline social dimension to gaming practices. In fact these networks in some cases have an overtly disciplinary role, Taylor demonstrates a variety of ways that guild hierarchies have used modding tools in *World of Warcraft* to enforce commitments about when and how to play, and punitive responses to breaches of these 'community' standards.[50] The ne-cessity of the players' action to enable the execution of the game, either through the demands of the linear rhythm of the game, or the community which has emerged from its play, establishes a dynamic where the player under a compulsion to act, and act in a certain way, to maintain the eurhythmia of the situated ecology.

Adaptations
In a control society characterized by the monitoring and management of everyday life, digital games have a pivotal role in negotiating compulsion and adaptation. Digital games demonstrate not only that the binary opposition of work and play are problematic in the control society, but that

the clear division between training and practice is also blurred. Digital games exemplify an ambivalence towards training and practice that amplifies the importance of the process of adaptation in the context of game play that reflects the centrality of adaptation in the control society. An ambiguity is highlighted in the slippage between the two categories: How does training become practice? And, conversely: how is practice a form of training? This situated approach to examining game play—which connects people, objects, places and ideas—provides a suitable framework for analysis of these slippages, which are highly dependent on the contexts of the cultures of use. This ambiguity is thoroughly imbricated in the process of adaptation to the control society and can be found in digital games earliest cultures of use.

The historic emergence of digital games is typically marked by either the development of *Tennis For Two*, by William Higinbotham or *Spacewar!* by Steve Russell and his colleagues at the Massachusetts Institute of Technology's Tech Model Railway Club. Without entering this debate, what is salient is that they are both examples of adaptation; as they turn the administrative, scientific, rational project of computation technology to the field of play.[51] Higinbotham, who worked on the Manhattan Project during World War Two, developed *Tennis for Two* as an exercise in public relations for the nuclear energy industry in the post-war period. Discouraged by visitors' nonplussed responses to the huge mainframe computers at Brookhaven National Laboratory's annual open day, he set out to write a program that allowed visitors to interact with the computer, utilizing its five-inch visual display screen. In an interview towards the end of his life he recalled: 'I knew from past visitors' days that people were not much interested in static exhibits... ...so for that year, I came up with an idea for a hands-on display—a video tennis game'.[52] This instance exemplifies the close ties between the origins of computers (and therefore computer games) in the Cold War military-industrial complex, which is so often stressed by scholars. However, Higinbotham's desire to give these massive machines—which in the 1950s were only accessible in the context of the military/industry complex—a 'friendly' interface is a case of adaptation in the face of compulsion, the carving out of practice from necessity. As a field of endeavor, the technological development of digital games was an unexpected consequence that arose from Higinbotham's (and others) attempts to humanize computers.

Spacewar! grew out of an educational environment—the Massachusetts Institute of Technology—although rooted in quasi-military program modeling space flight.[53] J. M. Graetz describes how it was produced by a collective of academics and technicians working with computers, and was approached as a puzzle or challenge that they solved over a number of years. Graetz foreshadows his discussion of the technical process of developing the game by emphasizing the influence of Dr. Edward E. Smith's science fiction series *The Lensmen* on Steve Russell and himself when they were conceptualizing the game that eventually became *Spacewar!*[54] Academics, students and technical workers transformed their compulsive time, the time spent at the computer screen working; and the computer, the dominant tool of the control society, into the (playful) production of play, and eventually to play itself. The process was not only guided by the needs of the emerging discipline of computer science, nor by the challenge of simulating spaceflight, but also as Myers has noted, by the demands of entertainment.[55] Adherence to the principles of simulation was moderated in favor of producing a 'fun' experience that was as concerned with capturing the spirit of the pulp science fiction of 'Doc' Smith as it was with the technical problems of zero gravity propulsion.

Both *Tennis for Two* and *Spacewar!* were widely distributed across the fledgling APRANET, where they became a part of computer culture, along with other early games like *ADVENT* and *Hamurabi.*[56] As they were distributed through various institutions using a variety of hardware, different individuals and groups adjusted and optimized the games for their particular situations, and were inspired to develop their own versions of the games, or to devise completely new games based on their own predilections, or on difficult programming problems or challenges that they wished to solve. Playing digital games in this early phase of the development of the medium often led to play with the game. Rosenberg describes his experience of playing a version of *Hamurabi* in 1975, stating:

> Within a couple of days of play I'd exhausted the game's possibilities. But unlike most of the games that captivate teenagers today, *Sumer* [the version of *Hamurabi*] invited tinkering. An yone could inspect its insides: The game was a set of simple instructions to the computer, stored on a paper tape coded with little rows of eight holes. (The confetti that accumulated in a plastic tray on the teletype's side provided nearly as much fun as the game.) It had somehow landed among my group of friends like a kind of frivolous samizdat, and we shared it without a second thought. Modifying it was almost as easy as playing it if you took the couple of hours required to learn simple Basic: You just loaded the tape's instructions into the computer and started adding lines to the program.

> *Sumer* was a blank canvas — history in the raw, ready to be molded by teenage imaginations. My friends and I took its simple structure and began building additions. Let's have players choose different religions! What if we throw in an occasional bubonic plague? Barbarian invaders would be cool. Hey, what about catapults?[57]

Rosenberg's experience occurred against a background of the commercialization of computer-mediated play—the birth of the contemporary digital game—that occurred during the seventies. The first commercially available game, *Computer Space*, released in 1971 in the form of what is now commonly known as an arcade game, was in fact a dedicated version of *Spacewar!*. A year later, in 1972, the first privately owned digital game consoles the Magnavox Odyssey came with a version of *Tennis for Two*, called *Tennis*. The Magnavox game was widely copied, famously by Atari in the form of *PONG*.[58] However, legal proceedings were instituted by Magnavox to obtain licensing fees from Atari, and various other companies that had produced *Tennis for Two* clones. Magnavox's right to royalties as creator of the game endured even in a challenge by Nintendo in 1985, which argued and demonstrated in court that Higinbotham was the original creator.[59] In the process of shifting from adaptations to, to products of, the society of control; the collaborative, creative, experimental and innovative elements of digital games were challenged by attempts to establish digital games as discreet proprietary objects.

There has been a long history of the digital games industry turning to the creative practices of players to develop new forms of commodification. This is exemplified by 'modding', which Julian Kücklich describes as gaming's quintessential act.[60] Modding typically refers to the practice of players' developing and distributing their own versions of commercial games. First done only at a small scale, the practice took on a new significant in the 1990s following the open source release of various graphics files for *Doom*. This coup by id software secured the value, success and longevity of their product, because the players' could continue to generate and through the rapidly increasing scale of the internet, distribute new content for the game. By the end of the decade a new phenomenon had emerged: *Counter-Strike* is a multiplayer, team-based mod of a successful single player game *Half-Life*. Developed by two North American university students—Minh Le and Jeff Cliffe—the mod was successfully acquired by *Half-Life*'s developers Valve Software, and published for PC and Xbox. As a commercial release it sold over 550,000 units, despite having been made available for free on the internet since June 12, 1999 by its original developers.[61]

The status of digital games as adaptations of the technology of the society of control is currently eclipsed by the more pervasive re-adaptation of digital games into the system of compulsion. Lefebvre acknowledges that the process of adaptation involves transforming compulsions into products.[62] By adapting computers to play, new products were formed, which allowed the digital game to be rapidly reabsorbed into the system of capital. The system puts constraints on the types of experiences of play that are developed, as shareholders and corporate investors demand high returns on their investments. Adaptation remains, but it is either incorporated into the system of capital, like *Counter-Strike* or directed into increasingly defined, jejune, and non-threatening activities, like avatar design in *Demon's Souls*. By making practice a necessary part of play, adaptation is re-conceptualized as a new form of compulsion, which further amplifies the ambiguity between training and practice.

Lefebvre, in his celebration of the role of play and games in restoring the balance between adaptation and compulsion notes that there is a danger that creative experiences may be turned into ones that are passive, or escapist, which are compulsions rather than adaptations.[63] The digital game industry is in a position where it can mount a similar threat to play, as it moves to domesticate practices established through creative cultures of use by channeling practice into areas from which they can profit. Galloway's, concepts of protocol and algorithmic culture demonstrate the adaptive functions of the control society.[64] While Galloway and Thacker suggest that there are still modes of operation that avoid this totalization.[65] The threat to the practices that emerge within, and tangentially from, digital game play is that the act of modulation absorbs all emergent creative acts and redirects them within the systems of control. This inverts Lefebvre's notion of adaptation, shifting it away from the notion of style through individual creative acts that are carved out of times and spaces that are characterized by necessity.

Dressage
Imbricated in this movement between compulsion and adaptation is the notion of training, or dressage. Kinder maintains that digital games acclimatize children to interactivity in other mediums, they: 'help prepare young players for full participation in this new age of interactive multimedia—specifically, *by linking interactivity with consumerism*'.[66] This argument has been made in numerous other contexts, by other commentators, including Ronald Reagan, who believed that digital games would be effective in training a new generation of warriors.[67] This point is explored extensively by Halter, starting with the use of the digital game *America's Army* by the US army as a recruiting tool, and then proceeds to trace the role that the military has had in the development of the digital game industry.[68] Kline et al., have argued at length that this connection has had a serious impact on the types of experiences that are provided in commercial digital game play.[69]

However, while there is a pedagogical frame which insinuates players into an environment which both links consumption with freedom and choice and naturalizes play as a commodity; it is also important to acknowledge that players' responses to this are varied, and include a variety of capacities: cooperation, either thorough sharing knowledge or other forms of reciprocal exchange like item trading, real money trading or leeching; as well as creative acts and inventions, like Machinima, mods, game art, even new maps, objects, or skin designs, which may be distributed and used on individual and collective scales.

Training or, as Lefebvre prefers, dressage, is not education. It is not about specific content, but acts on the level of attitude and initiative.[70] Lefebvre describes it as the process of human breaking themselves in; being trained in how to hold their body, move, gesticulate. Dressage is based on repetition.[71] It has its own rhythms, and the trained body is produced through imbrication in rhythms. What does a digital game train people to do? They train people in the rhythms (timings, movements, patterns, positions) of digital games, in the gestures, and postures appropriate to play. The player becomes familiar with watching the screen, but—unlike the television viewer, who is frequently distracted—with a type of intensity that reflects a high stakes engagement. Manipulating and acting upon objects on the screen, and crucially regarding the screen as something that may be acted upon, becomes second nature. The player becomes familiar with sitting in front of the screen for hours on end. Taken together this produces a situation akin to what Manovich describes as the 'cybernetic workplace'. He characterizes this contemporary workspace as a constant engagement with overwhelming amounts of information, establishing 'a constant cascade of cognitive shocks that require immediate interventions', which he explicitly compares to the playing of a digital game.[72] For Manovich the rhythms of play are similar to the rhythms of work. This eurhythmia between work and play foregrounds the role of digital game play as a site of training for work in the knowledge economy, not necessarily in direct application, but in terms of approach, attitude, initiative, and procedure.

Many approaches to play annex or subordinate it to work. The binary division of the times and places of work and play, may be broken and blurred by the shift to the control society, but work still is the dominant force, but the role of creativity in the economy is increasingly acknowledged and exploited. Play does not disrupt work. Rather, it segues into it, opening a pathway that invigorates work with a sense of creativity, intensity, liveliness, and purpose. Friedrich Nietzsche encapsulates this movement with this maxim: 'Mature manhood: that means to have rediscovered the seriousness one had as a child at play'.[73] To understand play in this way is, in the framework of rhythmanalysis, to suggest the rhythm of play exists in a comfortable eurhythmia with the overarching rhythm of work. Computers are central in facilitating the smoothness of this shift. Digital games have emerged as an adaptation of computer technology, and that adaptation is reincorporated into the system of capital. If play is annexed to work, then this oscillation is an example of eurhythmia, or in the terms of society of control, modulation. Adaptations are channeled into pathways that ensure their smooth transition into productive practices by nurturing strong institutional awareness of the practices of digital game players, in order to produce new commodities or forms of commodification out of their adaptive practices.

Conclusion
Digital game play must be construed in a wider context. By focusing on the centrality of the body

in the enactment of play it is possible to trace the activity across a wider network of affordances and constraints. This challenges the smoothness of concepts like cybernetic subjectivity and algorithmic culture that rely on understandings of digital game play that do not attempt to account for situated gaming. The measure of digital games training, and creative, currents should also be considered in relation to the situated ecology of play; the assemblages—both virtual and material—that are constructed, or otherwise arranged, by players in order to produce play.

Lefebvre's three concepts of adaptation, compulsion, and dressage provide a useful framework for thinking through the tension between training and practice in the digital game ecology. The gaming body oscillates between adaptation (practice) and compulsion (training), but is always subject to dressage, making the question of practice and innovation profoundly ambiguous.

Notes

1 Amis, M. (1982). *Invasion of Space Invaders: An Addict's Guide to Battle Tactics, Big Scores and the Best Machines*. Hutchinson: London: p.57.

2 Amis, *Invasion of Space Invaders*: p. 29.

3 Amis, *Invasion of Space Invaders*: p. 29.

4 King, G. and Kryzwinska, T. (2002). 'Introduction'. In G. King and T. Krzywinska (eds.). *ScreenPlay: Cinema/videogames/interfaces*. London: Wallflower Press: pp. 26-27.

5 Morris, S. (2002). 'First-person Shooters – A Game Apparatus'. In G. King and T. Krzywinska (eds.). *ScreenPlay: Cinema/videogames/interfaces*. London: Wallflower: pp. 84-85.

6 Yates, S. J. and Littleton, K. (2001). 'Understanding Computer Game Cultures: A Situated Approach'. In E. Green and A. Adam (eds.). *Virtual Gender: Technology, Consumption and Identity*. London: Routledge: p. 120.

7 Taylor, T. L. (2006). *Play Between Worlds: Exploring Online Game Culture*. Cambridge: The MIT Press: p. 156.

8 Crogan, P. (2004a). 'Games, Simulation and Serious Fun: An Interview with Espen Aarseth'. *Scan: Journal of Media Arts Culture* 1.1.

9 Satre, J-P. (1965). *Situations*. Greenwich: Fawcett Publications.

10 Jappe, A. (1993). *Guy Debord*. Berkeley, University of California Press: p. 149.

11 Rodriguez, H. (2006). 'The Playful and the Serious: An Spproximation to Huizinga's Homo Ludens'. *Game Studies: the International Journal of Computer Game Research* 6.1.

12 Laso, P. W. (2007). 'Games of Pain: Pain as Haptic Stimulation in Computer-game-based Media Art'. *LEONARDO* 40.3: p. 239.

13 Laso, 'Games of Pain': p. 240.

14 See: Chesher, C. (2004). 'Neither a Gaze Nor a Glance, but a Glaze: Relating to Console Game Screens'. *Scan: A Journal of Media Arts Culture* 1.1: p. 5; and Galloway, A. (2007). 'StarCraft, or, Balance'. *Grey Room* 28: p.87.

15 Wood, J. (2001). 'Images in Paediatric Medicine: The "How!" sign – a Central Palmar Blister'. *Archives of Disease in Childhood* 84.4: p. 288.

16 Warren, J. (2006) 'A Wii Workout: When Videogames Hurt'. *The Wall Street Journal*.

17 Lefebvre, H. (2004). *Rhythmanalysis: Space, Time and Everyday Life*. London: Continuum: pp. 12 and 15.

18 *South Park*, season 10, episode 8.

19 Bahktin, M. (1984). *Rabelais and His World*. Bloomington: Indiana University Press.

20 Flynn, B. (2003). 'Geographies of the Digital Hearth'. *Information, Communication and Society* 6.4: p. 571.
21 Flynn, 'Geographies of the Digital Hearth': p. 559.
22 Lefebvre, H. (1984). *Everyday Life in the Modern World*. New Brunswick: Transaction Books: p. 54.
23 Lefebvre, *Rhythmanalysis*: p. 23.
24 Lefebvre, *Rhythmanalysis*: p. 16.
25 In most MMORPGs this kind of cooperative large-scale action is called a 'raid'.
26 In the context of *World of Warcraft* (and its expansions) a talent is an ability that a character acquires when they achieve a new level. The player has some flexibility in choosing their characters' talents, which are organized according to class, and advance in a hierarchal fashion (e.g. talent x must be acquired before talent y may be acquired). The system of talents provides a further method of establishing distinction between characters.
27 The Café had no official name like many other such cafés in Venezuela, but it was referred to be the owner and employees as 'Cybercafé Avila'.
28 Marx, K. (1977). *Capital, vol. 1*. New York: Vintage: p. 548.
29 Benjamin, W. (2003). *Selected Writings, vol. 4, 1938-1940* (eds. H. Eiland and M. W. Jennings). Cambridge: Bellknap Press.
30 Marx, *Capital*: p. 548. Also, in Harvey's (1990: p. 105) commentary on Marx he suggests that for Marx the factory laborer was reduced to a mere appendage of the machine.
31 Benjamin, *Selected Writings*: p. 321. Emphasis added.
32 Lefebvre, *Everyday Life in the Modern World*: p. 53.
33 Lefebvre, *Everyday Life in the Modern World*: pp. 89 and 159.
34 Lefebvre, *Everyday Life in the Modern World*: p. 24.
35 de Certeau, M. (1984). *The Practice of Everyday Life*. Berkeley: University of California Press: pp. 24-28. Original emphasis. De Certeau (1984: 25, original emphasis) writes: 'La perruque may be as simple a matter as a secretary's writing a love letter on "company time" or as complex as a cabinetmaker's "borrowing" a lathe to make a piece of furniture for his living room'.
36 Lefebvre, *Everyday Life in the Modern World*: p. 87.
37 Lefebvre, *Rhythmanalysis*: p. 40.
38 Foucault, M. (1995). *Discipline and Punish: The Birth of the Prison*. New York: Vintage Books: pp. 136-137.
39 Foucault, *Discipline and Punish*, pp 131-144.
40 Lyon's (1994) work on how cotemporary surveillance exemplifies and amplifies Foucault's (1995) notion of the panopticon is demonstrates one way in which everyday life is disciplined outside of institutions.
41 Lefebvre, *Rhythmanalysis*: p. 40.
42 'Addicted: Suicide Over Everquest? Was he Obsessed?' (2002). *CBS News*.
43 Naughton, P. (2005). 'Korean Drops Dead After 50-hour Gaming Marathon'. *Times Online*.
44 Loftus, G. R. and Loftus, E. F. (1983). *Mind at Play: The Psychology of Video Games*. New York: Basic Books: pp. 109-110.
45 Coughlan, S. (2006). 'Just One More'. *BBC News Magazine*.
46 Networked society originates from Castells (1995); Hypercomplex society from Qvortrup (2003), the use of 'knowledge' and 'information' has become standard. All gesture towards Touraine's (1969/1971) concept of the post-industrial society.

47 Galloway, A. (2006). *Gaming: Essays on Algorithmic Culture*. Minneapolis: University of Minnesota Press: p. 2.

48 *Galloway, Gaming*: p. 5.

49 *Galloway, Gaming*: pp. 10-11.

50 Taylor, T. L. (2006b). 'Does WoW Change Everything? How a PvP Server, Multinational Player Base, and Surveillance Mod Scene Caused Me Pause'. *Games and Culture* 1.4: pp. 318-337.

51 For descriptions of the development of *Tennis for Two* and *SpaceWar!*, see: Burnham, V. (2001). *Supercade: A Visual History of the Videogame Age 1971-1984*. Cambridge: MIT Press.

52 Burnham, V. (2001). *Supercade: A Visual History of the Videogame Age 1971-1984*. Cambridge: MIT Press: p. 28. See also Mäyrä (2008: pp. 40-41), for an account of the development of *Tennis for Two*.

53 Myers, D. (2003). *The Nature of Computer Games: Play as Semiosis*. New York: Peter Lang: p. 4.

54 Graetz, J. M. (2001). 'The origin of Spacewar!'. In V. Burnham (ed.). *Supercade: A visual history of the videogame age 1971-1984*. Cambridge: The MIT Press: p. 42. See also: Kline, S., Dyer-Witheford, N., and de Peuter, G. (2003). *Digital\Play: The Intersection of Culture, Technology, and Marketing*. Montreal and Kingston: McGill-Queen's University Press: p. 89.

55 Myers, *The Nature of Computer Games*: p. 7.

56 Myers, *The Nature of Computer Games*: pp. 10-13.

57 Rosenberg, S. (2007). *Dreaming in Code: Two Dozen Programmers, Three Years, 4,732 Bugs and One Quest for Transcendent Software*. New York: Crown: pp. 1-2.

58 Kent, S. L. (2000). *The First Quarter: A 25 year History of Video Games*. Bothell: BWD Press: pp. 37-38.

59 Baer, R. (n.d.). 'Pong: Who did it first?'. In *PONG-Story*.

60 Kücklich, J. (2005). 'Precarious Playbour: Modders and the Digital Games Industry'. *The Fibreculture Journal 5*.

61 Keisler, J. (2007). 'The Top 100 PC Games of the 21st Century'. *Next-Generation: Interactive Entertainment Today*.

62 Lefebvre, *Everyday Life in the Modern World*: p. 88.

63 Lefebvre, *Everyday Life in the Modern World*: p.191.

64 Galloway, A. (2004). *Protocol: How Control Exists After Decentralization*. Cambridge: MIT Press; and Galloway, Gaming.

65 Galloway, A. and Thacker, E. (2007). *The Exploit: A Theory of Networks*. Minneapolis: University of Minnesota Press.

66 Kinder, M. (1991). *Playing with Power In Television and Videogames: From Teenage Mutant Ninja Turtles to Muppet Babies*. Berkeley: University of California Press: p. 6. Emphasis added.

67 The tendency for the experiment spaces of new digital media to be subjected to increasing regulation, and be redefined as commercial is discussed in: Benkler (2006); McChesney, (1999); Mosco (1997); Schiller (2000); and Terranova (2004).

68 Halter, E. (2006). *From Sun-Tzu to Xbox: War and Video Games*. New York: Thunder Mouth Press.

69 Kline et al., *Digital\Play*.

70 Lefebvre, *Rhythmanalysis*: p. 40.

71 Lefebvre, *Rhythmanalysis*: p. 39.

72 Manovich, L. (1996). 'The Labour of Perception'. In L. Hershman-Leeson (ed.). *Clicking In: Hot*

Links to a Digital Culture. Seattle: Bay Press: p. 185.
73 Nietzsche, F. (2003). *Beyond Good and Evil: Prelude to the Philosophy of the Future.* London: Penguin: p. 94.

CHAPTER THREE
SITUATED ECOLOGIES

> In the software, the global meets the local, as the games must of necessity be played by real people, in actual locations, using specific hardware—Mia Consalvo.[1]

This chapter begins a discussion of the ethnographic research that I undertook in Melbourne, Australia and Caracas, Venezuela between March 2005 and January 2006. These case studies illustrate the specificity of the digital game ecology and importance, of everyday life at the local level in shaping the experience of play. The two case studies stand only for themselves, any other two locations would have characteristics that are just as specific. The reason that the case studies are used, is to demonstrate that despite the specificity of the situated ecology in which individual instantiations of play take place, that the cultures of use that emerge share similar qualities which establish connections between otherwise disparate locations. This chapter describes the two situated ecologies, beginning with an account of the significance of the ethnographic method and how it was deployed. It then proceeds by providing a background of wider issues relating to media regulation, consumption, and production in the two locations. However, the latter—and larger—part of the chapter is devoted to describing the situated ecologies of Cybercafé Avila, in Caracas, and Cydus in Melbourne.

Method

I will start at the situation—the gaming situation—this entirely specific ecotone where the rhythms of everyday life and the rhythms of gaming overlap. Within this very specific overlap the gaming situation is highly heterogeneous supporting a wide variety of forms of digital game play that, according to the particulars of the situation, may be more robustly shaped by everyday life or the rhythm of gaming. Research on digital game play that takes account of the context of play should be informed by this heterogeneity. Recently, a number of scholars working with digital games have argued that a better understanding of digital game play can be garnered through the use of ethnography.[2] An ethnographic approach to digital game play, while not without its own set of problems, avoids the pitfalls of the 'cybernetic subjectivity' model of game analysis, and importantly examines games in their context, the everyday lives of the players.

The purpose of using ethnography to analyze digital games is to understand games as more than the hermeneutic objects that are played (and analyzed) in isolation. A situated ethnography of the digital game ecology—the meeting place of the rhythms of everyday life and digital game play—underscores the embeddedness of digital games in, and their dynamic relations with, the everyday. The ethnographic approach accounts for and examines the messiness and complications of the gaming situation, rather than ignoring it. This move away from a hermeneutic understanding of the player/game (or machine/operator) dynamic is the bottom line of 'situated gaming'.

The situated model of game analysis is in dialogue with models of digital game play that subsume play in discussions of control, like those of Galloway. The work of these scholars is an important critique of shallow emancipatory discussions of the 'potential' of digital games. The situated approach builds upon, and suggests that digital games have a particular, ambiguous relationship to the notion of control. The understanding of play as exemplary of algorithmic culture focuses on the interactions of a person with code is rather different from that of situated gaming; which perceives the gaming body within a web of connections to both the global and virtual that is grounded in the specificity of the local.

A key commitment of situated gaming is to examine the exercise of practice—creativity, innovation—in relation to imposed constraints. This chapter (and the he two following) illustrate how the situated approach provides a methodology that can register moments where such exercises occur. By shifting the object of study to digital games specific context in the everyday lives of their players', situated gaming is able to take a more nuanced approach; rather than conceptualizing digital games solely as an apparatus of control through the modulation of algorithms, it also explores play, the localized enactment of the game, as a process that demonstrates the possibilities of its own re-appropriation.

On the use of ethnography by digital games scholars, Williams remarks: 'ethnography should be a rigorous and systematic exercise and not the overused buzzword that substitutes for haphazard participant observation'.[3] This caveat is pertinent; but I do not advocate an approach that takes rigor so seriously that it is overly proscriptive. An ethnographic examination of play must retain its rigor whilst still capturing something of the spontaneity of play. In order to do this I went to the site of play, and engaged in play while also observing others engaged in the same activity. This is what people in public gaming spaces do anyway (minus the notebook). Then later interviewed some of the people that I observed playing digital games, five interviews—one a group interview—in Caracas, and six in Melbourne. The approach had certain benefits, and also certain limitations. By using participant observation 'the centerpiece of any truly ethnographic approach',[4] with supporting interviews, the data gathered was triangulated; but the primary benefit of this method is that it is live and dynamic. There was no preconceived notion of what kinds of participant observations would occur in the internet cafes I visited, until I got there and began observing what was happening. The interview subjects were selected from the people who were involved in what was observed who were also willing to be interviewed.

The main limitation of the situated approach is being able to draw out the specificities of the individual situated ecologies and make wider connections between the local and global, and the multiple localities of play. Cybercafé Avila was just one internet café in Caracas, ten minutes walk away at another internet café in the basement of Centro Parque Caracas everyone was playing *MU Online* when I wandered in looking for a place to do some photocopying. The specificity of these individual ecologies does not mean that there is nothing in common between them. Chapters four and five demonstrate through rhythmanalysis how tangible connections can be drawn between the two case study locations, while chapters six, seven, and eight discuss the ramifications and stakes of these connections.

Another limitation of ethnographic research is that the researcher inevitably impacts on the situation that is studied. This was more the case in Venezuela than Australia. In the latter case I blended in because I was "just another" New Zealander, but in Venezuela my English-speaking background meant I was often noticed and singled out; I could not avoid being a part of the situated ecology of the café, and I was often drawn into assisting in producing game play, by being asked to translate the gist of an English FAQ or strategy guide to Spanish, engaging in LAN games of *Counter-Strike* or *Medieval: Total War,* or blocking El Bebe's line of sight so that he couldn't cheat. But that is the point of using the notion of situated ecology: that people and things are drawn into individual acts of gaming to produce an experience that cannot be explained just by talking about algorithms, code, or protocols.

Background

Australia and Venezuela provide this discussion with remarkably different contexts of digital game consumption. This section focuses on the specificity of the contexts of the two digital game ecologies examined. But before I can delve into the specificities, it is necessary to establish a broader picture of the common pressures affecting these particular situations. The local situations are not mandated by global pressures, but rather by a peculiar percolation, mixture and negotiation of local and global demands. Australia and Venezuela are both unique countries with complex cultures and histories that are impossible to cover in extensive detail. This is also the case regarding the specificities of the metropolises of Caracas and Melbourne. This section briefly covers information that is particularly relevant as a basis for understanding the wider media ecology in each location, before moving to discussions of the individual internet cafés.

A situated ecology is one of any number of points in a digital game ecology where local rhythms of everyday life and the global rhythm of gaming produce eurhythmia. The term refers specifically to a point of interaction between the two ecologies: the global and virtual ecology of gaming, and the material conditions of the local. While the two situations discussed here are different, in many respects they are linked through the wider ecology of gaming. Nevertheless, the experience of digital game play in the two locations is significantly different. Game software like *Grand Theft Auto: San Andreas* is not played in the same way irrespective of location. The notion of situated ecology traces the material, virtual, and social currents that intermesh to produce situations where play is possible.

Digital game play in the two locations has substantially different stakes. This is based on unavoidable material conditions that establish key differentiations between the two situations examined. The context in which computers and the internet generally, and domestic and hand held consoles more specifically, are used in Australia is very different from Venezuela. Australia has one of the highest levels of internet access in the world, at 79.4% in June 2008 according the most recent Neilson ratings; while in Venezuela according to Conatel (Comisión Nacionale de Telecomunicaciones), in July 2008 only 24% of the population have access to the internet.[5] Furthermore, in Australia many households have a computer with dial-up or broad-band internet access, whilst many Venezuelans use privately owned, semi-public internet cafés—the most recent available statistics from the Worldbank in 2002—show that less than one in five Venezuelan households had domestic access to the internet.[6] There are also businesses in Australia that offer similar services to Venezuelan internet cafés, and people use them for a variety of reasons—they are traveling, need a fast connection, or because they want to use more than one computer—but usually not because it is their *only* option, as is the case for the majority of the population in Venezuela. This difference in the status of the internet café as a point of access to wider global culture through the internet demarcates the widely uneven stakes of digital game play between Venezuela and Australia.

Research that focuses on what is at stake in the public consumption of digital games in arcades, cafes, and various other contexts has indicated that it has strong consequences for even participation between genders.[7] Public consumption made it difficult for new players, particularly girls, to engage with games and gaming culture, largely because the spaces in which gaming takes place are male dominated spaces.[8] Thus, Cunningham argues that domestic console-based play is essential to create a niche—outside of the male dominated space of the public arcades—in which girls were able to explore digital games.[9] She also succinctly qualifies the stakes of their inclusion: 'it is vital that girls are included in these arenas where familiarity with new technology is established'.[10] In the case of Venezuela, this problem of exclusion is magnified as more gaming takes place in public. Console-based domestic play is not so readily available, so only girls and women who were inclined to participate in gaming in public are able to participate at all. Women and girl game players were clearly visible in Caracas; in fact the most visible example of digital games being played—as opposed to the ubiquity of the games themselves, as pirated copies in street stalls—were the numerous, mainly female, cashiers who would have *Solitaire*, open on their screen, and play it in-between serving customers. But in the internet cafés the girls and women playing would generally defer expertise to male players.

Venezuela's peculiar global status also impacts on the stakes on local digital game play. Since Hugo Chávez assumed the role of President of Venezuela in 1998 and implemented the *Revolucion Bolivariana*, he has become a prominent and controversial figure. He has spoken out against globalization, and US-Imperialism in Latin America and the Caribbean, on numerous occasions. Fitting this rhetoric, there have also been several policy moves by his government to challenge what they perceive as the pro-United States and anti-*Revolucion Bolivariana* stance of global and local media outlets operating in Venezuela. Chávez has acted to strengthen Latin America's region position as a producer of its own news media by organizing with the governments of Argentina, Cuba and Uruguay a strong regional Pan-Latino news network along the lines of al-Jazeera.[11] The resulting channel, teleSUR, is widely perceived in the USA as being a propaganda tool for Chávez, used to export the *Revolucion Bolivariana* across Latin America.[12] This investment in regional media infrastructure has been accompanied by a rigorous policy to roll back foreign control.

A policy of nationalization was introduced following Chávez's re-election in December 2006. Directly after the victory, plans to nationalize the country's telecommunications industries were announced.[13] The implementation of this policy has important consequences for the future of internet use and access in the country. The move to return the telecommunications industry to state control has been accompanied by a general crackdown on private media providers in Venezuela. Legislation that gives the government tighter control over television stations was introduced after Chávez won the 2004 recall referendum.[14] Since he has been in power the news media had become the de facto opposition.[15] The matter was brought to a head when local private television channels played a pivotal role in the temporary coup of April 2002.[16] Their refusal to broadcast Chávez's message to the people of Venezuela during the crisis,[17] was the final straw for the government, who began to impose severe penalties on media outlets that displeased them.[18] This environment of persecution culminated in the refusal to renew the broadcasting license for Radio Caracas Television—Venezuela's oldest private television channel—that expired March 2007.[19] This news was met by widespread protests in Venezuela, and attracted negative criticism from overseas, including a resolution condemning the closure from the US Senate.[20] The current conditions for media industries in Venezuela remains uneasy, however, much of the conflict has been focused on traditional news media channels and until recently, digital games have attracted little controversy.[21]

In contrast, the Australian media industries have become used to a more laisse-faire approach to regulation. Policy has shifted focus from a nationally oriented culture industry with only limited participation by private industry, to a conceptualization of the region's media industries as creative industries with a potentially global reach. The consolidation of the Film Finance Corporation Australia, the Australian Film Commission and Film Australia into Screen Australia in 2008 is an example of this new approach. However, the federal government still funds two national television and radio corporations (SBS and the ABC). The state-funded and commercial media outlets are both regulated by licensing conditions; including Australian Content Standards that dictate that 55% of the programming content between 6am and midnight must be produced in Australia.[22]

The general public may only purchase digital games, like other media content, after the Federal Office for Classification of Film and Literature (OCFL) has classified them. Unlike Venezuela, Australia has also fostered a small, yet growing, noteworthy digital game industry. The highlight of the locally produced games acknowledged by the Game Developers Association of Australia annual awards in 2009 was the iPhone title *Flight Control* by Melbourne-based Firemint; other Australian-made award winners were *Heroes Over Europe* and *PuzzleQuest Galactrix*. Many other locally owned companies operate in Australia, often within a specialty niche: Melbourne-based Tantalus Interactive focuses mainly on recoding games for hand held consoles; Transmission Games, also based in Melbourne has produced several localized versions of sports games; while Sydney-based Strategic Studies Group produces complex strategic war games. Overall, the digital game industry in Australia has met with some degree of success in the global market.

The Australian digital games industry's modest success is a major contrast between the two situated ecologies, and highlights unevenness in the digital game ecology. The major difference between the two situations being because of its largely unofficial status play in Venezuela remains play, while in Australia play may potentially become work. What is at stake in this difference will be discussed further in chapters six and seven.

Cybercafé Avila

The Venezuelan site of study is a small internet café in the capital city, Caracas. Cybercafé Avila is located on Avenida Avila, about two hundred meters south of the intersection with Avenida Galipan, a busy street heavily used by commuters and public transport. This section of Avenida Avila is almost entirely residential, with a mixture of large apartment buildings, smaller apartment buildings, and single and double story houses. The view up the street to the north is dominated by El Avila, the mountain that overlooks Caracas, and gives the street its name. To the south are the busy commercial districts of San Bernardino and La Candelaria, both of which are parts of

Libertador, a municipal division of the Federal District of Caracas. This part of San Bernardino was once a thriving middle-class district, characterized by wide mango-tree lined avenues and numerous open-air cafés and restaurants. European immigrants settled San Bernardino after World War Two, but the post war generation of prosperity has—like much of Venezuela since the 1980s—given way to urban decay, which is fueled by the districts proximity to several barrios or shantytowns.[23] Still one step away from poverty, the district is inhabited by a declining minority of European families, mostly from Portugal and Italy who live in the houses that their families had built in the district, and by the new generation of immigrants: some drawn to Caracas from the rural and provincial areas of Venezuela; but also first generation Columbian, Cuban, and Ecuadorian immigrants; and more recent immigrants from Haiti, and the Arab world.

Two factors were crucial in the decision to conduct ethnographic research in on digital game play in Venezuela. First, Venezuela was then, and is now an outsider from US-dominated global politics, suggesting that media products there would be received and contextualized in a rather different manner, from elsewhere. I recall strolling through Centro Comercial Tolón and noticing that the digital games shop there was called "The American Shop"; incongruous with this understanding of digital games was the painting of Nintendo's iconic Mario that also adorned the sign and the group of men outside the shop playing *FIFA Football 2004* on a Nintendo GameCube. Second, was that I had family—or rather my ex-wife's family—that could provide me with a place to stay, advice, and guidance; a primary concern for conducting research in an dangerous urban location like Caracas. The selection of Cybercafé Avila was made on the basis of its normalcy, and on its proximity to my apartment in San Bernardino. While several large LAN cafés were located in nearby La Candelaria, the typical internet café in Caracas was a small family-run affair, like Cybercafé Avila. The cafés usually just catered to the people in their neighborhood, and were thus located all over the city. As Cybercafé Avila was the internet café that was the closest in my neighborhood, my neighbors, and the other residents of my apartment building also frequented it.

The café is part of a building called Edificio Hilda that consists of two wings surrounding a central courtyard. The courtyard is separated from the street by an iron barred security door topped with barbed wire. The two wings on either side of the courtyard are accessed directly from the street and both have solid iron security doors. The northern wing has a street level entry but the other wing, where the internet café is located, is raised from ground level and requires ascent of three steps to enter the café. This means that the eye-level of a person standing outside the door is just above waist level with a person standing inside the room. Edificio Hilda is a boarding house, and the landlord of the boarding house rents out the two wings: the northern wing to a family, and the southern to Xavier (this and all othe names used throughout this book, are pseudonyms), a small businessman, who owns and operates Cybercafé Avila.

Figure 1. Exterior of Cybercafé Avila.

Xavier was assisted full-time by Maxim, a free-lance photographer who also lived as a boarder in Edificio Hilda, and part-time by 'El Bebe' a youth from a nearby apartment complex who worked every day after school, and all day on the weekends. Several others also worked there temporarily, Xavier's son and daughter worked there during their school holidays, and another assistant, David was also hired and worked for almost two weeks, before having to return to Barquisimeto for family reasons.[24] From time to time, when El Bebe was unable to work and the café was busy, Xavier would hire one of the other regulars to assist him for several hours. During the opening hours of the café—approximately seven in the morning to seven at night—the café would contain up to four employees, and as many as twenty customers, who often shared computers, or were present only to purchase goods or services provided by the café rather than simply use one of the available computers.

A locked, iron-barred security door blocked the doorway to the café; to enter the customer had to ring a bell. The door was watched from the main counter through a web-cam. This level of security was typical for such a well-equipped café located in a moderately dangerous neighborhood, cafés in safer locations—especially inside malls—lacked such overt precautions, while others in the poorer areas of La Candelaria were watched over by a security guard. Usually the door was answered promptly, other times quite slowly; a negotiation was sometimes necessary between the various workers in the café as to the relative importance of the tasks that they were conducting, before it could actually be decided who should open the door. This negotiation was sometimes lengthy, and occasionally a customer would take pity on the person waiting and let them inside, especially if it was raining. Usually the task of opening the door was left to El Bebe, or if he was not working that day, to another youth that Xavier has hired to perform the task.

The twelve computers in the café were put to a wide variety of uses. Many people came to the café during the course of the week to conduct these activities: chat, emails, and surfing. Students from the local high schools, and universities also worked on assignments and homework at the café. Some local business people conducted aspects of their business in the café, often with assistance from staff, usually just emails, but also power-point presentations, and printing. It was also common for people to listen to music, and watch movie trailers and videos. Digital games were also popular; at many times during the course of a day they would be the main activity in the café. The computers were equipped with headphones so the main sound in the café came from the stereo, which usually played Latin music or Reggaetón from CDs that the staff had burnt. Occasionally people would unplug their headphones from the computer so that more than one person could listen. This practice, and other loud activities—especially boisterous smack talk—were frowned upon and usually quickly stopped by Xavier if he was working, as he was prone to headaches. When he was not working the other employees, particularly Maxim, would allow these activities to continue unchecked, and also turn the music up several levels; causing discomfort to some of the café's clientele, who would later complain to Xavier, causing tension between the two.

The café consists of one long narrow room with a concrete floor, walls and ceiling. Most of the room is painted white but some features such as pillars and beams are painted either adobe or blue, while the floor is painted red. There is a large television mounted on one wall, which was seldom on, except during high-profile baseball games. Xavier eventually borrowed a stereo from his parents, and hooked up the television to the stereo to play DVDs. When I began the four months of fieldwork at the café in late March 2005 the walls were decorated with posters of cars, a film poster for *8 Mile,* a *Counter-Strike* poster, and an advertisement for inkjet printers. After Xavier got a Pepsi fridge in the café, he added posters advertising Gatorade and Seven-up. Along both of the longer walls were six computers on cheap chipboard desks, each with a plastic chair in front of it. The screens faced away from the walls, apart from the two computers which were the farthest from the door to the street, which were at right angles to the other computers, facing away from the entry door. These two also had slightly larger desks. Directly behind these two computers was the counter where people came to pay, at which were stationed two printers—one color, the other black and white—and the server. Behind this desk was a rack with snacks and candy, a refrigerator containing soft drinks and yogurt, and a shelf full of various supplies for the café, including a large number of boxes filled with CD-ROMs. The back wall had a concertina door with the sign '*prohibito el paso*' which led into what had once been a bathroom, but was now used for storage, mainly of cleaning products.

Figure 2. Interior of Cybercafé Avila.

Like most internet cafés in Venezuela, Cybercafé Avila provided additional services associated with computer use mainly printing and the burning of CD-ROMs. Although in many cases, these services were temporarily unavailable because only some employees knew how to perform them. For Cybercafé Avila in particular, these services were the major part of their revenue, and a reason that they were able to remain open while other local cafés were closing in the face of the competitive environment created by development of larger LAN-gaming cafés in La Candelaria that offered cheaper hourly rates for computers. Usually the services were provided to individuals, but also several local businesses—including McDonalds—used the printing/publishing resources provided at the café. Xavier also hired himself and his employees out for simple computer related tasks. Often Maxim or El Bebe would briefly help people who were using more complicated programs like Photoshop. The café also served as a workshop, where neighborhood computers were repaired and upgraded. Xavier would often be involved in this task in one corner of the cramped room. The prices charged for the services varied, and a non-cash economy was also at work; for example, on one occasion Xavier was paid by having his breakfasts and lunches cooked for him for one week. Another local businessman made repairs to Xavier's car in return for an upgrade on his computer. The customers' computers would often be left in the café for a week or more, and if Xavier was in the process of upgrading one of the café's computers he would replace it with a customer's computer and link it to the LAN so that customers could use it. One such computer had been there so long it had become a permanent fixture of the café. As it had been there so long -- and Xavier was hesitant to upgrade it at his own expense -- it had become the slowest machine and consequently the least desirable for gamers, which meant that usually it was used for chatting and surfing.

and drinks. The cafés that were located in the more wealthy parts of town like Chacao and La Castellana actually served coffee and desserts. Cafés in other areas served only cold soft drinks (Bebidas), candy and potato chips. But some also sold assorted US-style donuts, and one that I visited several times also sold empanadas.[25] Cybercafé Avila sold drinks and snacks, which constituted a key part of the business. Getting food and drinks while at the internet café was both an integral part of the regulars' use of the café, and the main way that passersby used the café.

Internet cafés around Caracas had varying prices, usually related to their location and the quality of the computers provided. The local mall, Centro Comercial Galerias Avila, had three cafés, two that charged 2000 Bolivars (bs.) per hour, but were not focused on gaming, and one other that was oriented more towards gaming—having at least *MVP Baseball 2005* and *FIFA 2005*, installed on the computers—that charged 1900 bs. per hour.[26] Cybercafé Avila, located in the same neighborhood, but in a residential area charged at two set rates, 1200 bs. per hour for casual, and 1000 bs. per hour for members. Membership involved paying for at least five hours in advance, and receiving a login and password that meant that the member could use any free computer without involvement from the staff.

Cydus

In Melbourne, the site selected was Cydus, a medium sized internet café located close to the city's central commercial district. Situated across Victoria Street from the high-profile Victoria market, the café is proximate to many restaurants, bars, and backpacker-style tourist accommodation. Victoria Street is a tram route between the center of the city and the northern suburbs of Melbourne, as is Peel Street that intersects Victoria Street approximately fifty meters west of Cydus. This makes the area readily accessible from the city center, and from the student accommodation around the University of Melbourne to the north and east, as well as the gentrified 'hipster' suburb of North Melbourne that begins on the far side of Peel Street. This area has a high proportion of immigrants, predominantly Cantonese speaking.[27] Most of the buildings in this area are older, dating from the 19th or early 20th centuries, although there is substantial redevelopment nearby.

I selected Cydus, in part, because it was proximate to where I lived, worked, and studied (the John Medley Building at the University of Melbourne). It was one of a dozen or so possible cafés in the area, and I chose to do observations there specifically because it had a reputation for being a gaming café. Many of the other cafés in the area focused on providing services to university students and backpackers. Cydus was also relatively dark and anonymous, and it had comfortable chairs (which I was grateful for after my three-month stint at Cybercafé Avila).

Cydus is in two adjacent shop fronts, which are connected internally. Along with the other shops and businesses on their block, the footpath outside is covered by a protective awning from which hangs a sign that promotes Cydus. The café may be entered through either of the shop fronts, although often the door to the right hand shop front was closed unless it is very hot. Heavy curtains black out the windows of the right hand side. The left hand shop front has the main door, and the window affords a view into the room: the counter and the coke fridge, with the computers lined up behind them.

While conducting my fieldwork at Cydus between late November 2005 and February 2006, I was unable to reach the level of camaraderie with the staff that I had achieved at Cybercafé Avila. Mainly I suspect that this was because Cydus was a much busier café, with more patrons and fewer regulars. Also the staff that worked there did not work as many shifts as the workers at Cybercafé Avila. However, several of the staff were notable. Tony, who focused on giving the computers technical upgrades, would often stop to reminisce with customers about games. For example, he would solict comments on *Sid Meier's Civilization* IV, and then ask how it held up compared to *Sid Meier's Civilization II*, in order to drawn people into a long conversation about the Civilization series. Another employee, Abby, often would play *Bejeweled 2*, and chat on MSN, while keeping an eye out for customers waiting at the counter. Conrad, however, would do his job meticulously, but would be in the café in almost all of the rest of his time playing *Flyff* or *Ragnarok Online*. While he was playing he would often help out around the store in various other tasks, including advising on tactics and strategies for the various MMORPGs that were installed on the café's computers.

The main entrance to Cydus is a single glass door—adorned by a *GunBound: Thor's Hammer* poster—that was typically open at daytime, but closed during the evening or in periods of inclement weather. A bar-height counter dominates the entrance; behind which the employees responsible for assigning customers to computers worked. Opposite the counter were large fridges with cold drinks and a rack of snack food, then an archway into the adjacent room (which could also be accessed from the street via the entrance on the other shop front). On the other side of the archway was a worn two-seater couch that was sometimes occupied by a sleeping person, and an old and empty pie-warmer beside a microwave on a bench against the wall. Because of the size of the café there were often several people in the entrance area, waiting to be assigned to computers, or to buy food and or drinks, or to look through Cydus's large collection of anime DVDs to select something to watch. Also because of the couch, and the employees stationed in the area, conversations often occurred in the entrance area. People would rise from their computers to come over and greet comrades as they arrived, before they became ensconced in their own games. Sometimes mixed in with the regulars in this area, were backpackers staying in cheap accommodation close-by who had come to the café as a group and were waiting for one or more of their number to finish using the computers.

Cydus consisted of two main rooms that were set up for different patterns of computer use. One room was designed as a LAN gaming environment, and the other for more general internet use, which includes online games like *GunBound* and *Counter-Strike*, and MMORPGs of both the subscription—mainly *World of Warcraft* and *City of Heroes*—and free to play varieties. This pattern was not rigidly enforced, as many of the computers were configured both ways, the user choosing which they preferred when they logged in. However, the technical set-up of each room suggested a clear division of activities, primarily through the inclusion of headphones with the computers in the room with the main entrance. This meant that the room was dominated by solo activities, whether it be YouTube watching, listening to music, viewing one of the many anime DVDs from the café's library, or playing a digital game. Consequently sound in the room was muted, dominated by commercial hip-hop and R & B music playing on the radio through speakers mounted on the walls of the room, and the sounds coming from the adjacent gaming room. The gaming room's computers played sound through speakers in the computers. This meant that the sounds of various games, and the play of those games would intermingle: the gangster patios from a cut scene of *Grand Theft Auto*: San Andreas, sounds of rapid fire from *Tom Clancy's Rainbow Six 3: Raven Shield*, armies clashing in *Rome: Total War*, the music score from *Warcraft III: The Frozen Throne,* and a matter-of-fact spoken world tutorial for *Age of Empires III*, enmeshed with human conversation, taunts and ejaculations in Arabic, Cantonese, English, and Vietnamese combined to produce a complex cacophony of noise.

The rooms were each decorated with their own game-related themes. The LAN room with a faux historical decor and the internet room with pulp science fiction murals. Both of the spaces had their aesthetic supplemented by posters, and cardboard commercial displays. The walls of the internet room were painted with murals depicting a science fiction solar system, complete with spaceships, ringed planets and stars. The exit to the toilet, keeping with the spirit of this theme, was clearly marked 'Emergency Airlock'. The gaming room is divided cross ways by a faux portcullis, which has been made by inverting a Victorian-era iron railing, and painting the beam that it is attached to gray, with black paint outlining the individual 'stones'. At each end of the archway this creates are lights that appear to be burning torches, the flickering flames simulated by orange cloth blown by fans coming out of the cone shaped base. The ceiling is covered with camouflage nets, and the walls have Australian, German, Japanese, US, and Welsh flags hanging on them like posters. A shield emblazoned with the St. George's Cross, with two crossed swords above it, is the room's final touch. The room's gestures towards the past are supported by a cardboard standing display for the game *Vietcong*. A similar display for *Warcraft III: Reign of Chaos* and a poster for *Ragnarok Online*, relate to the theme through their use of Tolkienesque quasi-medieval settings. The poster for *FIFA 2000*, however, was somewhat anachronistic. The science fiction themed internet room is decorated with similar posters—featuring *Diablo II, Age of Empires II: The Age of Kings, StarCraft, Half-Life* and *Tom Clancy's Rainbow Six: Rogue Spear*—although in these cases the posters were presented in frames. Another key difference between the two rooms is in the lighting. The LAN room is darkened because its exterior windows are covered by heavy curtains, which means that the only light in the room comes from the dim red light of the 'torches', and the light which comes through from the internet room, which is well lit because of the glass shop window that covers the whole of the wall that borders the street. It is elements like this, as well as decorations and activities that create different dynamics in the two rooms.

Cydus provided typical services, such as printing, scanning, and CD and DVD burning. The staff also assisted people with basic troubleshooting, but nothing like the highly personalized service at Cybercafé Avila. Prepaid game cards were also sold for *World of Warcraft* and *Ragnarok Online*. Some employees were able to go into quite detailed assistance about the mechanics and tactics with a number of games. Conrad, particularly, was able to provide expert advice on a number of MMORPGs, including commonly known 'exploits'. Beyond basic gaming and publishing facilities that they had installed on the computers, Cydus also maintained a large stock of imported DVDs. These mainly featured anime imported from Japan; a handwritten sign on the counter promotes the recent additions to their library. The food provided there was mainly of the potato chip variety, with hot pies and sausage rolls available on request, as the pie warmer was always empty.[28] A large amount of cold drinks were consumed there. The fridge was often almost empty, with the most popular brands of beverage completely depleted, an issue that was often brought up with the employees by the customers. Hot drinks (chocolate, coffee, and tea) were also available. More substantial fare could be found in many of the cheap takeaway restaurants on Victoria Street, or in the stalls and arcades across the streets at Victoria Markets.

The pricing at Cydus was on two scales, one for members and another for casual users. The members had to purchase membership for ten dollars, membership lasted one year, and during that time they could play for two dollars an hour. Non-members had to pay three dollars an hour, and would often be asked to leave a ten-dollar deposit at the counter to avoid people sneaking out without paying, which according to Tony, had been occurring with some regularity because people could leave from the exit in the LAN gaming room without the staff at the counter notic- ing them. Members had available two special offers for long periods of use, either the 'endurance pass' which allowed them five hours and a pie or bottle of coke for ten dollars; or the 'survival pass', which was ten hours for fifteen dollars. The latter was not available between 11am on Fri- day and 11pm on Sunday, the peak period of computer use at the café.

Conclusion

The situated ecologies of Cybercafé Avila, and Cydus, have markedly different rhythms. These differences can be traced back to the material conditions of play in the cafés. The background to these material differences is culturally, economically, and historically determined. Even as the situ- ated ecologies provide access to a global networked space, they operate in particular frameworks and constraints that are embedded at a local level. Each enactment, each location is inevitably different and this means that gaming experiences are rarely homogenous, although this does not mean that there are not significant connections and similarities between the two locations.

Notes

1 Consalvo, M. (2007). *Cheating: Gaining Advantage in Videogames*. Cambridge: MIT Press: p. 126.

2 See: Boellstorff (2006: 30; 2008; 2009); Stevens et al. (2008); Taylor (2006a); Williams (2005: 458-459); and Williams et al. (2006: 342).

3 Williams, D. (2005). 'Bridging the Methodological Divide in Games Research'. *Simulation & Gaming: An Interdisciplinary Journal of Theory, Practice and Research* 36.4: p. 458.

4 Boellstorff, T. (2008). *Coming of Age in Second Life: An Anthropologist Explores the Virtually Human*. Princeton: Princeton University Press: p. 69.

5 See http://www.internetworldstats.com/stats6.htm, for the Australian statistics, the Venezue- lan statistics are available at http://www.conatel.gov.ve/ (the information is reproduced in English at http://www.internetworldstats.com/sa/ve.htm).

6 While they are open to the public, people using the cafes were often scrutinized by security before being allowed entry, and in some cases were refused entry because they were considered to be suspicious, or undesirable.

7 See: Bryce and Rutter (2005); Cunningham (2000); and Lin (2008).

8 Bryce, J. and Rutter, J. (2005). 'Gendered Gaming in Gendered Space'. In J. Raessens and J. Goldstein (eds.). *Handbook of Computer Game Studies*. Cambridge: MIT Press: p. 305.

9 Cunningham, H. (2000). 'Moral Kombat and Computer Game Girls'. J. T. Caldwell (ed.). *Theo- ries of the New Media: A Historical Perspective*. London: Athlone.

10 Cunningham, 'Moral Kombat and Computer Game Girls': p. 221.

11 They have since been joined by Bolivia, Ecuador and Nicaragua, although Venezuela retains a substantially larger portion of the shares than any of the other shareholding countries. teleSUR also broadcasts in Brazil with Portuguese subtitles.

12 'teleSUR and Al-Jazeera Sign Deal' (2006). *BBC News.*

13 Kraul, C. (2006). 'Venezuela's Chavez Reelected'. *Los Angeles Times.*

14 The recall referendum is based on the current Venezuelan constitution, it requires that an incumbent President (or any other elected official) win a referendum, or be recalled from office. A recall referendum is called if 20%, or more, of the electorate petitions for it.

15 Gott, R. (2005). *Hugo Chávez and the Bolivarian Revolution.* London; New York: Verso: pp. 245-246; and Lemoine, M. (2003). 'How Hate Media Incited the Coup Against the President'. In G. Wilpert (ed.). *Coup Against Chavez in Venezuela: The Best International Reports of What Actually Happened in April 2002.* Caracas: Fundación Venezolana para la Justicia Global: p. 152.

16 Gott, Hugo Chávez: p. 245.

17 Indymedia Argentina (2003). 'Chronology of the April Coup'. In G. Wilpert (ed.). Coup Against Chavez in Venezuela: The Best International Reports of What Actually Happened in April 2002. Caracas: Fundación Venezolana para la Justicia Global: p. 213.

18 Gott, *Hugo Chávez*: p. 245.

19 'Chávez to Shut Down Opposition TV'. (2006). *BBC News.*

20 Santamaria, F. and Guillen, C. (2007, May 27). 'Chavez Closes Opposition TV Station; Thousands Protest'. *CNN International.*

21 In March 2010, a law was enacted in Venezuela, banning the sale and distribution of violent games and digital games. Hugo Chávez supported the issue, vocally condemning digital games on several occasions on National television and radio. A *Noticias 24* report from 17 January 2010 'Chávez la Emprende de Nuevo Contra la Muñeca "Barbie" y la "Play Station"', quotes Chávez's remarks on digital games where he singles out the Sony PlayStation (along with the Barbie Doll) as symbols of the capitalist system. He describes digital games as 'veneno' (poison) that encourage and teach children violent behavior, and inculcate them into capitalisms culture of violence.

22 Barr, T. (2000). *newmedia.com.au: The Changing Face of Australia's Media and Communications.* St. Leonards: Allen and Unwin: pp. 228-229.

23 Unlike the rest of the Spanish-speaking world in Venezuela barrio is not equivocal to neighborhood, instead it is used the term to refer to slum and shanty settlements.

24 Barquisimeto is the state capital of Lara, in western Venezuela; its population is estimated at 1.5 million.

25 A savory pastry filled with meat, cheese, or beans.

26 All the prices reported in this book are based on the currency prior to the redenomination of the Bolivar in January 2008.

27 See the City of Melbourne website, http://www.melbourne.vic.gov.au/info.cfm?top=66&pa=779&pg=782

28 This may have been because the fieldwork took place during the summer.

CHAPTER FOUR
THE SOCIAL MILIEU

At home I like them [digital games], but at the cyber you have communications with other people—Ajax, May 2005.

This chapter builds on the descriptive account of the ethnographic case studies at Cybercafé Avila and Cydus, by arguing that the social milieu of digital game play is an important common element of both situated ecologies. The social milieu, thus, provides grounds comparison for comparison between the two situated ecologies, and a starting point for drawing out the common rhythms of both locations. The connection between the locations can be found by examining the cyclic rhythms established by the patterns of use in each café. The social dimension stems from congruent rhythms between the situated ecology and everyday life. The social milieu of play is a general attribute of the digital game ecology, enacted in particular ways in the context of the local. Two social currents that are crucial in sustaining relations beyond the minimum required for digital game play: learning (and teaching others), and 'cheating'. These currents trace common themes emerging from the ethnographic research. However, there is a significant difference in the stakes that mark the peculiarity of the cultures of use in the two situated ecologies, stemming from the vastly uneven contexts in which play takes place.

This chapter uses, and develops the notion of 'gaming capital'.[1] Consalvo introduces the notion, which is a reworking of Bourdieu's notion of 'cultural capital', to mark how systems of differentiation within gaming culture are negotiated.[2] Gaming capital emerges from dynamic relations between gamers, 'information about games and the games industry, and other game players'.[3] The main virtue of the concept is how it highlights that meanings and values are produced through negotiation and contestation between various actors, importantly the players and the gaming industry.[4] The following exploration of gaming capital is intended to develop the notion by explaining how game capital impacts on the experience of play within situated ecologies.

Cyclic Rhythms

Each of the locations was characterized by its' own peculiar rhythmic flow of people. The rhythm of Cydus was more cyclical as it was open for twenty-four hours a day, and thus, could be accessed at any time; its lighter periods of use did coincide with more-or-less regular sleeping patterns. Cybercafé Avila was officially closed from 7pm each evening until 7am in the morning. Xavier—who was prone to oversleeping and also had problems with his neighbors blocking in his car—in practice often opened the café much later. The café also sometimes remained open past this point in the evening because there were so many people there that Xavier felt that he was pointlessly losing profits by enforcing the closing time. Usually, due to family commitments the 7pm closing time was rigidly enforced. A few of the café's trusted regulars had copies of the keys to the café, so that they could use the computers with their friends after hours. This only happened once while I was conducting my fieldwork, when Kermit organized a LAN party with his friends from high school for the evening following graduation. On occasion Xavier's friends prevailed upon him to open the café late in the evening, because they urgently needed to use the café for a university or work related task, and their home computers had failed them. This meant that effectively the hours at Cybercafé Avila were very flexible, but in the evening after dark usually there was little point in remaining open, because few people ventured out in San Bernardino after dark due to concerns regarding safety on the streets.

A typical weekday at Cybercafé Avila started with Maxim and Xavier, sweeping, then mopping the floor and booting up the server. While these routine tasks were performed the first clients of the day would arrive. These were usually youths attending a nearby high school—identifiable by their school uniforms—who waited outside until the opening routine was complete. In the hour following opening many other students would arrive to use the café on their way to the high school, often taking up all of the computers of the café. Other students would pause on the doorstep of the café in order to greet friends and acquaintances, or purchase a cold drink. Consequently, during this time of the day there were often several small groups of students talking outside the café. After this period of heavy use the café was quieter for some time, the next wave of clients being made up of parents dropping off their children at the primary school directly across the road from the café. These clients were recognizable because the school was restricted to children of the personnel of the nearby Command Center of the Venezuelan Navy. So after 9am the café could have three or four naval officers in dress uniforms using the computers, although they were emailing and viewing pornography, rather than playing games and chatting like the high school students.

During the course of the morning the clients at the café would have a variety of needs. At this time, many requests for printing and help with office applications like Microsoft Excel and PowerPoint were fielded, and if there was technical work or repairs to be done, Xavier would busy himself with them, while Maxim dealt with assisting software related requests. During the morning, students on their way to the afternoon session of the high school would start to trickle in, also using the computers for a variety of reasons, but in this time the focus was typically on individual rather than group activities, such as: downloading and listening to music, then burning it onto CDs; playing long sessions of single-player digital games like *Rome: Total War, Need for Speed: Underground,* or *Harry Potter and the Chamber of Secrets*; or lengthy periods of chatting on yahoo messenger, MSN messenger or *Habbo*.[5] The students from the afternoon session often lingered in the café mixing with students who were now on their way home from the morning session.

Early morning was definitely a down period for Cydus. Typically, the pre-dawn hours were used to play MMORPGs; by *World of Warcraft* players who had refused to shift to the newly introduced local realms,[6] and *City of Heroes* players who still lacked an defined Australian served. A few people would be playing other MMORPGs, taking advantage of the relatively empty café to utilize more than one computer so that they could play one character, and simultaneously 'grind' on another computer,[7] or using two or more computers to 'leech' by using multiple accounts. Occasionally there would also be a game of online poker going. Other people would be using the computers for IRC, both backpackers from the nearby hostels and local residents, communicating with friends and family in other time zones. It was not uncommon for one or more people in the café to be sleeping at this time, either with their head cradled in their arms in front of the computer, or more often on the couch in the main entry area.

During the course of the day more people would arrive in the café, most often to play World of Warcraft in one of the Australian realms, or one of the other MMORPGs that were installed on the computers.[8] Other people would come to play single player games; only a few groups arrived to play LAN games during the day. Such groups were more common in the evening, with the Warcraft III mod 'Defense of the Ancients' being particularly popular with LANers. Usually the evening was the busiest period, with more gamers playing MMORPGs and other games, as well as more people using the computers to surf and chat. During the period between 8pm and midnight the café would often be verging on full, but this was also the time with the highest turnover, as many people came to use the café quickly for a variety of reasons, including large groups for a few rounds of a LAN game like Counter-Strike.

In the hours after midnight Cydus got much quieter. The noisy LAN games, characterized by 'smack-talk' and punctuated with laughter, were usually over by this time.[9] The gamers who remained played in a quieter focused manner, although often in these hours groups of people would meet outside or in the entrance area to discuss the day's play. Some players would leave, while others returned to the computers, determined to get to some goal that they had set themselves. Others, previously engrossed in play would start to feel tired and order coffee or hot chocolate, or purchase Red Bull or another drink from the main counter. Sometimes a run down to the McDonald's on Elizabeth Street, or another nearby restaurant would be organized before it closed for the night, the money pooled and orders taken among groups of gamers. In contrast Cybercafé Avila very rarely stayed open past 7pm; Xavier would announce around 6:30pm that they would be closing soon, and at 7pm he would usher out the stalwarts, and with El Bebe and Maxim shut down the computers. During the fifteen minutes or so that this took, often several people would stand outside talking under the light of the street lamp, either waiting for Maxim or otherwise unwilling to return to their homes. While Xavier locked the doors of the café, Maxim and El Bebe would chat to the other regulars outside. Xavier would then either drive or walk El Bebe to his family's apartment, before returning home himself, while Maxim often remained talking with friends and locals outside the café for several hours.

The weekends were a little different. In Cybercafé Avila they meant that more adults would be using the computers, and that there was less ebb and flow of people, the café being instead consistently busy. Despite this Xavier insisted that the café remain closed until midday on Sunday, so that he had a chance to sleep in and then thoroughly clean the café with Maxim from around 11am. Eventually, the café's business in the weekends began to cause Xavier stress, and he raised the hourly rate for Internet use on Sunday, as well as introducing a one-hour minimum. This had little impact on the pattern of use at the café. The main difference in the weekend was that, as there were more adults using the machines, there was less play going on. However, the play that did occur was a little different because the weekend was without the organizing factor of school creating rhythms that meant people would be passing the café at a certain time and have the chance to meet each other for a LAN or online multiplayer game. Consequently, group play at the weekend was often organized around family groups, both adults with children, as well as siblings and cousins. Solitary play also followed a different pattern: without the need to be elsewhere players would play for longer, so rather than playing a quick game such as Counter-Strike,

GunBound, or *Vice City*, people would spend longer periods playing through *Age of Mythology: The Titans, Rome: Total War* or *The Sims*. The rhythm was different during the weekend at Cydus also. Mainly this meant that LAN games were more frequent from earlier in the day, and also later into the night. More gamers remained in the café over night playing MMORPGs, especially those involved in games with overseas servers. More small children came in during the weekend. Without adult supervision, such groups were typically attracted to games that they might not otherwise have available to them like *Grand Theft Auto: San Andreas*.[10] Other adults would supervise and assist the children playing, or in some cases play games themselves, either alongside or with the children they accompanied.

Clearly the cyclic rhythms of Cydus and Cybercafé Avila were shaped and influenced by factors outside of—yet integral to—gaming. While both situated ecologies examined had a public context of game play, the notion that gaming is open to outside influences is not confined to this public context. The situated ecology in which play takes place has a crucial impact on what digital games are played in a particular situation (an issue that will be discussed fully in the next chapter). The cyclic rhythm of an individual location, or multiple networked locations, is what determines the accumulation or mass of people that make the social milieu of gaming. Sociality initiated through gaming in many cases extends further than what is required for play.

Offline Sociality

The social currents of the internet cafés were conspicuously evident. The sociality of both sites extended beyond what is required for communication in multi-player games. It is the aggregation of bodies in the spaces, as well as the peculiar rhythms of digital games, that produce these relations between people. In Cybercafé Avila the social aspect of the café was evident from the moment that I entered; a series of negotiations between the person entering, staff and other users was necessary before a computer could even be used. First, gaining entry often involved distracting one of the staff members from their current task. Thus the appearance of a new customer at the security door was often meet by a complex series of negotiations, usually ending with El Bebe finally capitulating, by pausing, or in some cases quickly enlisting someone to take over, his game to open the door. Once inside, staff would inquire as to the client's intended use of the computers. This was done because the various computers had technical limitations imposed by their hardware and thus had specialties, which meant that when the café was crowded it was necessary to shuffle people around on the computers so that everyone could continue with their chosen activities. If this was impossible there was a space by the door that was used for waiting for a computer to become free, although often all the seats from that area were in use in other parts of the café so people could share computers.

The social relations at Cydus were less obvious, the business being larger and the process of getting a computer rather more simple and streamlined. Because it was a larger space with many computers, aside from times when it was very crowded—like Friday and Saturday evening—it was unlikely that anyone would be situated in close proximity to another person unless it was by choice. Cydus' large catalog of available games meant that few people ended up playing the same game, unless this was deliberate. At first sight, past connections, and prior association dominated social interactions in Cydus. However, over the time it became apparent that there were certain points of social contact and interaction that were established through the shared experience of play, particularly the discussion and comparison of various generic elements of MMORPGs, or in the case of games like *Sid Meier's Civilization IV* or *Age of Empires III*, the pros and cons of their historical iterations.[11]

Certain other material conditions reinforced the social milieu at Cybercafé Avila. The young game players, students in particular, developed many strategies to circumvent the expense of using the café, typically by sharing computers during play, either by taking turns or, in many cases, having one or two observers comment and offer advice while another played. As a result, there would often be more than 20 people in the small café, even though there were only 11—or sometimes 12—working computers. This situation sustained the sociality because not everyone was concentrating on using a computer at any given time, although they might have preferred to. The observers sometimes became bored with what their playing companion(s) were doing and started to observe other players, making comments and asking questions about the games and the strategies that were being used, sparking new connections and relations among the people frequenting the café.

Play in Cydus was more spatially isolated, and few people moved around to comment and observe others playing aside from employees. However, digital games did become points of contact between people. The more obscure strategy games that Cydus had on its computers meant that players could immediately recognize aficionados of games like *Rome: Total War*, which established common points of connection among players, leading to discussions of tactics, instances of both competitive and cooperative play, and to more general associations. In other cases, the shared experience of play would lead to discussion of events, such as the newly launched Oceania realms of *World of Warcraft*. The café in this case became a key site for negotiating new types of associations, in the form of online guilds, as players shifted to, or steadfastly ignored, the new servers.

A key element that sustained the social milieu was the smooth segue of rhythms between game play and game capital. Rather than taking place in a vacuum, digital game play occurs in the context of the culture of digital games.[12] Key to understanding the abundant culture of digital games and the notion of gaming capital is the paratext. Consalvo conceptualizes paratexts in a broad fashion, describing them as 'artifacts' that relate to gaming, without actually being gaming itself; this includes various forms of extra-gamic hardware and software, guides to games, websites, chat-rooms, and bulletin boards.[13] The use and knowledge of paratexts plays an important role in game capital by creating connections and distinctions between individuals, which establishes a key common ground for the basis of social relations formed around digital game play. The concept of 'gaming capital' must also extend to the lived culture of gaming itself, so that rather than simply focusing on tangible artifacts, the role of more ephemeral socially situated practices may also be accounted for. In the situated ecology of the internet café, gaming capital is distinct in that the contact, knowledge sharing, negotiations, and contextualization all have face-to-face and live components that engender social contacts extending outside of the time and space of play itself.

Common commercial paratexts like industry magazines, and commercially published guidebooks were unavailable at Cybercafé Avila: this established an environment where internet-based research and personal knowledge was pivotal to the accumulation of gaming capital. While entirely aware of the existence of the commercial paratext industry,[14] many people preferred to find the information for free on the internet, rather than using commercially available sources. Primarily this was because they felt that finding the information they needed in this manner was easier and cheaper. Interviewees in Caracas were asked if they used digital games magazines to find out more about digital games stated:

> Gabrielle (Caracas): Yes, but I usually to try to search for this information on the internet rather than in a magazine, because in magazine I cannot find exactly what I am looking for. The answers and the kind of magazine I need, I cannot find here in Caracas. So I go to the internet where I can find the answers to these questions.

> Kermit (Caracas): I don't use a magazine, because is expensive and they talk about games that I don't play. In those magazines they only describe new games that I cannot play on my computer. So I always go to look on the internet first.

Several players used their English language skills to increase their pool of potential information. The information would be disseminated among the other players eventually through word of mouth, increasing the game capital of those who sourced and shared the information.

The use of various paratexts, and the sharing of the information gained were less common in Cydus. The discussion was less likely to be focused on disseminating a cheat, or strategy, but on something relevant to play but outside it. For example, the nuances of particular player-designed maps for *Counter-Strike*, *Warcraft III: The Frozen Throne,* and *StarCraft* were often discussed, or the benefits of the various realms available for players in *World of Warcraft.* Game capital in these cases was demonstrated through knowledge of a particular game that came from a lengthy and committed engagement with the game, its various paratexts, and the community of players.

The social milieu of the internet café clearly extended into the street, as people congregated for extended periods on the pavement outside. In the case of Cybercafé Avila people would often be waiting there when the café opened at 7:00am and, at times, groups would remain on the steps talking after it closed at 7:00pm. The small groups that formed outside the café on the street drew in other passersby, as patrons recognized and hailed fellow students, friends, neighbors, and relatives. These groups melded with parents picking up children from the Naval school across the street; firemen taking their lunch break; street entrepreneurs peddling ice cream, *yuca*,[15] or *empanadas*; off-duty soldiers and grubby mechanics from the garage next door. People hung around outside Cydus in similar clusters. Usually driven outside by the need to smoke, or to make a phone call in a relatively quiet environment, small groups of people might be outside the doors of the café at any time during the day or night, talking animatedly in a variety of languages. The importance of these activities to digital game play in the situated ecology of the internet café was made apparent to me when the Cybercafé Avila was unexpectedly closed during a power failure. Although Xavier had been promised the repairs would take just thirty minutes, the café remained shut from just after 10am until almost 5pm. During this time some of the regulars still waited outside to meet their friends and acquaintances, and stayed there talking for hours despite the inclement weather.

Gaming capital is not the sole form of cultural capital in operation. The sociality that gaming engendered was not bound by the physical space of the internet café; both inside and outside the café gaming capital was entangled with other concerns. Discussions outside the cafés often turned to more general topics: families, gossip, homework, relationships, school, sports, and university. The interviews in Caracas emphasized that talk about digital games, and paratexts was usually confined to the moments and locations of play:

> Ajax (Caracas): Normally we don't talk about games because we are just trying to have fun on the street or at home. In the café of course, we always talk about games.

> Kermit (Caracas): Yes, but only just after the game we talk about the game. If we are doing sometime else we just talk about football, our girlfriend, whatever…

Interviews in Australia, however, suggested a much wider scope of contexts where games might be discussed:

> Grace (Melbourne): Then everyone starts talking about how much homework they have to do, and someone will say yeah but last night I didn't do anything because I was playing Defense of the Ancients, or whatever, then everyone else chimes in and we start to talk about games…

> Burgundy (Melbourne): I basically learn everything about the game before I even play it, just from listening to my brother and his friends.

Players in both locations emphasized that digital games were just one of many pursuits.

> Gabrielle (Caracas): I am skilled at playing digital games, but I also like to do something other things. I also play sports like soccer, basketball, and tennis. I have many skills and I like to pursue those skills.

> Premendra (Melbourne): I like sports, I study, spend time with my family; I try not to let *World of Warcraft* take over my life…

Other forms of cultural capital, apart from gaming capital, are operational in the internet cafés; digital games are just one among a variety of everyday leisure activities. While gaming capital shifted into other contexts more fluidly in Australia, both situated ecologies sustained a form of sociality that was, established and partially sustained by the relations formed in those locations.

This important social element of the digital game ecology follows Huizinga's observation ithat communities formed through play often endured after its cessation.[16] While the play itself is ephemeral, the community and sociality of play continues outside of its original context; into new contexts which, as the interview subjects intimated, were outside of the times, spaces and acts of play completely. Huizinga states:

A play-community generally tends to become permanent even after the game is over. Of course, not every game of marbles or every bridge-party leads to the founding of a club. But the feeling of being 'apart together' in an exceptional situation, of sharing something impor tant, of mutually withdrawing from the rest of the world and rejecting usual norms, retains its magic beyond the duration of the individual game.[17]

While in the strict sense play was confined to the virtual worlds of digital games, the sociality that emerged from the space of play took digital game play into new contexts and locations. Stevens et al. point out that the educational value of games comes not from any particular quality of the game world, but from the collaborative / hence social / environment that they established be tween players in the space that play takes place.[18] The social environment of play in the internet cafés that I witnessed was not always strictly collaborative; the sociality was also driven by a good deal of antagonism and competition. But it was obvious that a wide range of social rela tions occurred in the space that were organized around sharing different types of information, in particular two kinds of information: how to play the games on both technical and strategic levels, and how to cheat in them.

Learning to Play

Monday, April 4th 2005, 3:06pm: Three people use one computer to play *Vice City*. A young er girl (aged 8 or 9) watches the game quietly; she is listening to the game's soundtrack through the headphones. The other two youths, a male and a female, discuss the game; the male works the controls and the female gestures towards the screen, providing directions, advice, and commentary.

At the time that this field note was made I can recall thinking that this situation demonstrated a way of sharing the computer that reinforced a gendered understanding of digital games, and game capital. However, within the next hour something occurred that changed my opinion of this situation, and the situated ecology of the Internet café:

Monday, April 4th 2005, 3:50pm: The three people playing one computer have moved to diff erent computers, and now have one each. Both of the girls have started their own games of *Vice City*, and the male is playing another game I don't recognize [turns out to be *Tibia*].

Monday, April 4th 2005, 4:15pm: The male has just returned to playing on his computer after assisting the young female with *Vice City* for five minutes.

What I had originally appraised as a situation with a clear division between player and specta tors was, I realized, a more complicated relationship. While they shared the one computer, the male player had been demonstrating and explaining how to play the game, and whilst differently engaged with his activity, as they were watching play rather than playing, the two young women had been learning how to play. This power dynamic—boy with gaming capital teaches girls—repro duces a culturally gendered understanding of digital game play as a pastime; although it is worth noting that the situation challenges this kind of understanding also, because the young woman and girl were actually present, rather than involved in orthodox gendered play. However, this type of dynamic aside, in the situated ecology of the internet café learning how to play digital games is central to social relations.

The interviewees were asked if they felt that they learnt anything from digital games. While there were a few comments about content that they had picked up, like names of Greek Gods from *Age of Mythology: The Titans* or *Rome: Total War*, or historic information from *Civilization II*, most comments highlighted that what was learned was how to play the game.

> Gabrielle (Caracas): For example with the *Age of Empires*, I really learn many things, and when I have to play the *Age of Mythology* I have the skills I got from *Age of Empires*.

> Pramendra (Melbourne): By playing games I have learnt a lot of things, but I don't know… [laughs awkwardly]…I don't think… …these are useful things.

> Kermit (Caracas): Skills in computer technologies, you learn things just to play, but not for life. But I suppose if we have a war I will know some tactics [laughs].

> Burgundy (Melbourne): I don't know if I ever learnt anything useful, but playing means that I have spent more time with computers…

> Ajax (Caracas): [laughs] Yes I learnt many things from playing games, I use them to learn English, and I think games also make me think faster, because I usually play strategy games where you have to think and make plans.

In addition to learn how to play particular games several of the interviewees believed, like Gabrielle, that knowledge of how to play could be transferred effectively from one game to another. Kermit, for example, had been able to use his expertise in *SWAT 3: Close Quarters Battle* to his advantage in a number of other more popular first-person shooters, while Burgundy had "learned" how to play *Warcraft III: The Frozen Throne* through playing *StarCraft*. The claims in these cases were not absolute; rather that previous knowledge of the other game has put them in a better position than a complete novice. Pelletier and Oliver, for example, argue that players do transfer skills and skill-sets from one digital game to another. Game capital is cumulative: having capital in one game leads to skills in, and knowledge of, other games, and consequently even more gaming capital that is less tied to a specific circumstance.[19] Thus knowledge of how to play various games has practical consequences, because it provides players with the mobility and flexibility to insinuate themselves into a wider variety of situated ecologies of digital game play.

There are also a number of unquantifiable suggestions emerging from the interview comments. Kermit's half-joking comment about how games could be used to train people for war has a particular resonance with the controversy about games like *America's Army*.[20] Kermit and Burgundy also mention the issue of technology, and suggest that playing digital games have made them more familiar with computers. Missing out on this basic introduction to technology is one of the important consequences that stems from exclusion from digital game play, whether that is for cultural or economic reasons. If access to, and mastery of, contemporary computer technology is considered to be central to combating economic exclusion, then this means that to lack in gaming capital may be a factor that contributes to this exclusion; this issue is the central theme of chapter seven. Ajax's response attributes digital games to nurturing his self-described "fast thinking", and his growing English skills. Premendra's response indicates some doubt about whether the skills are transferable at all, other players happily speculate, while some—like Ajax—are adamant that digital games support a form of learning.

Rather than dealing now with what may, or may not, have been learnt, this section focuses on how the exchange of game capital among the players' of digital games is a method of establishing differentiation between players. The fieldwork notes from the internet cafes reflect a wide variety of practices of information sharing, the most common being simple requests for technical infor-mation, discussing play strategies, and sharing information about cheats or trampas.[21] The use of cheats was more prevalent, or at least more visible, at Cybercafé Avila, and will be discussed below.

Requests for help or assistance were often made between players. Inexperienced players would solicit specific information from other players who were demonstrating gaming capital while play-ing the same game. Such requests were numerous, although not always transparently answered, because sometimes the difference in gaming capital was so great that the person proffering assistance could not be effectively understood. This meant that the same request was some-times repeated to a number of different people until a response that addressed the questioner's specific lack of understanding adequately was solicited. Examples included requested like 'how do I trade items?' in Ragnarok Online, 'what do markets do?' in Rome: Total War, and 'how do I join the game' for a number of LAN based games. Other requests and comments reflected a so-phisticated understanding of the game in question and its paratexts; this type of exchange often involved demonstrations of gaming capital on the parts of both people involved in the exchange as they negotiated their relative status, rather than the acknowledgement the other player's ex-pertise that simpler requests involved.

Talk about digital games has a very important role in digital game play. Not only does it initiate sociality in the gaming ecology, it also plays a key role in the development of gaming capital, by creating a space of negotiation where the multiple actions, combinations, objects, and strate-gies of play may be contextualized. In heavily character-oriented games often the entry-point for discussion would be avatar design, and also the crucial decisions that were made when avatars 'power up' when players have to choose new skills and specialties. It was common for groups in the cafés to end up spending more time talking about the strategies involved at these crucial points in the game than actually playing the game. This occurred more regularly at Cybercafé Avila, where patrons would maximize their experience by watching others play after they had spent all their own money, either soliciting a commentary from the player(s) they were watching, or producing their own.

The circulation of information about gaming taking place in the situated ecology of the internet café establishes a hierarchy of gaming capital. While differences of opinion abounded, some people had demonstrably more gaming capital and they played a crucial role in the dissemina-tion of information about games in these spaces, consequently having a high impact on many players' experience, and playing an important part in sustaining the social milieu of play. In Cydus Conrad performed this role, when he was not working and dispensing advice on any number of MMORPGs, he was on the other side of the counter playing one of them. But the shift from work to play did not change his importance as a node in the circulation of gaming capital in that space, as people still stopped by to talk with him, watch him play, and ask him questions. El Bebe also had this kind of role at Cybercafé Avila, although his expertise was confined to *GunBound, Counter-Strike* and *Vice City*.

More respected was Johnny Lima, a resident of the neighborhood, and close family friend of Xavier's. Johnny only came to the café occasionally because he had a busy schedule, and also was affected by ill health. His arrival indicated that a substantial gaming session was to be undertaken. Unlike many of the other players in Venezuela, Johnny was clearly an adult, being in his early to mid-thirties. Several of the younger players would loudly greet him when he arrived, and Xavier would arrange for him to be next in line for one of the café's fastest computers. While he waited for his turn, he would inspect the other screens to see what was being played; approaching and questioning anyone playing a game he had not seen before. He also often brought copies of games with him for Xavier to install on some of the computers. Once Johnny started to play, he would often attract viewers, who would watch quietly, patiently waiting for any terse commentary that Johnny might provide. On one occasion he played *Age of Mythology:* The Titans for about four hours while Gabrielle watched him play, respectfully asking the occasional question. The next day Gabrielle was busy disseminating the information he had learned from his session with Johnny Lima among some of the other players who frequented the café. Over the course of the week I saw many games of *Age of Mythology*: The Titans, where the player was experimenting with the unique tactics required to succeed as the Atlanteans, as through Gabrielle the patrons of the café came to grips with Johnny's approach.[22]

The circulation of gaming capital in this manner helps to establish a social milieu for play, but it also has the potential to create new forms of homogeneity in the situated ecology. One of my Australian interviewees, Mel, had mentioned that she found the higher-level rooms of *GunBound* bizarre because everyone had exactly the same avatar, designed to maximize expedient play. Expert knowledge of the rules in this case had produced one particular combination that was universally acknowledged as maximizing the avatar's potential. But in addition to this homogeneity that was established through understanding the algorithm of the game, there were clear cases where game capital was used in a disciplinary manner. El Bebe in particular was a culprit of this kind of behavior, on several occasions openly mocking people who had purchased upgrades for their GunBound avatars that he saw as pointless. He did this mainly because the items lacked an in-game function and served only to individualize their avatar. El Bebe also made fun of Gabrielle and Ajax when they brought in, installed, and played role-playing games, *Blade and Sword* and *Dungeon Siege* respectively. Based on the nature of the remarks, in his opinion, such fantasy games were insufficiently masculine.[23] In Cydus this behavior was evident in the selection of maps for LAN games; particular maps were often popular, and most people would play on those maps, any suggestion of another map was met with criticism. Another point of conflict where game capital was prominent was in the evaluation of the avatars of other players in *World of Warcraft*. Some expert players had built up a very rigid idea of how each class should not only act in-game, but how the player should design the character, and configure their interface. The motivation of the expert players was to maximize the effectiveness of the avatars' class by distributing points among a pool of various talents as they increase in level. This led to many conversations where people would have their talent choices questioned and then have explained the 'ideal' combination for their particular class and level. In some cases the advice was accepted as genuine, but in other cases a difference that could otherwise be understood as based on personal preference would be framed by one person as the other merely demonstrating a lack of game capital.

Cheating

The two locations were different in how cheating during play was performed or executed, and how it was received by other players. In Consalvo's treatment of the topic of cheating, she argues which practices are constituted as 'cheating' in digital game play are entirely contingent on the situation and context in which the cheating takes place.[24] Thus, what is considered cheating in one situation may be considered normal in another; however, the concern in this section is not just to map how cheating varies between the locations, but also to examine what exactly it is about the particular material contexts of play being examined—the situated ecology of play—that makes certain forms of cheating emerge. While cheating is a common activity across the digital game ecology, by examining how forms of cheating are tied to particular situations, this section will also underscore the widely uneven stakes of cheating. Practices of "cheating" also established connections and similarities between the two cafes. In Cybercafé Avila certain types of cheating were more prevalent, especially the inputting of special "cheat codes" into the game that are designed to confer some advantage, or negate some disadvantage. These cheat codes are a part of the design of the game, and are distributed by the 'paratextual' industries. Cheating in Cydus was more focused on maximizing various 'exploits' in MMORPGs; rather than bending or breaking the rules these practices involve finding and then exploiting loopholes in the games design from which excess value—in the forms of experience, items, resources or gold—may be extracted.

Before midday usually there are only a few players at Cydus. One day in January 2006 I noticed one young man taking advantage of the many empty computers to use two of them at once. The simultaneous employ of two computers side by side was not that uncommon, I had noticed it before: Abby, an employee, would sometimes run a *Bejeweled 2* game on one computer while also chatting or surfing on the one next to her; others would also do this during the café's downtime, quickly looking at a FAQ, or website, without stopping the game that they were playing. This incident was clearly different; as I passed to log on to my own computer, I noticed that both screens were open to *Ragnarok Online,* and that the screen depicted—from slightly different perspectives—the same events unfolding. When I asked this gamer what he was doing, he reluctantly replied 'leeching'. Sensing that there was little more I would be able to get out of him, I turned to the bulletin boards of the *Ragnarok Online* community. The leech, it transpires is a controversial 'exploit' in the *Ragnarok Online* system, which allows vastly different levels of characters to party together, and share experience and treasure equally. This enabled the practice of leeching to flourish in *Ragnarok Online,* as characters join together to form a party, knowing that some will be leeches; that is they will not participate in combat, only receive the rewards from the other players' actions. The practice allows low-level characters to rapidly gain levels by leeching off more powerful characters. Often the leech will pay for their experience with in-game currency, or other items, however; in this case the player was leeching from himself by using two accounts simultaneously. While the rules and code of the game clearly permits the activity, many in the *Ragnarok Online* community feel that the practice harms the game, primarily because they believe leeching players do not know how to perform their roles once they achieve high levels. The rapid advancement in level means that they are not aware of the tasks required of them, based on their character's specialties, in team-based play.[25] However, the only way that this activity could be regarded as cheating in the context of Cydus is because the dual use of computers was cheating the café's system of payment. However, the activity was effectively tolerated, so long as it took place in the LAN room, and outside of peak hours.

Leeching as a practice was not common in my observations, but it was a part of a more general resistance to 'the grind'. That is the constant repetitive tasks that many MMORPGs devolved into at higher level, particularly when more experienced players were trying to 'level-up' new characters. At Cydus a common topic of conversation among MMORPG players is how to circumvent, or avoid 'the grind' altogether. Conrad would often complain about the process of leveling up or "buffing" in *Flyff*—another MMORPG commonly played in the café—on several occasions he used a five cent coin to jam down the key that he needed to press repeatedly in order complete the process. He used the freedom this action gave him to move about the café, grab a drink, and chat with other players. The general consensus was that the grind was something that could not be avoided; but the players who found ways of mitigating the boredom of the grind, either through an 'exploit' like leeching or Conrad's *Flyff* tactic, were not considered cheaters. Rather it was a form of gaming capital because it was acknowledged that their actions reduced the amount of time that had to be invested in a rather burdensome part of game play.

The main form of *Counter-Strike* cheating that openly took place at Cydus was the practice of 'ghosting'. This form of cheating relied completely on the café environment, and gave teams a distinct advantage. 'Ghosting' allowed eliminated players to continue to aid their team members by conducting in game surveillance to find enemy locations. While eliminated players were deliberately not able communicate with their fellows in game, this did prevent them from communicating to each other live in the café. In Cydus the practice was unquestioned, it was not cheating, just a normal part of the play of *Counter-Strike* (and other LAN shooters) in the café context. This practice, and leeching, represents the kinds of actions that are made possible in internet cafes through the aggregation of side-by-side networked machines and the multiplicity of screens.

Cybercafe Avila's situated ecology bred other forms of cheating. El Bebe was well known as a cheater in *Counter-Strike*. Not in any technical capacity, but rather because he would watch his opponents' screens to figure out their locations. Because his presence in the café was unavoidable, and he was a consistently strong (and willing) player, El Bebe was still often involved in games. However, steps would be taken to prevent his excesses. As he often played on a computer by the main door, because opening the door was one of his key duties, the other players in the game would organize to use the computers at the other end of the room. Or if that was impossible, they would turn their screens a little to make it harder for El Bebe to see them, and maybe enlist some of their friends among the various spectators to stand strategically, so they would block his view. If he started to cheat, it would rapidly become subject to good-natured abuse from the other players. This form of cheating worked, and was tolerated, because it was more or less

inevitable that it would occur unintentionally, and because it was easily remedied. At Cydus opponents could easily chose locations around the two rooms that meant their screens would not be
visible to anyone playing against them. Without the possibility of opponents accidentally catching
a glance at their screen this activity was considered taboo, creating a situation in Cydus where
the players could cheat by ghosting, looking at their own screen and telling others what they saw,
but not by looking at the screens of others and using that information against them.

The most common form of cheating at Cybercafe Avila was the use of the designed cheat codes
for games. This was also one of the primary points of discussion around games, especially *Counter-Strike* and *Vice City.* Knowledge of these codes was also an important form of gaming capital; individuals who knew the codes thoroughly were often enlisted to assist briefly during play by
reminding others of certain codes. When games of *Counter-Strike* began—as the map and host
were being chosen—the players also often briefly recapped the cheat codes, sometimes drawing
in other people, by acknowledging their gaming capital, to get the precise set of cheats straight
with all the players. If Ajax was at the café he would often be involved at this point, because he
was well known for having all the cheat codes memorized. The cheat codes commonly used at
Cybercafe Avila were shortcuts that enabled players to get new weapons and ammunition mid-
game without having to buy or capture them. But this practice of incorporating the use of cheat
codes into standard play of *Counter-Strike* was not the standard for all Venezuela. Towards the
middle of July 2005, a fifteen-year-old girl, Guadalupe, arrived in the neighborhood from Porlamar in Nueva Esparta.[26] After using MSN at the café for a few days, she hesitatingly joined in on
a few *Counter-Strike* games, and turned out to be a reasonably good player, except that she had
no idea about any of the cheat codes. Ajax began to sit beside her while she played, coaching her
on the cheat codes, after this she proved to be an expert *Counter-Strike* player, routinely 'pwning'
all comers on the café's LAN. The highly contextual aspect of this form of cheating created new
standards of expertise in the situated ecology. This approach to play—and cheating—was sustained in Cybercafé Avila because the relatively small community of players was able to establish
a more or less standard set of practices. Cydus supported a wider variety of play practices, even
around one game, because of the larger size of its location and clientele.

In *Vice City* the use of cheat codes was so ubiquitous at Cybercafé Avila that Xavier eventually
began to print out copies of the basic cheat codes and every morning would place a copy beside
each computer. Aghast at how rapidly they disappeared from the café, he began to print them
with a watermark that promoted Cybercafé Avila. Xavier remarked: 'If they are going to take them
to play in other cafes, people should at least know where they come from'. These cheat sheets,
a single A4 with the codes that Xavier had downloaded from the Internet were constantly in use.
While people occasionally brought in sheets like this for other games that they had printed, or
taken from, other locations, typically the use was confined to *Vice City.* The style of play was quite
recognizable, players looking from the screen, to the paper on the bench beside the keyboard
and then to the keyboard to place their hands in the right locations to execute the combinations
that were required. Usually people just tried to remember a few codes, like 'leavemealone', that
removed any tailing police. Other codes were used to skip through missions, unlock various vehicles, and open up parts of Liberty City.

The use of cheat codes was particularly important in the context of Cybercafé Avila because they allowed a flexibility of movement and actions in *Vice City* that was remarkably different from playing without the codes. Consalvo notes that the various concepts of 'cheating' are often simply a short hand for the player moving more quickly and flexibly between different areas or stages of the game than the rules of the game world might otherwise allow.[27] It is also important to appreciate that cheating in digital games is not merely instrumental, a way of getting to the end with the best result. In this context, players used the cheat codes to bypass and avoid constrictions on their activities, so that they could concentrate on exploring or mastering a particular part of the game. Players took a great deal of delight in the flexibility that the codes gave them, and would often spend time discussing various codes and demonstrating them to one another. Consalvo notes that cheating is also undertaken playfully.[28] The consequence of this type of playful cheating in *Vice City* is the expansion of the game. It creates new ways of playing through experimentation with the possible actions available in the game, for example: 'panzer' which allows the player to drive a tank, enabling familiar spaces to be reused in multiple ways. Cheating, thus allowed both a flexibility of movement through the game, and expanded the variety of actions available in that space.

Knowledge about when cheating was appropriate, and how to cheat, was central to the specific milieu of both locations. This knowledge constitutes an important aspect of gaming capital in a situated ecology. Consalvo argues that if players posses the right kind of game capital for the situation they may be able to shape the experience for other players:

> Game players possessed of the proper kinds of gaming capital – for their own gaming circle – are powerful in the sense that they can often dispense advice with confidence, are looked to as experts in some way, and can, through *their behaviour in game*, enhance or reduce opportunities for others.[29]

My observations in this section supplement Consalvo's point; the possessors of game capital do not only shape the experience through their in-game behavior, but also from their behavior and actions in the location that play takes place.

Cheating may be a 'universal' activity, but this examination of cheating that compares and contrasts two locations of play confirms that cheating has very different motivations and consequences from place to place. The acceptance of certain types of cheating at Cybercafé Avila was tied to the strong social networks and small size of that particular ecology. Despite the differences between the locations it is evident that there is a common motivation to use cheats to move through the game faster. However, even this common factor serves to highlight the uneven status of cheating as a form of gaming capital. In Venezuela the players used cheat codes to move through *Vice City* more quickly in order to find the part of the game that they enjoyed, while in Melbourne users leeched or used other exploits to develop high level characters more quickly. While both activities constitute a demonstration of gaming capital, only the players in Melbourne have the real possibility of using the gaming capital in exchange with another form of capital. Their digital game play is tangibly an asset, whereas that of a player in Caracas is not.

Conclusion

This examination of the rhythms of Cybercafé Avila and Cydus draws comparisons between them. The similarities suggest that the rhythm of the situated ecology of digital game play is always social, and the context of public consumption presents the possibility of 'live' paratextual engagements and demonstrations of gaming capital. The social milieu of the situated ecology is established through communication about games, either technical information, or gaming capital in the form of elaborate information about personal style or expertise. The sharing of this information establishes the basis for wider social interaction. Sociality in the situated ecology is demonstrated strongly in two ways—teaching and cheating—in both Cydus and Cybercafé Avila.

Notes

1 Consalvo, M. (2007). *Cheating: Gaining Advantage in Videogames.* Cambridge: MIT Press: p. 1.

2 Bourdieu, P. (1984). *Distinction: A Social Critique of the Judgment of Taste* [trans. R. Nice]. Cambridge: Harvard University Press.

3 Consalvo, *Cheating*: p. 4.

4 Consalvo, *Cheating*: pp. 184-185.

5 In this case it was not the Venezuelan version of Habbo that was being used. Depending on the whim of the player, the US, UK, or Spanish version was used. A Venezuelan version of Habbo was launched in 2006, as were regional versions for Brazil, Chile, Columbia and Mexico.

6 A 'realm' is in the lore of *World of Warcraft* a particular server, or server-cluster for the game. The Australian or 'Oceanic' realms were launched on the 8th of November 2005, about 3 weeks before the fieldwork at Cydus commenced.

7 In the context of gaming the 'grind' is boring, repetitive game play which is necessary to perform in order to play the game. Potentially, this is where games become completely 'ergodic'. This game element is commonly found in MMORPGs and other role-playing games, for example *Blue Dragon*.

8 The Australian servers are Khaz'goroth (Player versus environment) and Frostmourne (Player versus Player). They are served from the USA, but set to GMT +10 (Australian East Coast Time).

9 Smack-talk describes the lively banter of game players (on- and off-line) that involves the use of deliberately insulting, threatening, or otherwise inflammatory language. While it may be used to bully, distract, intimidate, or otherwise interfere with others, it is also often consensual. Because of its negative connotations, it is often strongly regulated in online virtual worlds.

10 The PC version was released in June 2005, seven months after the original PlayStation2 release.

11 Both games were newly installed on the Cydus computers when I began my fieldwork in late November 2005.

12 See Consalvo (2003b: p. 331; 2007: p. 184); and Newman (2004: pp. 57-58).

13 Consalvo, *Cheating*: p. 8.

14 Consalvo (2007: p. 38) notes that the paratextual industry, which has sprung up to assist players' in finding all of the secrets/Easter eggs in games, has become 'virtually indistinguishable' from the digital games industry itself.

15 Indigenous sweet potato.

16 Huizinga, J. (1970). *Homo Ludens: A Study of the Play Element in Culture.* London: Paladin.

17 Huizinga, Homo Ludens: p. 31.

18 Stevens, R., Satwicz, T., and McCarthy, L. (2008). 'In-Game, In-Room, In-World: Recconecting Videogames to the Rest of Kids' Lives'. In K. Salen (ed.). *The Ecology of Games: Connecting Youth, Games and Learning.* Cambridge: MIT Press: p. 53.

19 Pelletier, C. and Oliver, M. (2006). 'Learning to Play in Digital Games'. *Learning, Media, and Technology* 31.4: p. 340.

20 A border incident involving Columbia, Ecuador, and Venezuela, which occurred on 01-03-2008 altered the context of Kermit's flip comment. But aside from minor boarder disputes, Venezuelan troops have not been involved in conflicts outside of the National territory since the War of Independence.

21 This term is used in Venezuela to describe cheating in game play that is enabled through a password or combination of actions. *Trampa* translates literally as trap.

22 The Atlantean faction requires a different approach to resource management, because of the different abilities of the 'Citizen' unit and attributes of the 'Town Center' building. The Atlantean gods also had unfamiliar powers that had peculiar strategic uses.

23 The games were—according to El Bebe—marico, which is the common colloquial term for homosexual, but in this context the equivalent would be 'sissy'.

24 Consalvo, *Cheating*: p. 127.

25 As discussed by drsvss and others on the Legend: Ragnarok Online Forum February-April 2008.

26 An island state of Venezuela, that is very isolated from the metropolitan areas of the country.

27 Consalvo, *Cheating*: p. 172.

28 Consalvo, *Cheating*: p. 104.

29 Consalvo, *Cheating*: p. 123. Emphasis added.

CHAPTER FIVE
LOCAL RHYTHMS, GLOBAL RHYTHMS

> … games hinge on a dynamic experience that oscillates between doing and not doing. In each game there are periods in which the player is in control of gameplay and at others not, creating a dynamic rhythms between self-determination and pre-determination. This rhythm is present in most games…—Tanya Krzywinska.[1]

Rhythms and rhythmanalysis provide scope to analyze digital games on a number of scales, and to trace connections between those scales. The global ecology of digital games has its particular rhythm, which is enacted in and through the material conditions of a particular location: the situated ecology. The situated ecology has its own rhythm, which produces eurhythmia with some games and arrhythmia with others. The rhythms of the situated ecologies produce the variances and differences within the digital game ecology. However, despite these obvious differences digital games remain part of an overarching ecology because they have common rhythms that connect various situated ecologies, a dynamic exemplified through the case studies of Cybercafé Avila and Cydus. The digital game ecology is contradictory; while its homogeneity is challenged by the wide variety of individual and unique cultures of use, the common elements of these heterogeneous enactments of play also suggest that digital games can be spoken about in a general fashion. This contradiction illustrates a point that has constantly resurfaced in scholarship on digital games, a desire to address the specificity of digital games, yet at the same time use that specificity to talk about the medium in general.

This chapter examines two games and one game genre that are played in both of the case study locations that demonstrate this contradiction of enmeshed connection and disconnection between situated ecologies. This supports the importance of the location of play as a key site of negotiation between the rhythms of global ecology of digital games and the local rhythms of everyday life. If the rhythms are eurhythmic, a situated ecology is produced: a localized enactment of the global digital game ecology. The first game discussed, *Grand Theft Auto: Vice City (Vice City)*, illustrates how the rhythms thematically connect digital game play to other parts of the globe, while simultaneously remaining embroiled in the local situated ecology. This is followed by an examination of the online multiplayer game *GunBound: World Championship (GunBound)* that highlights how games are used deliberately to maintain social connections between different locations. The final section examines free-to-play MMORPGs, which demonstrates that national cultures and boundaries have an important role in establishing local communities of gamers.

Imagining Miami: From Caracas to Vice City

Vice City is a game with a clear narrative progression. The narration unfolds through a mixture of in-game missions and animated 'cut-scenes'. This interplay of action and inaction is common in the narratives of big-budget digital games, with the non-interactive 'cut-scene' often serving the purpose of explaining the significance and stakes of the actions that the player will be taking in the following interactive sequence. In the situated ecology I noticed that players reacted indifferently to these narrative sequences, they often used them as a chance to look away from the scene, to observe what others were doing, and make conversation with others at the café. This break in the rhythm of the game, established a connection to the social rhythm of the situated ecology. It also allowed players to integrate play with other online activities like IRC and general surfing; activities that were often turned to when cut scenes interrupted the player's actions.

There were two instances in which I observed the narrative sequences being followed with complete attention. The first case was in an internet café in Porlamar, this particular café had *Max Payne 2: The Fall of Max Payne* installed on the computers, and the players watched the 'cut-scenes' carefully because they contained valuable information. Rather than being simply explanatory, or tension building, the cut-scenes in this game move through the space in order to show the players where their enemies where located, and how and where to find objects necessary to complete the level. This is not an uncommon use of the cut scene; the same technique is evident in many other high-budget games like *Tomb Raider: Angel of Darkness* and *Beyond Good and Evil.* However, *Vice City* used 'cut-scenes' to emphasize the element of parody in the game through comedic references to popular culture.

The second case where I observed close attention to detail in the cut scenes was at Cydus. This incident occurred over several hours as two pre-adolescent boys aged played *Grand Theft Auto: San Andreas.* The boys played side by side on different computers. As each cut-scene unfolded both boys would watch the scene, one player pausing their game to watch the other's screen. They would then repeat various lines from the scene, imitating the slang and accents as authentically as possible, to great merriment. In this case, part of the pleasure of play came from the encounters with various taboo adult topics (like race relations, sex, crime, liquor, drugs, and especially bad language) that were expressed through the cut scenes. This illicit element made the cut scenes a key part of play for these two boys, it being quite possible that in another context they would not be able to play this game because of its MA15+ rating in Australia. This type of engagement was not as straightforward in Venezuela. Despite being readily available *en Español,* only the technical instructions for the game were actually in Spanish; the narrative sequences in *Vice City* were exactly the same as they were in the English version, just accompanied by Spanish subtitles. The language was moderated through translation and this, combined with the minor importance of the sequences in terms of game-play, and created a context where the 'cut-scenes' were widely ignored in Cybercafé Avila.

Vice City, despite its prominent and controversial cut scenes, is not a game where this element is essential to play. Perron points out that:

> What makes the success of such a driving-shooting-action-mission-simulation game is that there is as much for the gamer that has specific missions to accomplish to do as there is for the player who wants to wander the city and just go on committing various criminal acts.[2]

Perron's statement encapsulates the two major playing styles of *Vice City.* One extreme is a commitment to following the narrative trajectory that the game establishes, the other to ignoring it completely and exploring the space of the game, and the actions possible within it. This allows the game to fit into a variety of play-styles; both the extremes demarcated by Perron and multiple styles that rest somewhere in-between. Because it suits such a wide variety of play styles the game also suits many different situated ecologies of play. The case studies in Cybercafé Avila and Cydus suggest that there is a strong connection between the style of play in a particular location and the material conditions in which it is played. The particularities of the location will often set the agenda for what games will be played there. This is because the games played must have a rhythm that is able to initiate and sustain eurhythmia with the rhythm at the location. Games that have flexible play-styles and rhythms can be played in many situated ecologies. It also means that each situated ecology will produce specific play styles of such games that are formed by the process of developing eurhythmia between the local rhythm of the situated ecology and the rhythm of the game.

Play of the game *Vice City* was common at Cybercafé Avila, and a particular style of play had developed that was based on the relationship between the rhythm of the game and the everyday rhythms of the situated ecology at Cybercafé Avila. *Vice City* is exemplary of what Juul describes as an 'open and expressive games'.[3] Open and expressive games are: 'games that let the player use them in many different ways, games that for allow many different playing styles, for players pursuing personal agendas'.[4] This section demonstrates that the play of this game in Cybercafé Avila has numerous diverse styles. However, these styles are not solely based on the openness and expressiveness of the game, but are also examples of tactics and 'making do' adapted by the players to use that flexibility in order to produce a state of eurhythmia between the rhythm of the game and the rhythm of the café. The overall rhythm produced is thus not only based of the flexibility of the game, but the particular restrictions that are established by the material conditions in the site of play.

The first feature of *Vice City* that allowed players to establish eurhythmia with the situated ecology of Cybercafé Avila was the flexibility of the game's rhythms. This flexibility was accentuated by the ease that players had in deciding how the game is played, particularly with modulating between the missions set by the game, and activities that they devised themselves. Playing through the narrative of the missions accumulated progress along a determined route; however, because the players could move easily between this linear style and an open style of play, a greater variety of activities could be undertaken, irrespective of each individual's skill in, or progress through, the game. There are many opportunities for players to explore the various criminal elements of the game, robbery and murder among them. However, while these activities were being explored, other less controversial activities also unfolded. As one player or another would find a new discovery, often a simple series of jumps for a car or motorbike, the location of a beach buggy and some sand dunes, or a helicopter, ice cream van or taxi, which introduced new actions or movements into play. Then other players would take up the activity; discussing and exploring it: What happens when you use a bike on those jumps? Can the ice cream van weave through those palm trees as easily as other vehicles? Can you jump out of a helicopter?

The open style of play that the game allowed encouraged the sharing of information between parties in the cafe. Cheat codes were often the main point of discussion, and thus were an important element in establishing eurhythmia between the game and the social rhythms of the cafe. When exploring new activities caused pedestrian deaths or other collateral damage, 'leave-mealone' was used in order to reduce wanted levels. But in addition to the use of the cheat codes to thwart an unwanted element of the game, in some cases the cheats themselves would become central to play. Players explored parts of the game that were enabled only through cheating: 'seaways', allowed car to drive on water; 'comeflywithme', enabled the players' to fly cars; 'the-lastride' unlocked a drivable hearse. The game's open and expressive features, combined with the many different cheat codes, facilitated socialization; as there were so many possible actions and spaces to explore players were often curious about how other people were playing the game. It also mitigated the perceived difference in gaming capital between expert and novice players, as by using the cheat codes novice players could move around the game space with a similar degree of flexibility as an expert player. This is because when playing *Vice City* in this manner it is just as important to know 'where to go', as it is to know 'what to do' when you get there. The former type of information was shared easily, as navigating the game does not require explanation, because of the street map in the game's HUD. An occasional glance over to the other players' screens and maps sufficed to allow players in close physical proximity—like those in Cybercafé Avila—to engage in the same game action, albeit in different versions of the same game. Despite being a single player game *Vice City* sustained a communal form of play in this particular context that is eurhythmic with the social rhythm of the situated ecology.

The above analysis illustrates how situated gaming provides a strong account of the social prac-tices of the digital game audience. The benefit that is gained through exploring individual 'cultures of use',[5] is twofold: it avoids the homogenous understanding of digital game play that occurs with a formal analysis, while focusing on the emergent and dynamic practices of gamers, rather than the 'intended use' of the software. Situated analysis provides a useful counterpoint to formal analysis of game software because by focusing on particular situated practices it is able to ac-count for heterogeneous 'cultures of use'. It is also, by connecting the rhythm of the situated ecol-ogy to the rhythm of the game, able to suggest how this heterogeneity occurs. Situated analysis also suggests that, games may be used, or played, in a manner that was not intended. This allows games to elude the proscription of designer controller interpellation, and also to be directed into forms of adaptation, creativity, and practice based on the players' whims and predilections.

This margin of adaptation, creativity, and practice, that is suggested by situated analysis of games, is further exacerbated by the burgeoning popularity of the genre of open-ended or sand-box games. The open style of play that *Vice City* allowed was of particular importance in another context that is specific to the situated ecology in Cybercafé Avila. While specific, this point is important as it highlights how the context of play shapes how games might be played. While games might be open and expressive, particular contexts might shape their play in a manner that restricts and narrows their capacity for expression. People playing in Cybercafé Avila—and more broadly in any public form of game-play—had difficulty in saving their games. To complete a game like *Vice City* it is necessary to save the periodically. Saving games, while possible, was a problem in the public space of the café, as players had difficulty accessing the same computers when they returned, and had no guarantee that their game had not been erased or overwritten in the meantime. As a consequence, playing with an open flexible style towards the game became even more attractive.

The open and expressive style of play that *Vice City* allowed provided players in Cybercafé Avila with a viable alternative to saving the game. This meant that players continued to return to the game repeatedly, despite the fact that they could not proceed from the end-point of the previous session. Game designer Will Wright believes that the player's use of the save function in a digital game is an effective indicator that they have an investment in that experience; that the game is good enough to continue playing beyond on individual session.[6] This form of investment is effectively closed to players at internet cafés, making games that involve accumulative narratives difficult to sustain in such a situated ecology. However, the open style of play that *Vice City* permits establishes a relationship to the game that is less about progression through a narrative and more about exploring and experimenting with the possibilities of the game-space. This means that the players can return to the game many times without having to save it, because the player is—often with the aid of cheat codes—able to move through the space and pick up the game where they left off, or start exploring another area or aspect of the game without consequence. Juul argues that the save function has been a crucial factor in the evolution of digital games because it allows games to increase the size and variety of challenges while still catering to different skill levels among players.[7] The save feature may be key to digital games' technical progression and development over the years, but in terms of access to technology the requirement for a game to be saved in order to be played creates a marked differentiation between ecologies characterized by public and private consumption of digital games. While players in Cybercafé Avila were able, due to the open and expressive play style that the game allowed, to play *Vice City*; the restrictions established by the space of play meant that it was more effectively played in particular ways. The open and expressive elements of the game allowed it to be modulated into a particular rhythm of play that suited the social and technical demands of the space. However, while it highlights the specificity of the situated ecology at Cybercafé Avila, the play of Vice City also establishes connections between this cafe and numerous other situated ecologies where the same game is played; albeit with different styles that are appropriate to the peculiar context of those situated ecologies.

Vice City also has a particular resonance in Venezuela that stems from the relationship between that country and the fantasy world presented in the game. Through its available actions, themes and aesthetics, the game suggests that it is set in an imaginary version of 1980s Miami. Bogost and Klainbaum argue that Liberty City is a 'symbolic representation' of 1980s Miami.[8] *Vice City* draws upon many representations of Miami from U.S. popular culture, in particular the film *Scarface*, and the 1980s television series *Miami Vice*.[9] The game also uses more general imagery of Miami, associations with crime, drugs, and—importantly—the creolization of U.S. culture. Bogost and Klainbaum earmark this hybridity, noting that Miami is presented as 'a glamorous tropical gateway' between the 'streets of New York and the jungles of South America'.[10] For Miami, the 1980s were characterized by a creolization of culture caused by a large influx of immigrants from Latin America and the Caribbean. This cultural transformation rejuvenated the city's cultural and creative industries to take on the status of 'cultural capital of Latin America'.[11] Miami, at this time, was an important symbol of the growing importance of Latino culture in the Americas.

In the context of Venezuela, Miami also has a great deal of significance because of the close ties that have existed historically between the locations. The historic setting of the 1980s reinforces the connection, for two reasons. First, because of a widespread general nostalgia in Venezuela for the 1980s, which were the last years of the oil wealth and good relations with the USA.[12] Second, because the 1980s were the last period when it was common for wealthy middle class of Venezuela to take holidays to Miami to go shopping for clothes and electronics. This heyday is long gone for all but the most elite of Venezuela's wealthier class, and since Chávez has come into power, many wealthier Venezuelans have relocated to Miami. The fantasy 1980s Miami postulates a complex amalgam for the global imaginary of Venezuelans: nostalgia for better times, a place of refuge, a tourist resort and a cultural centre. Even so this is tempered by the obvious fantastic elements of the depiction.

The depiction of Miami is further complicated by the game's thematic focus on negative elements of US culture. Redmond argues that the game 'shine[s] a spotlight on the dark underbelly of the US Empire'.[13] The critical portrayal of the decline of inner cities in the United States that shows them as dystopian urban spaces dominated by violence, crime, and urban decay, takes on a rather different context in Caracas. Galloway points out that for a game to be realistic there must be: 'a special congruence between the social reality depicted in the game and the social reality known and lived by the player'.[14] Caracas, in particular, is a city that is troubled by violent crime, political unrest, and a sharp division between rich and poor. Although the fantastic and satiric elements of Vice City are unmistakable, in this context the game takes on different stakes. The social reality depicted in the game resonates more strongly in Caracas. In the latter case, the depicted social reality remains controversial, but due to the strong elements of comedy and parody, it is understood as a fantastic depiction of urban decay. In Caracas, where urban decay is displacing whole suburbs, the—still clearly present and understood—parody provides less room to maneuver around the more unpleasant congruent rhythms of everyday life and the game-world.

GunBound and Global Rhythms

GunBound is a free to play online game that is played in many areas of the world. It is served locally in Brazil, China, Europe, Indonesia, Japan, Taiwan, The Philippines, the USA/Canada, and Vietnam. It also has 'Latino' and International servers, distinguished by the language used: Spanish and English respectively. Aside from Counter-Strike, GunBound was the only game that was installed on both the computers at Cydus and at Cybercafé Avila. This direct connection between the two situated ecologies demonstrates that, despite major differences in the situations, the rhythm of both locations accommodated GunBound; the rhythm of both situated ecologies and the rhythm of GunBound produced eurhythmia. This established a global rhythm that connected the otherwise disparate locations. However, while the game was being played in both locations, the eurhythmia between the games and the situated ecology in Cydus and in Cybercafé Avila stemmed from completely different factors.

GunBound was a key part of the digital game ecology at Cybercafé Avila, and featured to a greater or lesser extent in the situated ecologies of all the cafés that I saw in Venezuela. Along with Vice City, it was the main game that was played at Cybercafé Avila. The key reasons were the cost and relative technical simplicity of the game. As the game is free to download and play, all that is required to play is a computer and an Internet connection. While other commercial games were easily accessible through piracy, they were, as often as not, developed for high-end computers with the latest sound and graphics processors. This meant they would either not perform optimally, or even at all.[15] GunBound was the only game that could work on all of the computers at the café because of its technical simplicity, having Manhwa style graphics and simple turn-based game play.[16] Despite this simplicity it was well regarded in Cybercafé Avila, but this regard came with a caveat. On GunBound Kermit stated: 'well it is not such a good game, but for free it is a good game'. This statement demonstrates two of the key points about GunBound play in Cyber-café Avila. First, even if the game is valued in terms of gaming capital as a 'good game', this value is entirely contextual and based on it being accessible online for free. Second, the players were acutely aware of the compromise or 'making do' that playing the game involved. This was because understanding that it was the best of the games available, implicitly involves acknowledging and apprehending the limiting factors in the situation. Both these suggest the importance of the context of the situated ecology in establishing which games are played, and even what constitutes a 'good game'. This demonstrates the importance of context in the experience of play, what games will be played and how those experiences will be valued in terms of gaming capital.

GunBound is a game that involves several stages of preparation before actual play. This distinction between preparatory activities and actual play was clearly evident from the different behaviors of the players in the various steps. It was also apparent to the players themselves; when I asked which game a group of people was playing Ajax responded, rather curtly: 'we are not playing now, right now are designing guns'.[17] Skill in the game, and therefore possession of gaming capital, was also attributed to the various preparatory configurative steps that occurred before play. This meant that avatar design and development, and gun or mobile selection, were included in addition to the skills and tactics needed to play the game successfully. When I questioned Ajax about his skill relative to another player, he replied: 'he is not so good, he doesn't know how to change the avatars for shit'. When I pressed him to explain, he elaborated:

> Ajax: [laughs] With this game, you need to know more than to play a good game, you need to know how to handle the website, and how to get the things you need to play the game to move through the game.

Each element of the game required different sets of knowledge; however, these different forms of knowledge were not unrelated. They each had their own impact on the play, and together formed a complete body of gaming capital in relation to *GunBound*. Players had different strengths and weaknesses based on their knowledge of the game and its multitude of paratexts. This added a great deal of nuance to the strategies of what would otherwise be considered a rather straightforward game, and it provided players with a large repertoire of actions, conflicts, goals, and knowledges to use in order to demonstrate their gaming capital.

Avatar design and mobile selection were the two segments of pre-game configuration that involved careful preparation. The players' avatars were persistent and remained with the account; the reward of successful play was the chance to use the gold earned in-game to buy special abilities, or unique features for the avatar. This meant that either the end of a session of play, or the start of a new one, could involve a lengthy engagement with the pre-game segments as players decided how to allocate their gold to buy different abilities. This configuration of the avatar was often done in consultation, either with paratextual information from the internet, or with other players. Avatar designs or customizations that were considered to be ill informed—a Columbian flag, a pink parasol—were subject to derision, particularly items which only changed the appearance of the avatar without giving them an in-game benefit. This pre-game segment was strongly tied to gaming capital, and its demonstration. To make good choices about avatar design the players needed to have a detailed knowledge of the next pre-game segment as well as the actual play. Players were recognized as having gaming capital by making choices during this phase that demonstrated this knowledge. The emphasis that was placed on making choices in the segment which had an impact on the actions available to the avatar in the coming game, rather than aesthetic grounds, suggests that in terms of gaming capital the importance of the pre-game choices were ancillary to the actions taken in the game.

The other pre-game step was to choose a 'gun' or mobile for the avatar to use. The mobile could be changed from game-to-game, and each of the nineteen possibilities has three individualized weapons, each with their own unique trajectories and effects, and specific strengths and vulnerabilities. Successful use of the various mobiles required different levels of familiarity with the game, and also the players' skill was salient, as some of the mobiles, like the ArmorMobile and Grub, are much easier to handle; because the aim of their primary weapons is less affected by weather conditions. Accurate aim was particularly important with a few of the available mobiles: the Boomer and NakMachine. Competency with such mobiles was a clear demonstration of game capital. This step also proceeded with much discussion. The exception here was that it was not simply the various nuances of the choices that were being evaluated, but also the combinations that the abilities of the various mobile would create when used together in team play. This meant that often a discussion would ensure between team-members that anticipated what tactics they wished to use in the game, and consequently which mobiles would be more useful in such a case. This phase was more oriented towards the game play that immediately followed than the avatar design. Even in this configurative phase, in-game actions were central to gaming capital.

The configurative steps took place in a "zone", a kind of general-purpose portal, where pre-game tasks could be performed which also included a number of chat channels, which allowed players to communicate. This was also important for the final configuration: organizing the game itself. One player would set up the game by opening a "room" and giving it a name, and then others would join the room either as team members or opponents. Usually this would involve a short wait, as more players joined the game from other locations. The waiting period was a particular point of consternation with some players, who would leave the room that had been set up in order to pursue one-on-one play which had much shorter wait times to find opponents. But this also suited the social milieu of the café, as waiting players would continue their conversations about issues that had arisen during the set-up period, or speak with others in the cafe about more general topics. The wait and the various steps of configuring the game established eurhythmia between the game and the sociality of the situated ecology. The social context of digital game play in Cybercafé Avila was entirely suitable for games like GunBound that had nuanced contents worth discussing, and times within them for discussion to occur.

The zones themselves were organized in two ways: according to the ability of the player measured by the experience and gold they had earned with their account, and according to the way that avatar abilities could be used. The zones are designated as beginner, free, and newb-free, which roughly represent a division in terms of gaming capital; although primary concern from a design perspective is the level of the player's avatar, not the skills or accumulated gaming capital of the player. The beginner zones are closed to players after they have accumulated a certain level in the game, and the newb-free are only accessible after a certain level has been obtained.[18] The zones were further divided into 'avatar on' and 'avatar off' zones, which more clearly reflect a division in the kinds of gaming capital that are in operation. The 'avatar off' zones established a mode of play where the abilities assigned to the avatar through the accumulation of gold or purchased with money do not have any tangible impact on play; gaming capital in this context was about pure skill, performance and action. The 'avatar on' zones are played with these avatar abilities in operation; game capital in this zone is focused on the accumulation of powers and abilities for the avatar. The key consequence of this division is that the 'avatar off' zones are in theory—but not necessarily in practice—smooth or even playing fields, where establish advantages based on wealth could not impact on play. The evenness is only in theory because both of the zones still proliferate with people using purchased aimbots and other cheats or hacks. However, the 'avatar off' feature is particularly important in a country like Venezuela, where many people lack the financial means to purchase avatar components online.

The game design of *GunBound* includes two key levelers that make it possible for players with free accounts to play and enjoy the game on an equal footing with those players who paid (either completely or partially) for their avatars. First, by creating an 'avatar off' zone the designers allowed players to chose a game-space which rendered purchased—and earned—equipment irrelevant. This meant that players could compete on an equal footing in a game purely based on gaming capital, without interference from other factors established through economic disparity. Second, by allowing players to both earn currency through play as well as purchase currency with real money, they created the possibility for players with different economic backgrounds to compete in the 'avatar on' zones. While there are very clear distinctions in terms of labor between having developed an avatar through purchase from in-game rewards and by simply buying the same avatar with money, it was possible with determination and skill for the former type of player to enter this space and compete effectively with the latter.

GunBound was eurhythmic with the social rhythm of Cybercafé Avila. Often the discussion of various options for avatars and mobiles, coordinating the zone and room for a group of people would take a considerable amount of time. From my field notes, it was common for players to spend as much as fifteen minutes preparing the game. In some cases players would log onto the site just to do research, or assign abilities to their avatars, leaving the café without actually playing the game at all. But this time spent in the avatar shop or choosing the mobile was not solitary, players would chat with the other people that were playing with, and the conversations about the coming game often drew in other people, El Bebe, and occasionally Maxim, were asked for advice in these stages, and also occasionally during play itself. The desire to discuss and contextualize the options of play in GunBound smoothed the transition between the processes of configuration and actual play, and nurtured the local, social rhythm of the café.

The play of GunBound involves the players in short but intense turns that cycle around the participants. Each lasts for thirty seconds, each game has between two and eight players, so the turns could be as infrequent as every four minutes. This created a great deal of time within the game for other activities. Often team members having taken their turn would begin to discuss tactics with their teammates, focusing on providing advice for the member of their team that was to take their turn next. If they were playing against others in the café, then this might also include tactics to distract the enemy player from taking their turn, or other lighthearted banter and 'smack talk'. Some players would use the gap between turns to quickly search the Internet or to conduct a brief flurry of IRC exchanges using MSN and/or Yahoo Messenger. Other players used it as a chance to explore what else was happening at the café, watching other games on the screens of nearby computers. The turn-based play established a rhythm that allowed online play and the offline sociality of the environment to be smoothly harmonized. The time between turns was utilized in much the same way as the cut scenes in *Vice City*, but with a greater frequency and predictable rhythm. Although, sometimes this comfortable state veered towards arrhythmia when players got so interested in other activities that they overlooked their commitments in *GunBound*, and missed their turn, or had to take their shot so quickly they did not aim true.

GunBound also provided scope for avoiding the problem of saving games. As the game was account based, each player saved their account online, and was thus able to save their customized avatar and the gold and experience that they had earned. Often players would share accounts, or allow a more experienced player to play their account for a while to get them a new item, or to build up the avatar so that it was strong enough to play in another zone. Huxley and Kermit both often played others' accounts, Kermit would play those of his cousin and younger sister, and Huxley would use ones belonging to Xavier's daughter or one of the other regulars at the café. Huxley was a soldier who worked at the school across the road as a security guard and custodian, he was dating a woman that lived in the house next door to the internet café and he would often come in to pass the time playing *GunBound* while he was waiting for her. Because he was good at GunBound, it was easy for him to find someone who would let him use their account for a short time: all the benefits that he accumulated would remain theirs.

In Melbourne, one interviewee, Nadia gave a similar description of account sharing. She described her own efforts in GunBound, and how she had eventually allowed her ex-boyfriend to play her account for so that she could get an avatar item that she really wanted. In the end he had:

> Nadia: ...paid money to buy the points (gold) so I could get new hair and other purely cos metic modifications

She was quick to point out that she would never actually have paid money for it herself. In none of these cases of account sharing was there any indication from the players that what they were doing might be considered cheating. In fact, more distaste was demonstrated towards the idea of buying avatar items with real money. While Nadia had clearly allowed her boyfriend to do this as an indulgence, she was equally clear in her caveat that the items purchased were cosmetic only. Buying an avatar item that impacted on the game play was implicitly disdained because *GunBound* was, to her, such an inconsequential and quaint game. While not explicitly mentioned by Nadia, part of the general disdain by many players towards purchasing items in a game like *GunBound* is because a particular premium is placed on how players perform in 'avatar off' zones. Gaming capital in this case is based purely on skill in the game, and not on the powers or appearance of the players' avatar. Paying for avatar abilities, while allowed by the game, is regarded as demonstrating a lack of gaming capital. While not regarded as cheating *per se*, it is perceived as not understanding the 'spirit' of the game. While this attitude is not universal—*GunBound* is characterized by a wide variety of attitudes towards play among its players—it is crucial in establishing a style of play and form of gaming capital that allows evenness between otherwise disparate locations. It is also the root of its ongoing global popularity, and a key point that the rhythms of Cydus and Cybercafé Avila connect.

It is precisely the global scope of *GunBound's* rhythm that is key to its continuing popularity in Cydus, and other locations. *GunBound* was clearly played less frequently in Cydus than it was in Cybercafé Avila, but somehow it remained popular, in the sense that it was a common point of experience for many people.

> Nadia: Sometimes I will play *GunBound*, you know, like all night. Then the next day when I tell my friends [laughs] they tease me for playing… …'what *GunBound*!?' You know they laugh at me… but then we start to talk about the different things in the games, the bots [mobiles] and avatars…

Nadia had played *GunBound* with her friends in Malaysia before she came to study in Melbourne, and while she did not play it as much now, she made a point of playing with her friends in Malaysia when she did play it in Melbourne. Burgundy, who lived in China before studying in Melbourne, described a similar situation, while she rarely played *GunBound* anymore, when she did it was to spend time with her brother who was studying in Adelaide, and they would often catch up with friends while playing the game.

> Burgundy: Sometimes I just talk all night; it's good because if I get bored of talking, or my friends go away I just concentrate more on playing.

The game, as it did in Cybercafé Avila, was able to facilitate social relations, although in this case it was not so much played because of its compatibility with the situated ecology but with the global rhythm of gaming. Burgundy played the game because it allowed her to indulge in play, while at the same time connect to friends and relations in other locations. In the case of Cydus, it is the restrictions and limitations facing the people at the other end of the network that are especially relevant. While *GunBound* connected them, Cydus was an environment where the game was played by choice or preference, rather than as a way of 'making do', while in the situated ecologies to which it was connected this was not necessarily the case. By choosing to play *GunBound* in order to connect with family and friends across the globe players are valuing the social element of play over other pleasures

This interest in the global reach of the game put an emphasis on playing on the International server. In terms of gaming capital, playing on the local server was regarded as insular and a demonstrating of a poor grasp of the game, especially by the interviewees in Australia. They believed that players on the International server were much better players and to play there was desirable primarily because it meant being exposed to a wider range of tactics.

> Nadia: I play in the international server, there is no Malaysian portal, but I wouldn't use the Malaysian portal anyway it is better to play with more types of people, the more strategy, so you learn more I think

Playing on the local server was okay if the series of games was to be played with a group of friends. The advantage being that the local server was less busy and experienced less lag. Burgundy described how she and her friends would often play together on a local server to hone their skills and teamwork, before shifting to play on the International server. This emphasis on International play further demonstrates that the gaming capital involved in *GunBound* is closely tied to its global access. The audience of players for a game like *GunBound* is large enough to sustain a variety of styles of, and motivations for, play. However, similar attitudes in both Cybercafé Avila and Cydus indicate that it is the global rhythm of the game; its ability to connect people around the world and redistribute gaming capital based on skill, which is central to its appeal.

Real Time Rhythms

Despite the existence of globally connected gaming networks there are still strong decentralizing forces which mean that while they are global in scale, they are more strongly connected at local, national, and regional levels. This section discusses two key decentralizing factors, national and regional identification, and the more primordial issue of balancing the synchronous time of the network society with the cyclic rhythm of the planets and stars. However, the tendency towards the splintering of the digital game ecology into multiple local ecologies is not only inspired by the national, but is also mitigated by it. While the nation becomes an organizing principle in gaming communities that emphasizes the local in the global networks, permanent and temporary movements of people also establish diasporic communities in various locations; and gaming—particularly online gaming—becomes one way that the community is maintained across national boundaries.19 This contradiction suggests that shared gaming practices are an important indicator of the connectivity between individual locations within the global network.

The national establishes divisions in the digital game ecology in a number of ways. The role that governments and institutions have in shaping the experience of gaming will be discussed more thoroughly in chapters six and seven; what is salient here is how the abstract idea of the nation figured in the experience of play, and in the accumulation and exchange of gaming capital. The national clearly comes into play in *GunBound*, particularly in relation to identifying the avatar as belong to a particular nationality, or in some cases, linguistic background. In the former, case this could be done with the acquisition of an identifying items for the player's avatar, in the form of a flag or other national symbol. The latter case requires a more deliberate deployment of language in the chat and game space. This may be either to establish a particular linguistic conformity in the play-space, e.g. the 'No Beaners' game room.20 Or it might also be used to create the possibility of communication in a public forum that only some people can understand, thus opening new channels for cheating—by using a public space to conduct private chat that could not otherwise occur in the game—and new potentials for 'smack talk'; for example this complaint about Latino players on *GunBound*:

> Mel (Melbourne): I don't mind if people don't speak English but I really don't like it when they curse at you in their own language… they get rude and then leave, it is like a way of taking a cheap shot at you.

For these reasons, many online games enforce linguistic conformity in their public chat channels, although players may address each other in whatever language they choose in their private talk.

Public communication in many online games is English by default, unless the game is popular enough to be served in a variety of different languages, or is one of the many games originating in Asia that is deemed to have limited appeal outside of the region.[21] This creates a proliferation of various versions of online games, publications that are matched to particular nations, or linguistic groups. As a consequence, even if multiple versions of a game may be accessed from anywhere in the world, in many cases the local version is selected. Language is an important influencing factor here, but often also the peculiar histories and cultures of the local have established a bi-lingual or multi-lingual tradition that allows people to connect with and operate in more than one of these versions. At Cybercafé Avila, Ajax would often play the English (for people from the United Kingdom) version of *Habbo*, choosing it over the Spanish (for people from Spain) version because he wanted to practice his English. This was a palpable demonstration of how cultural capital, in this case his knowledge of languages, could be exchanged for game capital, as Ajax because of his knowledge of English had more options available to him in terms of what games to play. But it also meant that he could use the games for different purposes; that is to develop his language skills in addition to the social networking that typically characterized *Habbo*.

Other online gamers at Cybercafé Avila used international servers to play *Tibia* and *MU: Online*. Gabrielle, played *MU: Online* on both the local and International servers, while his guild was transnational, it was entirely Latin, made up mainly from Venezuelans and Ecuadorians, and a few Argentineans and Colombians. While the opportunity to play with people from other countries online was a part of the appeal of *MU: Online* to Gabrielle, he was—unlike Ajax—only able to form social relations with other individuals that spoke Spanish. This cultural restriction also limited his access to gaming capital.

The gamers at Cydus were attached to different regional networks. The Latin American networks that were sustained in *GunBound*, *MU: Online*, and even in websites like www.latingames.com had little relevance to many people at Cydus who were enmeshed in other regional networks. The two regional networks that were important in Cydus were Asian regional networks, and networks that linked primarily English-speaking countries. These networks connect Australia to other nations through the movements of people, the English-speaking network historically and the Asian network more recently. In the case of the latter, its influence was apparent at Cydus, which had many Chinese and Korean online games that are popular in China and South-East Asia installed on the computers: *Flyff*, *Hero Online*, *Ragnarok Online*, and *ROSE Online*. Asians and Asian-Australians were not the only people playing these games; people from a variety of different cultural backgrounds played them. They were aware of the games' origin, as well as the cultural background and location of the majority of players in the game spaces.

Many of the players of this group of Korean and Chinese online games played the games for the same reason that *GunBound* remained popular: to connect with friends and acquaintances in various parts of the world in a real-time live globally-accessible environment. The large amount of International student accommodation in the area around Cydus created a consistent demand for these games to be available. Demand was such that the café stocked prepaid game cards for *Raganarok Online*—when they were available—so that players could renew their accounts without using credit cards; notably this was the only game apart from *World of Warcraft* for which Cydus stocked prepaid game cards. The management and employees of the café also went to some lengths to follow new developments in this genre of games. For example, during my fieldwork period at Cydus, one day in December 2005 I discovered that *ROSE Online* had been installed on the café's network overnight. The game had just been released in North America and was being served internationally; previously it had only been available from Indonesia-based servers in Indonesia, Malaysia and Singapore.

Regulars who had ties to those regions already knew about the game, and it quickly became a part of the situated ecology. It is because of these close ties between disparate locations established by the movements of people that the ecology of the café was closely attuned to developments and gaming trends originating in Asia. While this was primarily adopted as a policy of the café as a way of attracting and maintaining patrons from those regions, it also introduced nuances to the situated ecology at Cydus that impacted on patrons from other backgrounds. The popularity, and proliferation, of MMORPGs meant that the café carried the major commercial games of this genre—*City of Heroes, Guild Wars,* and *World of Warcraft*—all of which are to some degree transnational products. *City of Heroes* is designed by a US-based company, but is published globally by NCsoft a South Korean game publisher who also publishes *Guild Wars,* which is designed by their US-based subsidiary ArenaNet. Blizzard Entertainment, a US-based company that has found a great deal of success in South Korea, develops *World of Warcraft.* These games are distributed in a traditional manner, in the form of a CD-ROM or DVD, although they may also be downloaded from their company's websites. These games all have transnational audiences of players that are focused in Asia, North America and Europe. Through these games—and being in an environment where the games were played and discussed—local players became familiar with the global audience of games, and particularly the preponderance of gamers from Asia, and the importance of Asian gaming culture in the digital game ecology.

In addition to these top-tier commercial releases, many other games of the genre have been released, simply as free downloads, with a pay-to-play subscription model. The games that were available at Cydus were all originally produced in Asia, although some of them had been modified for publication to a global audience. This factor, combined with the strong Asian connections of the major MMORPGs, established eurhythmia between the gaming rhythm at Cydus and Asian-driven global gaming developments. This connection was strengthened by the, more or less, synchronized cyclic rhythms of the time zones of Australia and Southeast and East Asia. Australia shares time zone(s) with other major online gaming markets like China, Hong Kong, Indonesia, Japan, Malaysia, Philippines, Singapore, South Korea, and Taiwan. While Cambodia, Laos, New Zealand, Thailand and Vietnam also have relatively similar cyclic rhythms. This means that players in Cydus, in addition to playing games directed at Asian markets, also played with other gamers from the wider region. The rhythmic coupling of Australia with Asia erodes cultural and national boundaries.

The cyclic rhythm of Cyber café Avila was less strongly connected to Asia. Its strongest connection was to the other countries in the region with which it shared common heritage and language as well as similar time zones; Hispanophone South and Central America, and the Caribbean islands. Korean-made games like *MU Online* and *GunBound* were also popular there, but for different reasons. While individual Venezuelans certainly play subscription based online games like many Australian players, the games were not so popular that they were installed on the computers at Cybercafé Avila. This meant that the only MMORPGs that were available to play in that situated ecology were Korean-designed *MU Online*, and German-designed *Tibia*. Rather than being one element of a broader suite of digital games—from a variety of prices—with both a transnational and trans-cultural audience of players, these games were the only way that the players in the situated ecology of Cybercafé Avila had of participating in this global rhythm of gaming. These particular games were popular because they allowed players to create free accounts that did not require subscription fees. Their use was more a case of 'making do' than the use of similar games at Cydus. While economic factors undisputedly played a large part in this situation, another noteworthy difference between the use of these games in Cydus and Cybercafé Avila is the cultural homogeneity of the players in the latter situated ecology. A part of the situated ecology of Cydus was the cultural diversity of the players, which helped to establish a general interest in a wide variety of Asian-made MMORPGs.

The movements and rhythms of people across the globe have an important impact on the situated ecology of gaming. Internet cafés cater to the needs and demands of their patrons, and particular games are expected. In the case of Cydus, the situated ecology demonstrates clear trans-cultural influences, as the games available come from a variety of different locations. This, combined with the multi-cultural composition of the patrons of the café and the sociality and knowledge sharing that the internet café engenders, created a dynamic where the play of Asian online games at Cydus constituted an important form of gaming capital.

> Conrad (Melbourne): [*World of Warcraft*]… …is boring, its full of newbs, everyone plays it. I got sick of it, now I just like to change around. At the moment I'm playing Flyff, its cool be cause it has some little differences like combos [a kind of attack] and pets, and everything has like a very Japanese aesthetic… …like manga.

Part of the curiosity towards Asian-made MMORPGs was based on their aesthetics, which were clearly based on generic codes established through manga and manhwa. This made them clearly distinct aesthetically from North American designed online games that, generally speaking, have a much greater investment in the aesthetic of realism. However, thematically the games were often rather similar, *Ragnarok Online* and *Flyff* both take place in quasi-medieval European fantasy worlds, just like *World of Warcraft, Guild Wars* and may other popular online games. *Hero Online* is an exception to this, as it is based on a series of historical novels set in 6th Century China. The games also follow an extremely uniform set of conventions, wherever they happen to be developed. Usually, it is the graphics, and minor differences—like those cited by Conrad—that makes these games distinct. Players like Conrad, and others in Cydus, accumulated gaming capital through playing these games because they were perceived as being cooler, quirkier, more underground and exclusive. Of course this perception was completely contextual, and the prominence of Asian popular culture in Australia has an important influence on how the games were regarded. The high status that these games have allowed important exchanges based on gaming capital to take place between Asian, Asian-Australian, and gamers of other backgrounds. These exchanges involved an acknowledgement of expertise between these gamers of different cultural backgrounds, as well as even exchanges of game-centered information between parties with uneven language skills.

The status of this genre of games in Cydus points to a key difference between the two situated ecologies. In Cydus, playing games like *Ragnarok Online* was a matter of personal choice, a way of demonstrating gaming capital by playing a obscure, 'cool' Asian game, unlike all the 'newbs'. Whereas in Cybercafé Avila a similar game—*MU Online*—was played because it was free, the cost being a major barrier to participation in a standard commercial MMORPGs in Venezuela. This does not mean that playing it demonstrated a lack of gaming capital; in the context of the café it was considered in relation to other games, and the players also made a variety of distinctions about ways that the game could be configured and played. However, the shift from preference or personal style, to necessity is a major one, as the importance of the economic dimension of gaming capital underscores the uneven stakes of global participation in digital game play.

Conclusion

Despite the major differences between the situated ecologies of Cydus and Cybercafé Avila, the two locations shared a variety of features that indicated they were both a part of the global rhythm of the digital game ecology. This is demonstrated by the mutual games played—*Vice City* and *GunBound*—and the MMORPG genre, and also by the contrasting practices of the patrons. The interaction of the global rhythm of gaming and the local rhythms of everyday life in the situated ecology set particular rhythmic parameters for digital games. Games are played that suit the rhythms of the situated ecology and produce eurhythmia between the material, social, and cultural concerns of the situated ecology and the actions of play and configuration. The digital games played in the situated ecologies are similar, but the difference in styles or approaches to play demonstrates the material unevenness between them.

Notes

1 Kryzwinska, T. (2002). 'Hands on horror'. In G. King and T. Krzywinska (eds.). *ScreenPlay: Cinema/videogames/interfaces*. London: Wallflower: p. 207.
2 Perron, B. (2003). 'From Gamers to Players and Game Players: The Example of Interactive Movies'. In M. J. P. Wolf and B. Perron (eds.). *The Video Game Theory Reader*. New York: Routledge: p. 251.
3 Juul, J. (2008). 'Without a Goal: On Open and Expressive Games'. In B. Atkins and T. Krzywinska (eds.). *Videogame, Player, Text*. Manchester: Manchester University Press: p.191. Original emphasis.
4 Juul, 'Without a Goal': p.191.
5 Sassen, S, (2006). Territory, Authority, Rights: Global Assemblages. Princeton: Princeton University Press.
6 Salen, K. (2008). 'Toward an Ecology of Gaming'. In K. Salen (ed.). *The Ecology of Games: Connecting Youth, Games and Learning*. Cambridge: MIT Press: p. 12. Will Wright is most famously the designer of the SimCity and The Sims series of games, and the more controversial Spore.
7 Juul, J. (2005). *Half-Real: Video Games Between Real Rules and Fictional Worlds*. Cambridge: MIT Press: p. 111.
8 Bogost, I. and Klainbaum, D. (2006). 'Experiencing Place in Los Santos and Vice City'. In N. Garrelts (ed.). *The Meaning and Culture of Grand Theft Auto*. Jefferson: Macfarland: p. 165. The

name 'Liberty City' is also a reference to Miami, as one of the city's neighborhoods shares the name.

9 Bogost and Klainbaum, 'Experiencing Place in Los Santos and Vice City': p. 171.

10 Bogost and Klainbaum, 'Experiencing Place in Los Santos and Vice City': p. 170.

11 Yudice, G. (2003). *The Expediency of Culture: Uses of Culture in the Global Era*. Durham: Duke University Press: p. 196.

12 Márquez, P. C. (1999). *The Street is My Home: Youth and Violence in Caracas*. Stanford: Stanford University Press: p. 23.

13 Redmond, D. (2006). 'Grand Theft Video: Running and Gunning for the U.S. Empire'. In N. Garrelts (ed.). *The Meaning and Culture of Grand Theft Auto*. Jefferson: Macfarland: p. 104.

14 Galloway, A. (2006). *Gaming: Essays on Algorithmic Culture*. Minneapolis: University of Minnesota Press: p. 83.

15 Grand Theft Auto III: San Andreas and Rome: Total War would only work on two of the Cybercafé Avila's computers, while neither Lord of the Rings: The Battle for Middle Earth, nor Star Wars: Knights of the Old Republic II: The Sith Lords would operate on any of the computers at the café to the chagrin of many patrons. Medieval: Total War worked only with a nasty lag on several of the computers, a problem which was exacerbated in LAN battles.

16 *Manhwa* is the traditional aesthetic of Korean comics, which is often compared to, and clearly influenced by, the Manga aesthetic of Japanese comics.

17 In the official language of *GunBound* what Ajax refers to as his 'gun' (translated – firarma) are described as 'mobiles'. These are weapons that the players' avatar rides and fights in during play.

18 'Newb' is the GunBound slang for beginner.

19 See: Androutsopoulos (2006: p. 529); and Failkova and Yelenevskaya (2005: p. 92).

20 A 'Beaner' is a pejorative term for Mexicans/American Spanish Speakers originating from the USA.

21 South Korean games like *Lineage II: The Chaotic Throne* and *Ragnarok Online* are played by people across the globe, while other games like *Nexus: Kingdom of the Winds* are only popular in South Korea

CHAPTER SIX
SEGUES: PLAY RHYTHMS / WORK RHYTHMS

That's the beauty of college these days Tommy. You can major in Game Boy if you know how to bullshit!–Droz in *PCU*.[1]

In *PCU*, the suggestion of academic research and teaching in the area of game studies is used as an example of 'political correctness' taken to far. The comedy of Droz's statement is rooted in the notion that digital games are trivial and thus not a fit subject for rigorous academic study. While the belief that digital games are trivial still endures, many commentators, most significantly Prensky, have noted the increasing significance that digital games have in contemporary education and training.[2] The connection between digital games and learning is one of the themes that emerged from the fieldwork observations in chapter four. The process of acquiring and sharing knowledge of digital games in the internet cafés amounts to what Consalvo has described as the exchange of gaming capital. This chapter examines how this learning is put to "work".

This chapter explores three areas where robust connections can be drawn between digital game play and forms of labor. Each of these areas is one where the digital games industry has been conceived in a non-traditional manner. The first model is the creative industries; an industry model that has been important in periphery development markets, like the UK and Australia; the *Tomb Raider* series represents one of the more significant successes of that policy in the UK. The second model is the 'serious games' industry, a niche but still commercial industry, that develop games—often in partnerships with other institutions—that have a message to get across. The final model examined is the various practices collectively known as 'game art'. These three areas of segue also exacerbate the ambiguity between training and practice that characterizes digital game ecologies. The notion of counterplay is introduced in order to develop this ambiguity further.

The collapse of clearly defined categories of work and play is a phenomenon implicitly identified by Deleuze in his discussion of the reduced importance of institutions that break up individual's time and activities into clearly distinct categories in the control society. Furthermore, Deleuze also maintains that in the control society nothing is ever finished, but rather remains in a coexisting, open, metastable state.[3] Work, then is able to coexist with play and vice-versa. Rather than taking on a discreet career after finishing some form of training or education, people are expected to have a variety of careers during their lifetime, and also potentially long periods of training and study to re-skill themselves in order to move between different jobs in an ever-changing and fluctuating job market. Digital games figure not only as a leisure activity that also affords the possibility of acquiring new technological skills, or as providing skills for children and youths that are primarily developmental, but also as an effective ongoing-training method for the contemporary workplace.

The rhythm of play has not become the rhythm of work. Digital games—or rather some digital games—have a polyrhythmic capacity that provides the flexibility for a variety of rhythms to coexist. This means that neither rhythm is entirely subsumed in the other, so while play may be a form of training in some contexts, this is not always the case, and vice versa. Individual games do, of course, fit the digital games-as-training model; the highly successful *Cooking Mama*, for example, shows little variance from the notion of training, to succeed in each minigame the player must follow the recipe exactly. Training, however, need not necessarily be confined to content. Lefebvre's notion of dressage includes comportment and attitude, as well as more conventional notions of training. Digital games, as demonstrated in the case studies in Caracas and Melbourne, establish situations where peer-based learning and collaboration take place. But whilst this occurs, the players are also being trained in how to hold their bodies, memorize hand positions on keyboards and controllers, and techniques for scrutinizing and using interfaces. To take the notion of dressage a little further, they are also being trained at how to attend to a computer, and to maintain and modulate an algorithm.

How can we understand the significance of the vastly different stakes that the accumulation of gaming capital by players has in Australia and Venezuela? The major point of contrast is the flexibility of exchange. Gaming capital need not necessarily remain simply gaming capital, but may—particularly considering the fluidity of the segues between play and work—be exchanged for other more tangible forms of capital. This possibility is explored in relation to the movement from game playing, into forms of labor. For this kind of movement to be made it is necessary for a smooth pathway to exist between digital game play and the industry. Kücklich suggests that this pathway is the mod.[4] Conventionally defined as: 'amateur modifications of existing games',[5] the mod provides key segues between playing digital games and making them. Kücklich argues that the mod has become a meta-act in gaming that unites players with industry practitioners; for while play become more like modding with the inclusion of development tools in commercial releases, modding has also taken on a central role in digital game design because of the standardization of game engines and middleware.[6] The boundary between playing the game, and playing with the game is not as clear at it might otherwise appear due to the increasing commercial introduction of modding into many digital games. This means that many players will become involved with modding without consciously making a decision to do so, simply by exploring the possible designed engagements with the game.

Counterplay

This chapter reflects on, and expands, de Peuter and Dyer-Witheford's notion of 'counterplay'. Originally the term was used to describe audience practices that were commercially reiterated by the digital games industry; a process they dubbed the 'capture of counterplay'.[7] The 'capture of counterplay' pinpoints how innovative gaming practices are harnessed by the games industry to produce new forms of play. By isolating counterplay, practices of digital game players' can be examined outside of the context of appropriation. Counterplay is an important concept for digital game scholarship as it does not privilege the compulsive element of play, instead providing an account of play that emphasizes how the relationships between players and digital games oscillates between compulsion and adaptation, training and practice. This conflict and ambiguity is central to counterplay. Counterplay challenges the validity of models of play that suggest digital games compel the players' to play according to encoded algorithms, which they must follow exactly in order to succeed. Instead, it opens the possibility of an antagonistic relationship between the digital game and player. An antagonism that is considerably more high stakes than the player overcoming the simulated enemies, goals and challenges that the game provides, rather it is directed towards the ludic rules that govern the digital games configurations, processes, rhythms, spaces, and structures.

Counterplay is evident where during the course of play the player produces results that were otherwise unanticipated during the design process. These results could be the outcome of varia-tions to the programming of the game, or of in-game actions; but as long as they are in-play—or in support of play—they are counterplay. By reasserting the adaptive element of play, counterplay suggests that the stakes of digital game play cannot be reduced to 'it is just a game'. Digital games are experiences of control, discipline, modulation, and training, but these elements are tempered by the possibility, and search for, innovation and practice, in: actions, configurations, modes, polyrhythm, rhythms, strategies, styles, and tactics.

Counterplay occurs in the virtual spaces of digital games, but in order to expand play, counter-play may leverage the situated. It is enacted in the local, and may mobilize the gaming body, the: hardware, people, and the spaces through which play is embedded and produced. Counterplay explores the material limits of digital games: the actions, actors, artificial intelligence, and objects of the virtual space, and may even involve cataloging a game's bugs and glitches. But this doesn't necessarily involve players knowing or learning how to code. Counterplay is not hacking; it simply involves understanding and using the limits of the virtual space of game play.

The Creative Industries

Digital games fit into the general concept of creative industries without controversy. While spe-cific definitions of the notion are difficult to come by, generally the defining element of the crea-tive industry is: 'an industry where brain work is preponderant and the outcome is intellectual property'.8 The British Government's Department of Culture, Media, and Sports describes the creative industries as:

> Those industries which have their origin in individual creativity, skill and talent and which have a potential for wealth and job creation through the generation and exploitation of intellectual property.9

The emphasis on the development of intellectual property fits well with digital game development. For example, the state government of Victoria—the state where Melbourne is located—specifically couches their financial support of the local game development industry through Film Victoria's Digital Media Fund, as focused on establishing locally produced intellectual property.10 Hartley elaborates the emphasis on intellectual property by earmarking the significance of the creative industries in enhancing the value of new media technology within the 'knowledge economy'.11 This section explores how, through the notion of the mod, the creative industries approach to digital games ameliorates the ambiguity between adaptation and compulsion by conceptualizing the adaptive process of playing a digital game as a form of training.

The ambiguity that digital games establish between adaptation and compulsion is resolved in the logic of creative industries. Crucial to this is the observation that digital games blur the boundary between work and play, by 'subordinating play to work'.12 In the context of creative industries it has been established that the 'work' of the players adds tangible value to the game.13 The key issue with this blurring is that players who have added value to the game should be acknowledged by the industry as stakeholders in a collective project, rather than merely consumers of products.[14] At stake for the players in this blurring is their ambiguous status as either consumers or citizens of game-worlds. The ongoing denial that the work done by players during the course of play should give them some kind of 'rights' to the management of the game, and game community, demonstrates the exploitative element of the subordination of play to work in the games industry.[15]

Several case studies that suggest the possibility of a more equitable relationship between the games industry and players have focused on the game Trainz.[16] This game, developed by the now defunct company Auran, allowed players to retain control of the intellectual property of the objects and items that they designed for the game.[17] Through this relationship, it was believed that Auran was able to profit from the close allegiance of the game community who, because of this incentive, continued to produce content that established the game's longevity. However, it is also suggested that this close and equitable relationship may have led to Auran's downfall, due to the critical and commercial failure of FURY. While Auran's CEO Terry Hilliam blamed the games lack of commercial success on the company's failure to 'find a viable business model'.[18] Other commentators attributed the commercial failure of the high budget (13.2 million dollar) MMORPG to Auran's close relationship with their fan-base during the development of the game, which they suggest led to the creation of a game that had little appeal outside this select group.[19] This indicates that a close relationship between the producers and consumers of a game may not necessarily benefit the producers of a major commercial project.[20]

However, it is accepted that the success of the digital games industry is the close relationship it has established and maintained with players. This relationship is demonstrated through the industry's practice of using audience members to beta-test games during the development process. Beta testing is the practice of allowing people to play uncompleted versions of the game, and using their comments and experiences to locate any bugs or game-balance problems. Kline et al. describe beta testers as: 'cadres of digital knowledge workers who are encouraged to blur the lines between labor and leisure'.[21] This 'blurring' does not stop when the game is released, as often games are updated by after their commercial release by 'patches' designed to fix problems that players have located.

Beta testing demonstrates how play is used to add value to digital games. The activities of the community or audience of players' is of interest to the creative industries model because having large and active communities of players will increase digital games longevity, quality, and profile; and hence profit. But players rarely begrudge the work that takes place under the guise of play. While it is usually unpaid, contributing to a game by participating in beta testing, generating para-texts and patches, or even creating product, like new maps or items, is highly rated as a form of game capital in most gaming communities.

This industry practice, of capitalizing on the free labor of the audience in order to increase the value of their intellectual property, also exploits the ambiguity between consumption and citizenship that characterizes players of digital games. This ambiguity has led to a strong industry focus on the cultivation and management of game communities practices, that has been lionized in some creative industries scholarship as the logic of 'harnessing the hive'.[22] This concept suggests that new media platforms such as digital games are: 'the bleeding edge of massively networked innovation'.[23] The role of the innovative entrepreneur is to coalesce the 'collective intelligence' of virtual communities.[24] Bruns points out that the process is not necessarily commercial, pointing to the manner in which various aggregation services link the 'blogosphere' as an example of how 'harnessing the hive' may provide non-profit, benefits to the community of participants.[25]

The creative industries model of 'harnessing the hive' ignores the ambiguous relationship between the players of digital games, and industry. While it uses the language of 'potential' and 'libratory' practices that suggests a form of grassroots democracy, the process of community building also involves a high level of scrutiny, and modulation, of players' activities. 'Harnessing the hive' and 'the capture of counterplay', while emerging from different debates and contexts, provide a remarkably similar description of the centrality of the player and their activities in the continuing profitability of the digital games industry. There are numerous cases of the digital games industry 'harnessing the hive': the release of *The Movies* in the wake of the widespread recognition of Machinima, the commercial release of games that were originally conceived as player-made mods like *Counter-Strike*, and the foregrounding of the role that the virtual economy would play in *Second Life*, following the 'discovery' of virtual economies in other MMORPGs. These developments demonstrate the stakes in the distinction between 'harnessing the hive' and 'the capture of counterplay'. 'Harnessing the hive', suggests that the zeitgeist of contemporary gaming relies on a synergy between the industry and players. However, 'the capture of counterplay' underscores how the industry has been able to profit from the creative actions of players', by recognizing them, and subsequently re-structuring individual games as well as elements of the gaming industry to make those actions into features, products, or services.

In the context of the two case studies, the creative industries model indicates several key differences in the global digital games ecology in the area of industry/player relations. Venezuela lacks the institutional synergy and government support to establish a thriving local game development industry.26 The Australian digital games industry, however, receives a degree of support at the state level from the governments of Victoria and Queensland, which includes support in the form of higher education degrees at state-funded TAFEs (vocational education providers) and Universities. There are also a growing number of private institutions catering for students that wish to enter the games industry. Overseas companies—like Atari Creative Assembly, and Pandemonium Studios—by locating studios in Australia have also nurtured the growth of this sector.

The creative industry model provides segues from play to work in the digital games industry in Australia, but this is not the case in Venezuela. The digital game players are 'harnessed', their practices are 'captured', but the industries efforts do not extend globally. While the digital gaming ecology is global, the relationship between players' and the industry that the creative industries position as being central to the success of the digital games industry is only realized in select locations.

'Serious' Games
'Serious' games are a new genre, or category of digital games that both demonstrates, and emerges from, the developing respect that the medium is garnering in educational and pedagogi-

cal contexts. As a genre it is difficult to clearly define, because it is applied to games that have been developed in a number of different contexts, for example: advertising, education, journalism, and public relations. While diverse, the genre is united by a sense of purpose. Play of serious games has deliberate stakes; it is neither play as an escape from everyday life, nor as the development of ill-defined general skills (coordination, strategic thinking, etc.). Serious games propose purposeful play with meaningful outcomes; they aim to bring an issue, or issues, to the players' attention through play. The primary significance of this sub-industry of digital games is that it positions the communication of ideas and persuasion through play as an essential, rather than periphery, design concern.

Serious games are developed for heterogeneous purposes, this suggest that what is at stake in their play varies greatly. For example, the Australian-made serious games *Escape from Woomera* and *Reach Out! Central*, both deal with serious issues through play, but have entirely different agendas. The stated aim of Escape from Woomera is to highlight the plight of refugees in Australian 'detainment' centers, by: 'offering an interactive, immersive glimpse of life within one of the most secretive and controversial places on the Australian political and geographical landscape'.[27] While *Reach Out! Central,* although it shares a concern for human well-being, is directed at helping youths 'improve and learn skills for life' with an emphasis on providing information on 'depression, anxiety, self-harm, independence and body image'.[28] The latter game aims to extend the support provided to at-risk youth, while the former proposes an explicitly political intervention on a particular topical and controversial issue. However, the variety of entry-points into the serious games industry through various partnerships—which the above examples only begin to demonstrate—also suggests that serious games as a sub-industry is open to a wider scope of participation, from a greater variety of stakeholders, than the commercial games industry.

The "impact" of serious games, has yet to be effectively measured. In many cases, it appears their role has been more effective through the coverage of the games themselves in other mainstream media, than through play of the game. However, this is not always the case. The widespread coverage of *Food Force*, was accompanied by over three million downloads of the game in the years after its initial release.[29] The much discussed *Howard Dean for Iowa*, while attracting a great deal of attention from mainstream media, was also downloaded over 40,000 times in the two weeks following its online release.[30] Co-designer of *Howard Dean for Iowa*, Ian Bogost argues that irrespective of hard figures that index the number of players, the success of the project could be measured by the impact of the game on the blogosphere in the form of discussions about the ways that games represented rules and rule-based systems.[31] Here, Bogost makes two important points. The first, is that the test of a games' impact should not be defined solely by a figure based on sales, players, or downloads, rather if and how a game resonates outside of the times and spaces of its play is also significant. This point highlights the importance of situating the play of digital games, and use of the paratextual industries, in relation to the digital game, and general media, ecology. The second point Bogost makes, suggests that the 'effectiveness' of serious games does not stem from their engagement with serious issues, *but from their willingness to take games seriously.* The measure of success for serious games is that they encourage reflection on the representation of systems and processes in games, this invites critical thinking about games themselves as well as meditation on the particular issues presented.

This perspective on serious games, suggests that the 'serious' element of the game is in how they represent systems and procedures. *Howard Dean for Iowa's* other co-designer Gonzalo Frasca argues that digital games can convey ideas about the world through the rules that define the simulation: 'narrative may excel at taking snapshots of particular events but simulation provides us with the tool for understanding the big picture'.[32] Many serious games follow this logic, and represent the serious issue through the rules and process of the virtual world that are encoded in the games' algorithm. Frasca suggests that the strength of digital games as a communicative medium is that they can represent processes, causes and effects, and that because they are compossible, players may explore a variety of outcomes. His work establishes how digital games may be used to convey a serious message, and what kind of messages they might be better at conveying. Most importantly Frasca presents the cornerstone of the serious game: that the message must come from the process of play: the interaction of player, machine code, and the wider digital game ecology.

In Frasca's argument the importance of simulation over narrative is established by examining digital games as process-based computer code. By communicating at the level of process, Fracsa suggests that through simulation digital games are able to connect events to their underlying causes. Thus, digital games function as 'epistemic tools' as well as more tangible training simulators.[33] Frasca is not alone in suggesting that it is playing with the procedural system of digital games that establishes new possibilities for knowledge. For Salen knowledge of systems, and the multiple ways that they can be configured and transformed constitutes a new form of literacy.[34] Other scholars introduce similar terms—algorithms, procedural, and unit operations—in order to highlight the break from narrative that is established by coded simulation.[35] These approaches all examine digital games as configurative systems. Salen's definition is different, she emphasizes that knowledge of a system also involves knowing how to change the system.[36] This is the goal of the serious game, to channel players' into a particular understanding of a system, and to persuade them to a particular position on how that system should be changed. This suggests that counterplay offers, and affords, players the opportunity to: deliberately 'resist' or ignore coded messages, create aberrant outcomes, and even to change the message. This form of adaptation is not without complication, as it takes places within a system that is designed for configuration.[37]

However, games can have serious messages, without necessarily being serious games. They may advocate change through their narrative rather than through the processes that they simulate. For example, the Venezuelan-developed game *Mazinger Z Salvo a Venezuela* has a politically motivated narrative and agenda.[38] But, these elements of the game are not a part of its rules or simulation. The critique is not explored through play and configuration of the game; rather the critique is implicit in its theme. *Mazinger Z Salvo a Venezuela* is a sideways scrolling fighting game where the actions focus on battles between a giant robot that is controlled by the player, and the Venezuelan military forces and their allies (evil giant robots). The battles take place at prominent landmarks around Caracas, such as Plaza Altamira, Parque Central, and Plaza Venezuela. Mazinger Z—the giant robot that is the players' avatar—is the main character from a cult anime of that name created by Go Nagai in 1972 that has a large following in Venezuela. The premise of the game is that Mazinger Z must save Venezuela from other marauding evil giant robots, and the army that has been turned into cyborgs and are now the evil robots' minions. Despite the explicitly fantastic milieu, considering the current political situation in Venezuela the game can be read as an implicit critique of Hugo Chávez. However, the effectiveness of this critique is highly dependent on understanding its context. The background material provided on the back cover of the game's case, states:

"Nos robaron el referéndum"
Sólo dos jóvenes podrán detener
el imperio de terror.
Prepárate a salvar a Venezuela
y al mundo del imperio Mikene.

"They stole the referendum"
Only two youths can stop
the reign of terror.
Prepare to save Venezuela
and the world of the Mikene empire.

Produced during a period of political crisis, the cover message specifically mentions a key concern of Chávez's opposition: the plea "*Nos robarón el referéndum*", links the evil robots in the game to the alleged fraudulent election practices of Chávez. The actions against the army (who are dehumanized machines) in the game are also implicitly an anti-Chávez message, as the President is a former military officer, and is still closely associated with the army. The game clearly reflects a political agenda, and draws upon both specific local iconography and that from a cult Japanese anime, to address specific Venezuelan concerns.

While *Mazinger Z Salvo a Venezuela* is not a serious game, it does effectively illustrate the problems facing the implementation of serious game design in the Venezuelan context. First, is the issue of distribution, *Mazinger Z Salvo a Venezuela* is available on CD-ROMs in several computer shops in Caracas, and also through Mediatech's website. Typically serious games are available for free, either as downloads like *Escape from Woomera*, and *Food Force*, or playable in browser windows, like *September 12th*. This method of free online distribution ensures that the game can reach the maximum amount of people. However, this game has little appeal outside of Venezuela, and was never intended for global distribution. *Mazinger Z Salvo A Venezuela* is not intended to maximize peoples' exposure to an issue and influence their opinion on it. This is because the critique that it proffers relies on a localized understanding of events. Furthermore, the partisan position that the game takes means that it will only appeal to critics of the current government. It was not designed to change or influence anyone; it speaks to people who already agree with the position that it takes.

The insider status of the political message in *Mazinger Z Salvo A Venezuela* also suggests a strategy of flying under the radar. While the Venezuelan president has no overt record or policy of dealing with media critics in an unlawful manner, his supporters have allegedly been involved in a large number of documented acts of violence against supporters of the opposition. Chávez's policy towards the media has been to reduce their independence, by introducing legislation and new executive powers reinstating state control. The stakes of being widely noticed as a critic are rather high in Venezuela, with the real possibility of some kind of punitive action. Serious games function effectively when they have clear institutional support and may be distributed and played in repercussion-free environments. Local political situations vary and can create digital game ecologies where serious games are not a viable form of criticism.

Shifting the stakes of play outside of the virtual is the point of serious games. Rather than celebrating the virtual, serious games highlight the connections between digital games and the material world. The seriousness of serious games is highly context-specific. The concept of serious games refers not to the topic or content of the game, but to the manner in which the digital game is used to engage the player. However, the genre suggests an important way of understanding how digital games convey messages, based on the materiality of the computer code and the process through which the player enacts that code. The concept—and design strategies—of serious games have important consequences for counterplay; by suggesting that digital games are persuasive they offer a space for counterplay to negotiate the argument or ideological position presented in the game.

Digital Game Art

The term 'digital game art' is used to refer to a number of approaches to incorporating digital game technology and aesthetics into artistic expression.[39] Stockburger outlines the three main areas where digital games have become integrated with artistic practice: 'appropriation, modification, and production of original games'.[40] By 'appropriation', Stockburger refers to the incorporation of iconography and aesthetics from digital games into orthodox art practices. 'Modification' refers to the practice of modding, although in the context of artistic practice they are characterized as 'interventions'.[41] The final category, production of original games is, for Stockburger, equivocal with the serious game. The focus of this section is on artist-made mods of games. As an artistic intervention made into the game-space the art mod disrupts the smooth segue that the mod provides between amateur and professional modding. This is because the interventions that it makes often end up reducing or removing interactive game play.[42] It is for this reason also that many art mod projects are difficult to classify as counterplay, although they do suggest to Galloway the possibility of a new, radical approach to game design, that he dubs 'countergaming'. The purpose of this section is to contrast the possibilities of countergaming with those offered by counterplay.

Stockburger suggests that serious games may actually be a subset of digital game art.[43] In any case, serious games are games that have been made to highlight some issue in the world, whether that is youth suicide or mass starvation in Sudan.[44] Art mods are distinct from this as they are about examining the politics of the medium itself. Huhtamo's suggests a subtle agenda for art modding, that avoids being overtly political:

> A game patch [mod] artist may be motivated by ideological concerns, an urge to re-assert the role of the player as a (co)creator, or to subvert the prevailing gender relations, particularly the depiction of women as game characters. *Yet the political determination should not be overemphasized.*[45]

Huhtamo suggests that a problem with political interventions into gamespace is that by being overtly deterministic they operate on the level of propaganda rather than persuasion. By subordinating play to other extrinsic goals it becomes something other than just play. Huhtamo suggests that the most effective forms of modding a game are subtly political. They multiply the possibilities of play, while overtly political interventions potentially channel and constrain it. Serious games use gaming as a means to an end, but art mods often see gaming as the end in itself.

With the notion of countergaming, Galloway outlines a potential agenda for game art that suggests it gestures towards new forms and possibilities of digital game play. He acknowledges that countergaming is, as yet, an 'unrealized project', in which 'aesthetics are elevated over gameplay'.[46] However, Galloway argues that countergaming may in the future be realized as a form of gaming, rather than art made with games. He suggests that game art offers a new and radical language of game design.[47] In principle, it operates as a critique of industry game design, but the mod artists rely heavily on that industry for its materials.[48] Galloway describes the relationship between game artist and the digital games industry as 'symbiotic',[49] but to others it is 'parasitical'.[50] Although it relies on the materials that the industry provides, countergaming suggests that artistic and creative practices have a place in reimagining digital game play's potentials.

Countergaming and counterplay are not antithetical to each other; rather the notion of counterplay is complementary to that of countergaming. The latter's concern with developing new 'avant-garde' forms and genres of digital games suggests an activist grass-roots approach to changing and challenging the digital games industry, commonly held perceptions of what digital games are, their potential role in relation to politics, and the future of the medium. Countergaming mobilizes game designers and artists to create 'a new language of play'.[51] Galloway's discussion examines specific works made by artists using digital game mods to suggest a basis of, and future for, a radical language and politics of countergaming, one that he emphasizes is a unique response to the affordances of the gaming medium. In contrast, counterplay examines and explores already existing, localized, enacted practices of digital game play and how they use and exploit the fragile and retreating margin of play that digital games provide. By examining the innovative practices of the players, with particular interest in the points where these practices suggest forms of play that open its margin into new domains, counterplay indentifies *a reconfiguration of gaming from within* that may take gaming in a number of directions; from activism, for example projects like Delappe's *dead-in-iraq*, to regressive politics like those proselytized in the racist mod 'WPDoom'.[52]

Digital game art and art mods are congruent with forms of counterplay in two key instances. First, as interventions, mods may either reduce or increase the possibilities of counterplay, by removing or adding actions that the players make take. Second, in-game performances are also closely attuned to existing practices of counterplay, and by conceptualizing the intervention as art, focuses on the creative element of the performance, which otherwise might not be appreciated. Both of these types of game art share counterplay's concern with examining, challenging, and playing with, the material coded limits of digital games

Artistic forms of modding sit uneasily between amateur or playful mods, and professional or industry mods. This is because, despite having this practice in common, game artists use modding in a manner that is difficult to trace back to either in the modding practices of players', or in the industries use of modding during digital game development. Artistic approaches to modding are interventions, or interruptions in the eurhythmia of work and play that seek to turn modding into a conscious, deliberate, and political act. It is through highlighting the politics of modding practices that artistic modding suggests that it is not merely a process of playful tinkering that develops the 'creative' skills necessary for players to successfully segue into the creative industries. In a 2007 interview the art collective JODI (Joan Heemskerk and Dirk Paesmans) commented:

> I've read an article somewhere, where the game industry and the game makers explain it that it was better business to include the audience in the creative process than to just release their finished games... ...The industries know that a big part of the public more then just playing also likes to add to the game their own face or their own building or their own monster or their own car. So it becomes normal that a game becomes modified... ...What our interest in modifying the game was, we always worked in the style of abstraction.[53]

JODI's projects have explored the process of modding from a different perspective than that which is embraced in the eurhythmia of players and industry. They present modding as a form of counterplay that has no intrinsic value to the segue from game player to worker. Counterplay offers this critique of game play, digital games need not be valued for the way that the provide leverage into other activities. Counterplay is the struggle to carve out from the compulsive elements of digital games a space that allows for adaptation, creativity, improvisation, innovation, and reflection.

Mainly working with commercially released games JODI have produced a number of projects— *ctrl-space, SOD, Untitled Game* —that explore the layers of abstract data which produce the game interface. In Untitled Game, the collective produced a series of games on a scale of increasing aesthetic minimalism, which was done through modifying *Quake*. Each of the works in the series involves erasing more code, which produced incremental levels of minimalism, the apex of which was a white screen, where everything was erased.[54] *Untitled Game* focused on exposing the materiality of the digital game by bringing the code to the forefront of the experience.[55] New York-based artist Cory Arcangel's seminal *Super Mario Clouds* has a similar agenda, taking *Super Mario Bros.* as a starting point the artist erased code until just the background of floating clouds was left. While both projects involve reducing the possibilities of play, by turning the digital game into something that is unplayable, they also suggest something about play. Lines of code may just as easily be added to the game as they are removed. By reducing the possibilities of a game-world the projects make an important point about interactive spaces, just how open, flexible and non-linear are they? Despite the celebration of the rhizomatic and non-linear potentials of contemporary digital games, many games remain linear and hierarchical in structure; Fable, for example. *Super Mario Clouds* and *Untitled Game* both suggest that games have a rigid structure, which is a part of their material existence. This is highlighted by Corey Arcangel, who includes the hacked game cartridge of *Super Mario Bros.* in the *Clouds* installation. Counterplay shares this concern with the material; it may involve leveraging the materiality of digital games to produce play, or to create some form of advantage or distinction.

A key way in which counterplay is used in digital games is to increase the possible actions available to players. This is an area where player-modding practices and game art mods overlap. Not all art mods remove interactivity from games; some add new forms of actions. *The Velvet Strike* project by Anne-Marie Schleiner, Joan Leandre, and Brody Condon is an example of this type of art mod. Designed as mods for *Counter-Strike, The Velvet Strike* mods allowed players to spray paint graffiti, on the levels that they were playing, which could be read by players in other locations. The downloadable mods focused on anti-war-on-terror activism, people were also invited to submit their own mods of a similar vein. While clearly a politicized protest, *The Velvet Strike* project utilized pre-existing digital gaming practices as an intervention. In *Counter-Strike*, mods are commonly used to multiply the possibilities of play, by designing new maps for example. But this art project uses that practice as a platform for political intervention.

In these cases the link is conceptual; other game art projects are firmly grounded in actual play or play practices that actually mirror the counterplay practices of the community of players'. Nevada-based US Game artist Joseph Delappe describes his projects as: 'expanding the potential of what these [game] spaces could be about'.[56] Delappe's art is a performance described as an in-game protest or intervention. This involves the artist taking actions in the game as a player. This form of game art has taken on a new significance in the contemporary networked era due to the increasing prevalence of online gaming, either through specific networks like Steam or Xbox Live; or through MMORPGs like *World of Warcraft* or *Flyff*. This is best illustrated by Delappe's recent work, *dead-in-iraq* and *War Poets Online* which took place within preexisting commercial online multiplayer games, *America's Army* and *Medal of Honor: Allied Assault,* respectively.

Delappe's work involves making peaceful anti-war 'aesthetic protests' inside the gamespace during the course of play.[57] In *dead-in-iraq* this was done by typing a list of the names of the US casualties in the invasion and occupation of Iraq (2003-), into the chat channel of the game. *The War Poets Online* project had a similar modus operandi; Delappe logged into the game as 'Siegfried Sassoon' and typed in the war poems of the famous World War One poet. For the this project, he also took screen shots of the moment that his avatar was shot, which contrasted the hyper-realistic virtual portrayal of death with Sassoon's meditations on the horrors of war. While highly conceptual, Delappe's work resembles other forms of counterplay in online communities. For example, in *GunBound* players can chat during the game, and the text appears both in a chat box, and also in *Manhwa*-like style, as a cartoon balloon emit from the players' avatars. When a player's gun or mobile is destroyed the physically unharmed avatar floats out of the wreckage and disappears off the top of the screen. In this moment, many players' try to make a witty parting remark, which lingers behind them as a trace—a speech balloon, without a speaker—for a few moments after they have disappeared. Some *GunBound* players took great delight in this moment, using it to convey insults, compliments, or an in-joke. Delappe's project takes this kind of playful juxtaposition of chat text and image to produce a critique of, and reflection on, the playful and virtual depiction of war.

Both *War Poets Online* and *dead-in-iraq* resemble counterplay practices of digital game players. In-game protests have a long history in MMORPGs, they have occurred in *Ultima Online, EverQuest*, and *Star Wars Galaxies*.[58] Protests were also made in *World of Warcraft* after Blizzard had threatened to expel players promoting gay-friendly guilds from the game.[59] In another incident, dubbed 'The Gnome Tea Party', the Argent Dawn server was deliberately overloaded and crashed by naked gnome avatars that were advocating changes in the rules that would address the perceived imbalance in powers between warriors and the other available classes.[60] There was also a widely reported mass protest in the Chinese-made MMORPG *Fantasy Westward Journey.* The protest occurred when the mainly Chinese players mobilized against what they perceived as Netease implementing a heavy-handed policy towards in-game racism against Japanese.[61] These incidents suggest that in the context of MMORPGs counter-play is political, or at least, not a purely artistic issue. This form of in-game action is a key turning point; through play the consumer/player reconstitutes themselves as citizens of the virtual world.

Delappe's interventions differ from the above examples as they have a strong resonance outside of the gamespace, primarily because the invasion, and subsequent occupation, of Iraq by the USA remains a hotly contested, controversial topic. Delappe's methods share similarities with practices that have been used by online gaming communities. These practices are not considered artistic, but are understood as a form of protest. What they share with Delappe's practice is the use of in-game action to demonstrate dissent. However, Delappe has an agenda which is rooted in us-ing the virtual site as a way of drawing attention to real world problems; other forms of protest, while often involving issues parallel to offline concerns, like gay rights, are usually focused on issues involving play. Often they deal directly with resolving the ambiguity between citizenship and consumption that characterizes digital game play in the contemporary era, by challenging the authority of the owners and managers of the games and game communities to make decisions which impact on the players' experiences.

The reason why Delappe's art projects are significant is that they follow, and extend, established practices of counterplay. Disruptive behavior in virtual worlds is an historic form of protest among game communities, and his work suggests that in-game protest need not focus on maintaining the autonomy of the game world, and its players', from 'outside' influence; they may also bring the 'real' world into play, as a strategy for highlighting the arbitrary construction of the virtual. This indicates that counterplay, as a form of action, can establish resonations between the games and everyday life that elevate the stakes of play outside of the virtual.

Conclusion

Digital game play offers segues into 'real' world activities in a number of ways. None of them are entirely smooth; the ease of the segue is dependent on the context of play and the supporting conditions in the location of play. Together they suggest a global inequality between digital game players that will be discussed in the following chapter. The creative industry model suggested an approach to understanding digital game that centered on how play fostered creative skills that can be harnessed by the digital games industries. This model is highly dependent on location for its success, focusing on high tech clusters in creative cities; furthermore, the harnessing of the audience tends to focus on the digital game players that make productive contributions to digital game culture in some manner, consequently many players are marginalized by this model. The creative industries, while explicitly creative has an ambiguous understanding of digital game play. Digital game play is positioned as a kind of training in creativity that turns the practices of the audience into a major resource for the digital games industry.

While the serious games sector suggests a segue that is based on systems 'literacy', the genre also raises questions about the ambiguity between training and practice, as they suggest digital games may be designed to communicate a specific message they appear to emphasize training over practice. However, the model of digital game communication presented through serious games suggests that counterplay provides scope for practices that disrupt these serious 'messages' by using the resources in the situated ecology: the actions within the game, the gaming body itself; and the objects and individuals recruited to the assemblage.

Game art suggests a segue in forms of practice. Game art is also highly contextual, illustrated by the game art projects—like Delappe's *dead-in-iraq*—that make connections and establish resonance between the virtual world and real-world events. This chapter also argues that Galloway's notion of countergaming, the search for a new language and grammar of gaming, should be informed by the notion of counterplay, the unruly innovations and practices of game cultures that emerge from digital game play. Counterplay is more than the creative actions of the individual player during the process of adapting to the highly structured game environments, it also encapsulates the adaptation to compulsions that makes digital games a crucially important medium for the contemporary society of control.

Notes
1 *PCU* (Bochner, 1994) distributed by 20th Century Fox, starring Jeremy Piven as 'Droz'.
2 Prensky, M. (2001). *Digital Game-based Learning*. New York: McGraw-Hill.
3 See: Deleuze, G. (1995). *Negotiations 1972-1990*. New York: Columbia University Press; and Deleuze, G (2006). Two Regimes of Madness: Texts and Interviews 1975-1995. Los Angeles: Semiotexte.
4 Kücklich, J. (2005). 'Precarious Playbour: Modders and the Digital Games Industry'. *The Fibreculture Journal 5*.
5 Jenkins, H. (2006). *Convergence Culture: Where Old and New Media Collide*. New York: New York University Press: p. 289.
6 Kücklich, 'Precarious Playbour'. Note—game engines and middleware are software specifically designed for digital game development.
7 de Peuter, G. and Dyer-Witheford, N. (2005). 'A Playful Multitude? Mobilising and Counter-mobilising Immaterial Game Labour'. *The Fibreculture Journal 5*.
8 Howkins, J. (2005). 'The Mayor's Commission on the Creative industries'. In J. Hartley (ed.). *Creative Industries: A Reader*. Malden: Blackwell: p. 119.
9 Cited from: Lovink, G. and Rossiter, N. (2007). *MyCreativity Reader: A Critique of Creative Industries*. Amsterdam: Institute of Network Cultures: p. 253.
10 This issue is reported on by: Hill, J. (2006). 'Game Industry at the Crossroads'. The Age; and is discussed in: Apperley, T. H. (2008). Video games in Australia. In M. J. P. Wolf (ed.). The Video Game Explosion: A History from Pong to Playstation® and Beyond. Westport: Greenwood Press: pp. 223-228.
11 Hartley, J. (2005). 'Creative Industries'. In J. Hartley (ed.). Creative Industries: A Reader. Malden: Blackwell: p. 5.
12 Thomas, D. and Brown, J. S. (2007). 'The Play of Imagination: Extending the Literary Mind'. Games and Culture 2.2: p. 169.
13 Humphreys, S. (2005). 'Productive Players: Online Computer Games' Challenge to Traditional Media Forms'. *Communication and Critical/Cultural Studies* 2.1: pp. 37-51; and Taylor, T. L. (2006a). *Play Between Worlds: Exploring Online Game Culture*. Cambridge: The MIT Press.
14 Humphreys, 'Productive Players'; Kücklich, 'Precarious Playbour'. and Taylor, *Play Between*

Worlds.

15 This issue is common to many discussions of digital media. See Benkler (2006); Gillespie (2007); Grimes (2006); Rossiter (2006); and Terranova (2004).

16 See: Banks (2003); Banks and Humphreys, (2008); Fitzgerald et al., (2007); and Humphreys et al., (2005).

17 Humphreys et al. (2005). 'Fan-based Production for Computer Games: User-led Innovation, the 'Drift of Value' and Intellectual Property Rights'. *Media International Australia* 114: pp. 16-29.

18 Quoted from: Coalli, E. (2008). 'Auran shutting down FURY MMO'. *Worlds in Motion.*

19 VanOrd, K. (2007). 'Fury Review'. *Gamespot Australia.*

20 A researcher involved in the project has recently published an insider's account of the downfall of Auran. See: Banks (2009).

21 Kline, S., Dyer-Witheford, N., and de Peuter, G. (2003). *Digital|Play: The Intersection of Culture, Technology, and Marketing.* Montreal and Kingston: McGill-Queen's University Press: p. 215.

22 Bruns presents a number of different models, of which 'harnessing the hive' is one. See: Bruns, A. (2008). *Blogs, Wikipedia, Second Life and Beyond: From Production to Produsage.* New York: Peter Lang: pp. 31-33; and Herz, J. C. (2005). The concept is derived from: 'Harnessing the Hive'. In J. Hartley (ed.). *Creative Industries: A Reader.* Malden: Blackwell: pp. 327-342.

23 Herz, 'Harnessing the Hive': p. 328.

24 Innovation in this context, involves 'the construction of systems that leverage the million monkeys theorem' (Herz 2005: p. 328).

25 Bruns, *Blogs, Wikipedia, Second Life*: p. 32.

26 Lugo, J., Sampson, T., and Lossada, M. (2002). Latin America's New Cultural Industries Still Play Old Games: From Donkey Kong to Banana Republic. *Game Studies: the International Journal of Computer Game Research* 2.2.

27 *Escape from Woomera* Project Team (n.d.). 'Escape From Woomera Design Preview'.

28 *Reach Out Central* (2007) 'Reach Out Central'.

29 Rosenberg, T. (2005). 'What Lara Croft Would Look Like if She Carried Rice Bags'. *The New York Times.*

30 Tierney, J. (2004). 'The 2004 Campaign: Political Points'. *The New York Times.*

31 Bogost, I. (2007). *Persuasive Games: The Expressive Power of Videogames.* Cambridge: MIT Press: p. 327.

32 Frasca, G. (2003). 'Simulation Versus Narrative: Introduction to Ludology'. In M. J. P. Wolf and B. Perron (eds.). *The Video Game Theory Reader.* New York: Routledge: p. 228.

33 Thomas, D. and Brown, J. S. (2007). 'The Play of Imagination: Extending the Literary Mind'. *Games and Culture* 2.2: p. 156.

34 Salen, K. (2008). 'Toward an Ecology of Gaming'. In K. Salen (ed.). The Ecology of Games: *Connecting Youth, Games and Learning.* Cambridge: MIT Press: p. 8.

35 See: Bogost (2006; 2007); Galloway (2006); and Wark (2007).

36 Salen, 'Toward an Ecology of Gaming'.

37 Galloway, A. (2006). *Gaming: Essays on Algorithmic Culture.* Minneapolis: University of Minnesota Press.

38 The title of the game translates to Mazinger Z save Venezuela.

39 Bittanti, M. (2006). 'Intro – Game Art'. In M. Bittant and D. Quaranta (eds.). *Gamescences: Art in the Age of Videogames.* Milan: Johan Levi: pp. 7-14.

40 Stockburger, A. (2007). 'From Appropriation to Approximation'. In A. Clarke and G. Mitchell

(eds.). *Videogames and Art*. Bristol: Intellect: p. 29.

41 Stockburger, 'From Appropriation to Approximation': p. 32.

42 Cannon, R. (2007). 'Meltdown'. In A. Clarke and G. Mitchell (eds.). *Videogames and Art*. Bristol: Intellect: p. 41; and Galloway, Gaming: p. 108.

43 Stockburger, 'From Appropriation to Approximation': pp. 33-34.

44 *Darfur is Dying*.

45 Huhtamo, E. (1999). 'Game Patch – the Son of Scratch: Plug-ins and Patches as Hacker Art'. *Switch* 12.

46 Galloway, *Gaming*: p. 115.

47 Galloway, *Gaming*: p. 126.

48 Galloway, *Gaming*: p. 108.

49 Galloway, *Gaming*: p. 113.

50 Schleiner, A. (1999). 'Editorial Notes from Switch Art and Games Issue'. *Switch* 12.

51 Galloway, Gaming: p. 126.

52 WPDoom'–'White Power Doom'—is one of several racist games and mods described by the Anti-Defamation League. See: http://www.adl.org/digital games/default.asp.

53 Hunger, F. (2007). 'Perspective Engines: An Interview with JODI'. In A. Clarke and G. Mitchell (eds.). *Videogames and Art*. Bristol: Intellect: p. 152.

54 A process that echoes the work of Kazimir Malevich (e.g. *Black Square,* 1913), and the artists of the Letterist International, the forerunners of the Situationist International.

55 Galloway, *Gaming*: p. 115.

56 Winet, J. (2007). 'In Conversation Fall 2003: An Interview with Joseph DeLappe'. In A. Clarke and G. Mitchell (eds.). *Videogames and Art*. Bristol: Intellect: p. 98.

57 Winet, 'In Conversation Fall 2003': p. 98.

58 Chan, D. (2009). 'Beyond the "Great Fire-Wall": The Case of In-Game Protests in China'. L. Hjorth and D. Chan (eds.) *Gaming Cultures and Place in the Asia-Pacific*. London: Routledge: pp. 141-157.

59 Ward, M. (2006). 'Gay Rights Win in Warcraft World'. *BBC News*.

60 See the blog post by Abalieno (2005) 'These Screenshots Are Worth a "Ban"', on *The Cesspit.*

61 Lemon, S. (2006). 'Worldbeat – Chinese take Ani-Japanese Protest Online'. *Networked World.*

CHAPTER SEVEN
BLOCKAGES: CENSORSHIP, PIRA-CY AND PARTICIPATORY CULTURE

> A person's out-of-game status should not be able to affect their in-game status. For exam
> ple, a rich person should not be able to by their way in to a great character. My personal feel
> ing, and that of the rest of the team, is that it is something that could be harmful to the game.
> Grave harm? Probably not – but something we decided to take a stand on all the same—John
> Smedley, President of Sony Online Entertainment.[1]

Smedley's position raises an interesting question about 'status', and the digital game ecology. Moving away from *EverQuest* shifts the question from: 'should an individual's wealth affect their in-game status?' to: 'should a person's wealth or status affect their access to the digital game ecology?' This question is significant because access to the digital game ecology is not just about access to entertainment, it also has important implications for sustaining skills that are relevant outside of digital game play. This issue of unevenness suggests that the 'digital divine' has a significant impact on the digital game players, because it is a key factor shaping the situated ecology. However, while this establishes forms of exclusion, unevenness is also productive because precarious cultures of use emerge that draw upon forms of practice to take adaptive, creative, innovative actions in order to establish the possibility of play. The situated approach to digital game analysis is the best way to fully appreciate the creative and adaptive elements of players' practices, as they emerge from, and respond to, the specific conditions in distinct situated ecologies.

Building on the discussion of the segues between play and work, this chapter examines the blockages that impact on participation in the digital game ecology. The first two sections deal with issues that are closely connected: the national regulation of digital games consumption, particularly censorship, and the way in which piracy challenges regulation at the national level. Case studies from Australia and Venezuela illustrate that censorship of—and controversies over— digital games are about maintaining local standards at the national level in the face of erosion from outside influences. This issue marks the importance of 'local' concerns in shaping situated ecologies, but paradoxically the regulations themselves suggest common 'global' concerns about the impact of digital games on culture that cuts across national boundaries. Piracy, however, chal- lenges regulatory bodies, suggesting a form of 'global' gaming culture. Thus piracy plays a key role in mitigating blockages in the global access to the digital game ecology, not only in regard to local regulation, but also in terms of the 'digital divide'. The final section reflects on the stakes of inclusion and participation in the digital games ecology, arguing that the positive outcomes from inclusion that are considered beneficial in the developed world are experienced in a significantly different manner in Venezuela.

Censorship
Digital games are regulated for many of different reasons: in South Korea and China the concern

is that people are playing games for too long;[2] in Brazil it is feared that digital games are addictive;[3] in the United Kingdom and Australia some games are considered to be excessively violent, or to encourage other forms of criminal behavior; and in China, games have been banned for depicting sensitive issues, like an independent Tibet.[4] Local attempts to regulate digital games are embroiled in various panic discourses that surround digital games: they cause childhood obesity,[5] social introversion,[6] violence and crime,[7] that digital games are addictive,[8] or depict culturally inappropriate or otherwise bad moral values.[9] The truth or falseness of these allegations is not something that this book is interested in assessing; the significance of these regulations and these discourses is for the argument presented here, simply that they all operate on the presupposition that digital games are a medium that has a powerful impact and influence on peoples' lives. This section contrasts incidents of censorship and community outrage around digital games in Venezuela and Australia in order to argue that game controversies are underpinned by local concerns that suggest particular niches of privilege and exclusion within the global digital games ecology.

Mercenaries 2: World in Flames

Until recently digital games were not regulated in Venezuela. However, the release of *Mercenaries 2: World in Flames (Mercenaries 2)* catalyzed government opinion in favor of their regulation. Subsequent to the announcement in 2006 of the use of Venezuela for the setting of the 'sandbox' game *Mercenaries 2*, a number of prominent international news outlets (Fox, BBC, *USA Today*) reported on the official response from Venezuela. A spokesman from the Venezuelan congress, Ismael Garcia, in reference to the game, stated: 'I think the US Government knows how to prepare campaigns of psychological terror so they can make things happen later'.[10] Garcia suggests that the proposed theme of the game, invading Venezuela to oust a military dictator that threatened US oil supplies, is a deliberate part of the perceived US propaganda campaign against Chávez.[11] Pandemic's vice-president of commercial operations, Greg Richardson vigorously contested this claim denying any relationship between the company and the US government.[12] Pandemic's publicist Chris Norris downplayed the politics of the games by explaining that the designers were merely making a 'rip from the headlines'.[13] The choice of Venezuela as a setting is merely an attempt to contextualize the actions of gameplay within the contemporary geo-political concerns of what Pandemic perceives as their primary audience: the US market.

The controversy surrounding this game is surprising considering that there was no official response to the similarly themed Xbox version of *Tom Clancy's Rainbow Six 3*. In *Rainbow Six 3* the primary mission was to defeat terrorists who were endangering the US oil supplies; as it transpires the terrorists are in league with the newly elected president of Venezuela, Juan Crespo. The violence on Venezuelan soil in *Rainbow Six 3* is on a quantitatively different scale to the violence in *Mercenaries 2*, as the primary objectives of the game are presented as covert missions. Andrew Goldman, the co-founder of Pandemic Studios, describes the latter game as: 'taking destruction to the next level'.[14] The whole country has been modeled in the game, and its role is to be the setting for this mass destruction.

This example illustrates how arrhythmia between the local and global may emerge in situations where games present particular world-views that are dissonant with everyday life in the location of play. Game design that is presupposed by a particular geopolitical context may not always be smoothly assimilated into a situated ecology. Pandemic used the setting of Venezuela to contextualize the game to its major audience, hoping to facilitate the credibility of the diegetic world of the game by rooting it in the everyday life of its players, through their experiences of news head-lines and sound bites. However, this presentation of Venezuela resonates in a different manner with locals; a press release by the Venezuela Solidarity Network quotes Gunnar Gunderson, who states: 'I wouldn't want my sons to buy it and blow up neighborhoods that we can clearly recog-nize where their cousins, aunts and uncles live'.[15] Similar concerns by citizen and civic officials regarding the representation of their habitation or municipality as a playable environment have emerged from a number of other locations: the depiction of Las Vegas in *Tom Clancy's Rainbow Six: Vegas*;[16] mods of Counter-Strike that feature battles between police and street gangs in the *favelas* of Rio de Janeiro, that led to the banning of that game in Brazil;[17] and the original *Mer-cenaries: Playground of Destruction* was also banned for a time, along with *Tom Clancy's Ghost Recon 2*, in South Korea, because the games portrayed the conflict between North and South Korea, and crucially the North Koreans as generic enemies.[18] The dissonance that eventuates from these contexts demonstrates that at stakes in digital game play are notions of national, re-gional, and local identity, that have to negotiate with a hegemonic depiction of "global" concerns.

Escape from Woomera

In Australia, the issues of dissonant geo-political perspectives have yet to become an issue in digital games, probably because of the countries close alignment with US interests. However, the mod-art project *Escape from Woomera,* did briefly enter the media spotlight in the months before its release.[19] The developers used the mod to portray life inside Australia's notorious 'detention centers', used to house illegal immigrants. While clearly developed as a protest statement that would draw attention to the plight of detainees, various government officials criticized the game because it encouraged players to take illegal actions to escape from the detainment centers.[20] Like the situation in Venezuela with *Mercenaries 2*, this furor was concerned with the local sig-nificance of a game. However, the case of *Escape from Woomera* is distinct because the mod is locally produced with a relevance that is especially significant to Australia. The project, and the reaction to it, suggests that having local people engaging with local concerns in producing digital games, even just mods, can raise the stakes of digital game play in that location, in this case by highlighting a particularly contentious and greatly divisive political issue. It also suggests that members of the players who are engaged in making content as well as playing games have a greater expressive capacity in the digital game ecology. This distinction between having access to the freedom to easily move from player to designer, and participating in the digital game ecology as a player only, indicates a key blockage in the digital game ecology.

The controversy over *Escape from Woomera* follows the current focus of Australian game regu-lation on the legality and morality of the available actions within games. The Australian Federal body that determines ratings, the Office of Classification of Film and Literature (OCFL), has refused classification for a number of prominent globally distributed digital games. The conse-quence of being refused classification is that it becomes illegal to sell or distribute copies of that game in Australia. The main reason behind the large number of refusals is the lack of an adult rating for digital games. The highest rating that the OCFL may award in MA15+, a rating that indicates the game is suitable for mature people fifteen years and older. The remit of the OCFL requires that they consider any interactive sequence to be one rating higher than the same actions would be given if they were simply depicted in film. This requirement means that many games that portray sex, violence, and criminal acts are refused ratings, and thus effectively banned in Australia. Recent, banned games include: *Dark Sector, Left 4 Dead 2*, and *Soldier of Fortune: Payback*, which were all refused classification for excessive violence; *Blitz: The League* and *Fallout 3*, were both refused classification because of their realistic portrayal of drug-taking; and *Marc Ecko's Getting Up: Contents Under Pressure*, which was refused classification because of its portrayal of an illegal activity, in this case the making of graffiti.[21]

These punitive measures cause considerable consternation, and outrage, in the Australian gaming community. The OCFL is perceived as holding games to an outdated standard, and while various grassroots projects that seek to change the OCFL official guidelines exist, it appears that for the foreseeable future that such attempts will be blocked at the state level by the Attorney-General of South Australia, Michael Atkinson, who justifies his position in terms of protecting family values.[22] Atkinson's role in preventing change is pivotal because for a legal change to the OCFL guidelines, consensus is required from the Attorney Generals of all Australian States and Territories, as well as the Federal Attorney-General.[23] The lack of an adult rating irks the local players, who feel that the restrictions are out of sync with the contemporary Australian gaming audience, who have an average age of 28 according to a recent survey.[24] The inconsistency of the OFLC refusals also frustrates local players, for example the refusal of classification for *Marc Ecko's Getting Up: Contents Under Pressure*, is based on the games theme of graffiti-based resistance to dystopian totalitarian regimes. A theme that is extremely similar to the themes of the earlier game *Jet Set Radio Future,* which was given an MA15+ rating.

This officially enforced disjuncture from the global digital game ecology leads Australian players to look for alternative methods of participation. The following comments on the Gamespot news story, breaking the news that *Dark Sector* had been denied classification by the OCFL, suggest that a variety of avenues where still open to Australian gamers:

> Meh, we can still order it on E-Bay. Those crusty old bastards will never succeed in stopping me from playing any game I want.[25]

> BOOOOOOO.... Well stuff'em then!! I'll just download it for FREE then (this is by no means saying that "downloading games" is good, but if i can't buy it, what else am i suppose to do).[26]

The government can effectively regulate sales in Australia, but regulating credit card purchases from overseas vendors is more problematic, while online methods of exchange like file trading are more-or-less impossible to control. The blockages imposed on the Australian digital games ecology are ineffective, because the players have enough knowledge through the paratextual industries, to be aware of the variances between locations; and, in addition, they have a repertoire of resources available that enable them to access games from other locations. The government's efforts deter only those who are easily thwarted, either because they lack knowledge of how to use the global gaming ecology to mitigate the blockage, or they have no access to credit or an internet connection. This indicates that the efforts made to overcome this enforced arrhythmia, and establish and maintain global connections, adapt currents of counterplay; they involve understanding and mobilizing the affordances of the particular situated ecology in order to access and participate in the global digital game ecology.

In each of these examples the theme of the game resonates particularly strongly in everyday life through their close ties with specific local concerns. Gaming controversies are highly dependent on context, but these controversies are similar in the respect that the problems centered on in-game actions: in *Mercenaries 2* the players must invade (and possibly destroy parts of) Venezuela; and in *Escape from Woomera* the players must escape from a detention centre. Critics in Australia used this to argue that the games were suggesting that certain actions were appropriate, while Venezuelan critics argue that the actions available in the game implied that it was okay for the USA to invade Venezuela. This similarity is peculiar, but clearly, Venezuela is considered to be marginal enough to the digital games industry that they are unconcerned with any problems that Venezuelan's might games have with the game. This suggests that at stakes in the various blockages that impact on the access to the digital game ecology, are issues to do with the 'representation' of the local and the national as autonomous agents, and not as malleable and controllable locations, environments and populations. This issue is heightened when considering the global distribution of the privileged groups in the digital games ecology, which are able to use games as tools of expression. The sustainability this practice is of great importance for the self-expression of location specific and national issues in countries that lack a strong local digital game industry.

Piracy

This section expands on how digital game piracy ensures the global reach of digital games. In some countries the practice mitigates local limitations placed on digital game play through censorship and regulation. However, in other contexts like Venezuela, piracy has an important role in sustaining digital game ecologies. Through an examination of the role of digital game piracy in the situated ecology of Cybercafé Avila, this section argues that the practice mitigates unevenness caused by disparate access to technology. In this case, the stakes of piracy shift from just ensuring variety, to actually establishing the possibility of playing digital games. This highlights the importance of recognizing that the absolute criminality of piracy is disputed.[27] By considering piracy as tactic that mitigates divisions among players of digital games, it is apparent that in certain contexts piracy takes on stakes that outweigh its alleged criminality.

This discussion is limited to how piracy reduces the cost of software for people in Venezuela. Despite the existence of burgeoning mod and homebrew scenes, the costs associated with hardware cannot be alleviated in the same manner.[28] The use of pirated software has widely different stakes in Venezuela, than it does in Australia, which may be mapped onto other regions of the globe that are characterized by relative prosperity or poverty. Yar points out that the 'locus' of piracy is the developing world.[29] This marks an important division between those digital game players who do not rely on piracy (although they might use it) and those who are—to a greater or lesser extent—reliant on piracy to play digital games at all. The latter group has a particularly precarious status, due to the increasingly strong anti-piracy policies that enforces the current trend towards digital rights management, downloadable content and subscription models of payment.

In Venezuela media piracy was ubiquitous. On the streets, stalls selling pirated software, DVDs, PlayStation games, and music CDs—not to mention bootleg publications of popular books—were common, especially in the La Candelaria area of Libertador. The most common forms of pirated digital games were PC games that might be sold on either CD-ROM or DVD format. Some of the street stalls were small with correspondingly small collections for sale, while other large stalls, had a similar variety of games—both new and old—to what would be found in a chain store like EB Games in Australia. Some of the stalls are dedicated to digital games, but often they would sell other digital media also. Not many stalls were run by people who had an extensive knowledge of digital games; for most people it was just a business. However, those few with a passion for games would talk up, and promote, their newest products to passersby. One stallholder in particular, having recognized me as a kindred spirit, singled me out for his commentaries: on *Playboy: The Mansion*, 'hardcore man'; in relation to *Lego Star Wars: The Video Game*, 'its great for the kids'; and on *World of Warcraft*, 'over one million players!'.

Even away from the streets, piracy was common. Digital game stores were usually had little stock and few customers, unless they also had in-store console hire. Apart from this last variable—which usually meant that there were three or four Nintendo GameCubes, or possibly PlayStation2s set up, ready for players—the digital game stores in Caracas were remarkably similar, from the poorer areas of la Candelaria to high-class shopping districts like Chacao. The few original games were sitting in locked glass display cases, gathering dust. The attending clerks would respond to my inquiries about available games by producing a large folder or file from behind the counter that contained color-photocopied leaves of paper showing the covers of the various pirated games that they had available. Sometimes the covers would be reproduced at quite a small scale in order to fit a number of games on each page, any that were out of stock were crossed out with pen. From this 'menu' of pirated games, selections could be made, which would then be produced from the back room.

Only console games were available from digital game stores in this way. Computer games were easily copied and cracked across file-trading networks. The ease of obtaining computer games in this manner meant that, in Venezuela, the use of computers to download games was a crucial tactic for leveraging the situated ecology of the internet café to mitigate blockages cause by uneven access to software. The street-sellers of Caracas either obtained their supply of computer games from source that used file trading, or organized their own copies through the same networks. The gregarious stallholder mentioned above often complained about how late he had to work at night after the stall was closed in order to procure fresh product. Some businesses used a publish-to-order system, for example the innovative entrepreneurs *tu pana*, ran a business from home, downloading software, films and music to order, and delivering them anywhere in Caracas by motorbike.[30] These combined methods were efficient; the standard time for a new game to be available on the streets with a visible saturation was within 48 hours of its North American release, especially with much anticipated high profile games like *The Sims 2*.

Interview subjects described how they would examine the digital game stalls carefully when they passed, often questioning the attendants, in order to see if there was anything new which sparked their interest.

> Kermit (Caracas): I find out by watching the pirate sellers to see when they will start to sell the first copies of a new game. Sometimes I ask them if they have anything new right now.

Knowledge of what was available on the streets, and also being able to anticipate the arrival of new product was a way of displaying gaming capital. This involved integrating online research about new release digital games with a more streetwise knowledge of neighborhood locations.

Interview subjects were highly aware of that pirated software reduced their cost. However, they were still savvy to the variables that established different prices even within the pirated software market, particularly location. In 2005 most pirated computer games cost around 6000 bs. (approximately 3$ US at the time), although they would often cost more if they required more than one CD-ROM. DVD copies cost at least twice as much, where they were available.

> Gabrielle (Caracas): You can find very close to my house stalls selling cheap copies of com puter games. But if you go to the mall, the same copied games are being sold for three times the price.

Players also noted that buying copies was a good way to avoid being disappointed by lackluster games, which failed to live up to the expectations that their promotional hype promised to deliver.

> Ajax (Caracas): You can find a very expensive original game that is a bad game, but you can find a very cheap one with the street sellers, which is very good.

This approach to digital game piracy, suggests that, even in this context there is a current to piracy that operates as a critique of the digital games industry. The players reassert their agency by mobilizing the local situation against the digital game industry's discourse that equates newness with quality. This doubled moment of adaptation suffers from the ambiguity of being both a necessity and a critique. To be included in the global audience of digital games the players at Cybercafé Avila had to use pirated software, and through this inclusion they gained the knowledges, skills and game capital to recognize that a simply being an original did not affect a game's quality.

The use of copied games sustains the participation of Venezuelan players in the digital game ecology. Piracy, at this time is essential for the digital game ecology to have a global reach. But permitting and multiplying inclusion in the digital game ecology was not the only way that piracy influenced the situated ecology at Cybercafé Avila, it also enabled the experimental exploration of a greater variety of games than what might otherwise be considered appropriate, or found, at a internet café in Australia. The element of experimentation was sustained by the collective efforts of the patrons. Players described how they would buy their own copies of a digital game that interested them, even if they did not have a computer at home. They would take their copy to the internet café and give copies to staff, to make sure that it ended up on the computers there. The flexibility in purchase that piracy provided thus transferred across the community of gamers, allowing them to sample many new and obscure games in the internet cafés. Often new games would be installed and then just as quickly removed if they did not pique sufficient interest. But the appearance of some new games on the desktop would create a massive interest, which was often accompanied by a surge in the game's use across the community of players. This happen following the release of *GunBound*, and also after Maxim obtained a copy of *Age of Mythology: Titans*. Typically after a few days the general interest would subside, leaving a small community of dedicated players.

In the context of Cybercafé Avila, digital game piracy becomes a form of counterplay, regardless of the fact that the activity of piracy is completely non-diegetic and not a part of play. This is because it was essential for sustaining, and multiplying, the possibilities of play in that particular situated ecology. Piracy pushes at the edge of what can be construed as play and counterplay. Recalling the notion of the gaming body, counterplay, may involve drawing on a wide repertoire of objects and people. Counterplay is not solely playful and virtual, but may involve exploiting the materiality of digital game formats. This challenges the notion that piracy is simply getting something for free, as it repositions piracy as an adaptive practice that enables inclusion in global media systems. The creative practices in operation are revealed through investigation of particular situated ecologies, this demonstrates how examining particular situated ecologies complicates global accounts of gaming. The context of the local situation has an important impact on the stakes of piracy—which may be either, or both, opportunistic to necessary—that is smoothed over by global accounts of the criminality of piracy.

Global Participatory Culture

The precarious position of players that are reliant on piracy is further exacerbated by the notion of participatory or convergence culture. The aspect of participatory culture that is of particular concern is the shift the concept marks to the audiences' active involvement in both consumption and production of media. In this paradigm, media cultures are co-produced by the audience, who add to, and supplement the existing content. The interactive, paratextual, playful, productive and social elements of digital games, make them exemplary participatory cultures. Using digital game play in Venezuela as a case study this section builds on the discussion of segues between work and play found in the previous chapter to examine the global stakes of the argument that media which allows audiences to produce, as well as consume, content provides the audience with the skills considered crucial for participation in the knowledge economy. These stakes suggest the blockages that impact on players, and players' own attempts to mitigate these blockages, have a political and ethical dimension that needs to be addressed.

Digital Games and Knowledge Economies

Many contemporary discussions of convergence focus on the implications of the shift from the technologies of convergence—the 'black box fallacy'—to an understanding of the cultural impact of those technologies.[31] Jenkins reframes convergence as the ongoing processes that: 'alters the relationship between existing technologies, industries, markets, genres, and audiences'.[32] However, considering the impact that these changes have had on media industries and products is also important, because the shifting power relationships of convergence culture are still underpinned by the drive for the media industries to extract profit from the audiences' emergent uses of new technology. This change in the relationship between audiences and media industries reflects the shift from industrial to post-industrial or knowledge economies characterized by intellectual rather that physical labor. Particularly important for emerging convergent media industries is the control, distribution, and extraction of profit from user generated content. As previously discussed, critics of the digital games industry suggest that it is modeled on the 'capture of counterplay'. Similar metaphors are adopted by the industry's admirers—scholars like Bruns, and

Herz—who suggest that such a model is worth exporting to other new media industries with participatory audiences. Jenkins rightly argues that many of the emergent aspects of convergence culture are precarious; primarily due to the challenge that the productive audience of convergent culture leverages on corporate ownership of media content through user generated content. However, the global precariousness of participation in digital gaming is underscored by shifting this discussion of convergence culture to examine the impact of blockages caused by access to technology on Venezuelan digital game players, because it indicates that for many Venezuelan players their participation in the digital game ecology is—and under current regulatory systems, can only ever be—partial.

Some recent discussions of digital games have emphasized their potential for education. Not in the sense of teaching content, or rhetoric, but rather that digital games encapsulate a key encounter with developing a 'literate' command over new digital, interactive media. Zimmerman suggests that gaming literacy is a paradigm for new digital literacy.[33] Salen, begins to outline exactly what this literacy constitutes, she claims that the first step of gaming literacy is to understand digital games as systems, while the second step is to understand how that system can be changed.[34] Zimmerman extends this, arguing that gaming literacy also engenders a playful understanding of the various structures that individuals inhabit; and an approach to design that is about 'creating a set of possibilities'.[35] Gaming literacy also shares two important attributes with Jenkins account of convergence culture. First, the relationship between digital games and their paratexts is an example of how the convergent audience uses other media, especially the internet to collaborate on, conduct, and coordinate research. Second, the multiple and versatile, productive practices of digital game players—art, FAQs, Machinima, mods, walkthroughs—demonstrate the new mode of audience participation that involves engagement in the production, and the sharing, of user generated content. Jenkins suggests that convergence culture heralds a new era. He states, convergence culture:

> …may be the next step in that process of cultural evolution – a bridge to a new kind of culture and a new kind of society. In a hunting culture, kids played with bows and arrows. In an infor mation society, they play with information.[36]

Access to the digital game ecology affords valuable teaching and learning experiences. The experience gained through digital gaming that are relevant to contemporary society, and especially to the contemporary workforce include developing the skills to use digital, interactive technologies effectively, particularly to collaborate and produce new knowledge.

'Adaptation' is the common thread linking these somewhat intangible, but widely discussed skills. Digital games require that players adapt to compulsions and provide flexibility that allows people to turn necessities into creations. Leadbeater suggests that in contemporary 'creative', 'knowledge', or 'information' economies it is creativity, not knowledge that is the focus of learning.[37] The crux of Leadbeater's distinction rests on the difference between training and practice. By separating knowledge from creativity Leadbeater suggests that developing new innovative practices, rather than the replication of training drives the 'knowledge economy'. Digital games provide convergence culture with a smooth segue from play to a broader literacy that is relevant in many other spheres of activity. Jenkins construes the implications widely, he states: 'the *skills we acquire through play* may have implications for how we learn, work, participate in the political process, and connect with other people around the world'.[38] From some perspectives this training amounts to a form of training in precarious or immaterial labor.[39] However, whether described as literacy, skills, or training, it is evident that this phenomenon suggests strong consequences for those who are voluntarily or involuntarily excluded from digital game play. Lack of access to this type of use constitutes a form of blockage, as the "skills" acquired through digital game play involve engagement with the emergent communicative, connective, and productive elements of networked technology.

The concept of convergence culture must be understood in relation to unevenness of access. Global networks are not experienced homogenously; there is no global experience of digital game play, or convergence culture. Rather many specific experiences drawn from multiple local cultures of use. The US is considered a very important location for convergence culture, because of its preeminent economic position, and substantial political freedoms, many technological and cultural practices of the 'early adopters' of convergence culture occur there.[40] However, Jenkins positions these practices as important by suggesting that broadening the scale of participation will have important implications. Expanding the scale of participation to the global level necessitates addressing the issue of access to technology. On the level of the individual this means not just access as a reader, but also as a producer of information.

The consequence of uneven access to digital games ecology is that a large sector of players lack experience in the intangible adaptive skills—the practices—that they foster. In the paradigm of the knowledge or information economy the lack of such skills may mean full or partial exclusion from the mainstream economy. Zimmerman states:

> …in the coming century, the way we live and learn, work and relax, communicate and create, will more and more resemble how we play games. While we are not all going to be game de signers, game design and gaming literacy offer a valuable model for what it will mean to become literate, educated and successful in this playful world.[41]

The stakes that Zimmerman places on digital game play suggests that only partial inclusion in the digital game ecology will further exacerbate existing blockages, inequalities and unevenness.

The work by van Dijk and Hacker on the digital divide argues that while differences caused by lack of access to hardware may be solved relatively easily, the divide in terms of lack relevant of skills to make use of technology is likely to persist.[42] Padovani and Nordenstreng similarly urge that issues of access to technology are not regarded as merely technical issues.[43] They suggest that current purely technical understanding of full participation in the information society be balance with a political appreciation of the stakes of participation:

> Knowledge societies are supposed to be spaces in which citizens will be able to communi cate, interact and participate. But this risks remaining only rhetoric if transformations, chal lenges and political solutions are perceived as highly technical issues removed from the pub lic.[44]

This exclusion is likely to exacerbate existing inequalities between nations. Castells argues that the central role that information plays in the global networked society both establishes and entrenches regions and areas of inclusion and exclusion to the benefits of those networks.[45] This establishes a class of locations and people that are not valued. He states:

> There is also exclusion of people and territories, which, from the perspective of dominant interests in global, informational capitalism, shift to a position of structural irrelevance. This widespread, multiform process of social exclusion leads to the constitution of what I call, taking the liberty of a cosmic metaphor, the black holes of informational capitalism. These are regions of society from which, statistically speaking, there is no escape...[46]

The people all over the world play digital games, but there are clearly classes of players that have more value than others. Venezuela is structurally irrelevant by the digital games industry; it is not considered a market because so few units are sold there, thus the feeling of the Venezuela audience are not regarded, hence *Mercenaries 2*.

Productive Consumption and Citizenship

While new technologies, like digital games, establish new forms of global connections they also entrench old and create new forms of inequalities. The new form of inequality caused by lack of access to digital games, centers around the kind of training, learning, and creative opportunities that digital games provide. García Canclini argues that in the contemporary epoch access to information is the key to being able to act autonomously and creatively.[47] He believes that existing inequalities of access have had a significant role in forming a mobile transnational elite that has restructured understandings of national communities.[48] Digital games provide a more conceptual mobility, Jenkins' early adopters of convergence culture are also an elite group of consumers—those who produce content as well as consume it—who have restructured understanding of audiences. Clearly, the early adopters are an important sector of any audience, however, they by no means account for the entire audience, and by focusing on their activities other cultures of use are ignored. While the digital game ecology offers the possibility of being a part of contemporary global media culture it is apparent that inclusion is still uneven.

The work of García Canclini, radically reformulates the notion of citizenship to argue that human rights should be defined in the context of material consumption rather than abstract ideals.[49] The ability to think, act and make informed decisions is based on access to information that García Canclini argues belongs to the people by right. This reframing of access to media as a right challenges notions of media piracy, and in the context of convergence culture, suggests a right to access the digital technologies necessary to both consume and author content. By including the right to consume in the notion of citizenship, García Canclini presents a very different position from Jenkins on the relationship between citizenship and consumption. Jenkins argues that convergence culture is a return to the grassroots approach to democracy on which the USA was founded.[50] He suggests that through increasing access to participation, convergence culture will reinvigorate the public sphere, and hopes that as a consequence collaborative consensual politics will triumph over the partisan.[51] This formulation of the convergent democracy has very little to say about peoples' right to participate, in part this is implicit in Jenkins' argument due to the ease of access to technology in the context of the USA.

In the gigantic mall of Sambil, in the Caracas suburb of Chacao, the three shops selling digital games were mostly empty, but the strategically placed window displays attracted considerable attention. Televisions connected to Nintendo GameCubes, endlessly repeating the starting sequence of *Super Mario Sunshine*, or *FIFA 2005* for example, would often have groups of watching youths congregating outside the shops. Reduced to watching interactive media, these youths were, at that moment at least, locked out of participatory culture, readers in a world increasingly defined by the interplay of reading and writing, observers in a media paradigm characterized by action. Watching a game instead of playing it is one thing, and simply playing a game instead of playing it and producing content for it, is another. Jenkins points out that convergence has changed the notion of literacy to include production: 'we should not assume that someone possesses media literacy if they can consume but not express themselves'.[52] By placing this emphasis on expression, the existing inequalities between digital game players are obscured because the activities of some 'players' are increasingly 'structurally irrelevant', compared to the activities of player/designers or player/artists.

In Venezuela the publicly situated context of digital media consumption and production makes it difficult to develop this level of literacy. While users demonstrated competency in using fan resources—for example by finding maps for *Counter-Strike*, looking up episodes of *Charmed*, and searching for paratexts—there was no noteworthy incidences of formal production. Just the banal kind: PowerPoints for a homework assignment, designing an avatar for *Habbo* or *GunBound*, uploading photos to an MSN profile. Significant productions in the internet café environment focused on school and work. Cydus was similar; in this case, productive practices did not appear to take place in this public context. The main difference in Cydus is that most of the people using the café also had access to domestic use of both a computer, and the internet. At Cydus the people were there to play with others, productive play occurred in the domestic sphere; while at Cybercafé Avila people were there to play, often because it was their only way of playing digital games (or that particular game) at all.

This area constitutes a crucial unevenness for digital games players. The empowering possibilities of productive play are not readily available to participants in a country like Venezuela. This means that in many aspects of digital game culture they participate only as spectators. Participation is limited by sparse access to privately owned PCs, and despite the users' having highly developed consumptive literacies, production was focused on work-related activities rather than the playful production that characterizes engagements with digital games. The culture of use in Cybercafé Avila placed a premium on 'constructive' use of the short amount of time most users have at the computer interface. Thus they either threw themselves into work or play, avoiding the ambiguity between training and practice that is prevalent in productive play.

Audience production impacts on global power dynamics by challenging corporate ownership of their products. This challenge is localized. Venezuela has its own peculiar challenge to corporate ownership. Rather than the nebulous area of fan-production, the challenge stems from the clearly illegal way that most digital media is obtained in Venezuela. While media owners have pathways to asserting their legal rights, without the support of local government this is impossible. Importantly, this suggests a limit for the strategy of the 'capture of counterplay'. Garcia Canclini's argument implies that media owners who use copyright enforcement to prevent access to the digital game ecology by people in the developing world are in an ambiguous ethical position. This is exacerbated because the ownership rights are not used to shut down fan-based productions—as they are in the developed world—but to exclude large parts of the people in the 'underdeveloped' world from full access to the digital game ecology.

Conclusion

Censorship constitutes a key blockage to participation in the global digital game ecology. While incidents of censorship and controversies around games have reflected largely local concerns, they have also implicitly acknowledged the power of digital games as rhetorical and training tools. The heavy censorship in Australia has been largely ineffective because of the ways that typical Australians are connected to other parts of the world through global networks. Global networks also challenge economic blockages by sustaining software piracy, which means that piracy plays an important role in sustaining the global reach of the digital game ecology. Piracy also has a significant role in mitigating exclusion from full participation in the digital game ecology that is a consequence of these blockages. However, the reliance on piracy also raises the stakes inclusion in the digital game ecology, because total reliance on piracy is a form of inclusion that is extremely precarious. It is precarious because of its illegality, and the constant legal and technical challenges that are developed to prevent and limit it. While there are no legal rights for this underclass of players to participate in the digital game ecology, these rights could be established by turning to García Canclini's notion of citizenship based on the right to consume. Considering the high stakes placed on digital game play as a practice that engenders creativity, collaboration and computing skills that have clear segues into working in the knowledge economy in the first world; it appears that to deliberately exclude a person or group from the digital game ecology has heavy repercussions. It further entrenches the exclusion of those people from the full benefits of participation in the network society. The bottom line of full inclusion is not just to be able to play games, but to be able to participate in the productive paratextual industries, and also in the content creation and sharing that characterizes the contemporary digital game ecology. As it stands the precarious underclass are structurally irrelevant for the digital game industry, and it is the elite players of the global 'North' that sets the agenda for the digital games industries' program of the capture of counterplay.

Notes

1 Quoted from: Marks, R. B. (2003). *EverQuest Companion: The Inside Lore of the Game World*. New York, McGraw-Hill/Osborne: p. 75.

2 Anderson, J. (2005). 'Spot On: Korea Reacts to Increased Game Addiction', in GameSpot; and 'China Imposes Online Gaming Curbs' (2005). *BBC News*.

3 'Brazil Bans Popular Video Game Seen to Incite Violence' (2008). *MSN News*.

4 Cap, T. (2004). 'Interview with Joakim Berggwist'. *GamersHell*.

5 Schiesel, S. (2007). 'P.E. Classes Turn to Video Game That Works Legs'. *The New York Times*.

6 Matthews, A. (2001). 'Computer Games Make Children Anti-social'. *Telegraph.co.uk*.

7 Leung, R. (2005). 'Can a Video Game Lead to Murder? Did 'Grand Theft Auto' Cause One Teenager to Kill?'. *CBS News*.

8 Coughlan, S. (2006). 'Just One More'. *BBC News Magazine*.

9 Harlow, J. and Baxter, S. (2005). 'Hilary Opens Up Morality War on Violent Video Games'. *Times*

Online.

10 For a more detailed discussion see: Toothaker, C. (2006). 'Video Game Simulating Invasion of Venezuela Raise Ire of Chavez's Allies'. USA Today; and 'Venezuelan Anger at Computer Game' (2006). *BBC News.*

11 Allegedly Pandemic revised the appearance of the Venezuelan President during the production of the game so as to make the character resemble Chávez less (Venezuelan Solidarity Network, 2007). In an implicit reference to *Mercenaries 2*, on national radio Chávez remarked: 'Una vez hicieron uno con la cara mía' (They even made one with my face). See: 'Chávez la emprende de nuevo contra la muñeca "Barbie" y la "Play Station"'. (2010). *Noticias 24.*

12 The BBC story—at least—uncovered links between Pandemic and the US military; a partner that they had previously collaborated with in the development of *Full Spectrum Warrior.* See: 'Venezuelan Anger at Computer Game' (2006).

13 Toothaker, C. (2006). 'Video Game Simulating Invasion of Venezuela Raise Ire of Chavez's Allies'. *USA Today.*

14 From a YouTube interview with Goldman: http://au.youtube.com/watch?v=419vRevhdzY

15 Venezuelan Solidarity Network (2007). 'Grassroots Group Celebrates Delay of Game Attacking Venezuela'. *Venezuelanalysis.com.*

16 Jones, C. (2006). 'Terror on the Strip'. *Las Vegas Review-Journal.*

17 'Brazil Bans Popular Video Game Seen to Incite Violence' (2008, January 18). MSN News.

18 Brooke, J. (2005). 'South Koreans React to Video Games' Depiction of North Koreans'. The New York Times.

19 See: Apperley, T. (2008). 'Video games in Australia'. In M. J. P. Wolf (ed.). *The Video Game Explosion: A History from Pong to Playstation® and Beyond.* Westport: Greenwood Press: pp. 225-226.; and Swallwell, M. (2003). 'The Meme Game: Escape from Woomera'. *RealTime 55.*

20 Nicholls, S. (2003). 'Ruddock Fury Over Woomera Computer Game'. The Age.

21 *Fallout 3* was later classified MA15+, after Bethesda removed real-world drug references from the worldwide release of the game ('morphine' was changed 'med-x').

22 Moses, A. (2008). 'Fallout Continues from Ban on Game'. *The Age.*

23 Michael Atkinson resigned immediately following his 2010 re-election, where his seat was contested by Kat Nicholson for the political party 'Gamers 4 Croydon' on the platform of introducing an adult rating for games. While initially, this was hailed as a victory by advocates of an adult rating, it transpires that Atkinson's replacement John Rau does not see it as a high priority to revise the position of the South Australian Attorney General's Office.

24 Brand, J. E. (2007). 'Interactive Australia 2007: Facts about the Australian Computer and Video Game Industry'. Everleigh: Interactive Entertainment Association of Australia: p. 1.

25 streak000 (2008, February 13). Message posted http://au.gamespot.com/news/6186009. html?action=convert&om_clk=latestnews&tag=latestnews%3Btitle%3B0&page=6

26 Amtrkblue (2008, February 13). Message posted to http://au.gamespot.com/news/6186009. html?action=convert&om_clk=latestnews&tag=latestnews%3Btitle%3B0&page=6

27 Yar, M. (2005). 'The Global "Epidemic" of Movie "Piracy": Crime-wave or Social Construction?'. *Media, Culture, and Society* 27.5: pp. 677-696; and Yar, M. (2008). 'The Rhetorics and Myths of Anti-piracy Campaigns: Criminalization, Moral Pedagogy, and Capitalist Property Relations in the Classroom'. *New Media and Society* 10.4: pp. 605-623.

28 Modded hardware has been customized to allow copied games to be played. While 'homebrew' is used to describe user-developed software made for hardware that typically operates only

proprietary software. The two phenomena are often related, as consoles are modded in order that they might run homebrew software. See Cesarini (2004).

29 Yar, 'The Global "Epidemic"': p. 680.

30 *Tu pana* translates as 'your buddy' or in Australian English 'your mate'.

31 Jenkins, H. (2006). *Convergence Culture: Where Old and New Media Collide*. New York: New York University Press: p. 14.

32 Jenkins, *Convergence Culture:* p. 15.

33 Zimmerman, E. (2009). 'Gaming Literacy: Game Design as a Model for Literacy in the 21st Century'. In B. Perron and M. J. P. Wolf (eds.). *The Video Game Theory Reader 2*. New York: Routledge: p. 23.

34 Salen, K. (2008). 'Toward an Ecology of Gaming'. In K. Salen (ed.). *The Ecology of Games: Connecting Youth, Games and Learning*. Cambridge: MIT Press: p. 8.

35 Zimmerman, 'Gaming Literacy': p. 29.

36 Jenkins, *Convergence Culture*: p. 6. Emphasis added.

37 Leadbeater, C (1999). *Living on Thin Air: The New Economy*. London: Viking: p. 102.

38 Jenkins, *Convergence Culture:* p. 23. Emphasis added.

39 Terranova, T. (2004). *Network Culture: Politics for the Information Age*. London: Pluto Press: pp. 83-84.

40 Jenkins, *Convergence Culture*: p. 23.

41 Zimmerman, 'Gaming Literacy': p. 30.

42 van Dijk, J. and Hacker, K. (2003). 'The Digital Divide as a Complex Dynamic Phenomenon'. *The Information Society* 19: p. 322.

43 Padovani, C. and Nordenstreng, K. (2005). 'From NWICO to WSIS: Another World Information and Communication Order?: Introduction'. Global Media and Communication 1.3: pp. 264-272.

44 Padovani and Nordenstreng, 'From NWICO to WSIS': p. 270.

45 Castells, M. (2000). End of Millennium. Malden: Blackwell.

46 Castells, *End of Millennium*: p. 162.

47 García Canclini, N. (2001). *Consumers and Citizens: Globalization and Multicultural Conflicts*. Minneapolis: University of Minnesota Press: p. 45.

48 García Canclini, *Consumers and Citizens*: p. 45.

49 García Canclini, *Consumers and Citizens*: p. 5.

50 Jenkins, *Convergence Culture*: p. 20.

51 Jenkins, *Convergence Culture*: p. 256.

52 Jenkins, *Convergence Culture*: p. 156.

CHAPTER EIGHT
COUNTERPLAY AND ALGORITHMIC CULTURE

What makes a player a star is more than perfection of technique. Technical perfection merely makes a player most competent. To technical perfection the star adds something extra. Per haps a way of catching the eye of players on the opposite team to make them self-conscious and throw them off their game. Perhaps a feint added to every kick. Or an imperceptible spin. Little extras. Small but effective ways of skewing the potential movements composing the field. The star player is one who modifies expected mechanisms of channeling field-potential. The star player plays against the rules but not by breaking them. He plays around them add ing minute, unregulated contingencies to the charged mix—Brian Massumi.[1]

There is a tension between the society of control, or 'algorithmic culture' and counterplay: the emergent practices of digital game players. The configurative, modulating elements of digital game play is sometime taken to mean that the coded algorithms contain all potential meanings, allowing no space for critical reflections, or engagements, with digital games. This position mirrors the fluidity of the digital game industry as it reorganizes to accommodate for, manage, and commodify emergent practices and styles of digital game play. Counterplay and the ancillary concepts of the digital game ecology, the situated ecology and the gaming body illustrate how the modulation of algorithmic culture has a material limit; that to be played the algorithm of the digital game must align with the rhythm of everyday life in the location of play. The limit is demonstrated by counterplay, innovative practices that draw upon the process of play, the everyday rhythms, and the material concerns of the location in which play takes place. This chapter first discusses the stakes of digital game play in contemporary culture, then examines important emergent practices of play that suggest a free margin of play where forms of practice that are experimental, innovative, risky, unintended, and unruly emerge.

The subordination of adaptation to compulsion is the paradox of the capture of counterplay. The ambiguity suggested by this relationship is highlighted when the utility of digital games is brought into question. Attempts to reclaim digital games for 'higher' purposes place greater value on their compulsive or training elements. Once digital games are re-conceptualized as 'serious', for example, a sub–industry emerges that explores, examines and critiques serious issues with and through digital games. A similar phenomenon has followed from the re-conceptualization of digital games as art. This does not imply that such projects are misguided, rather that their cultivation is a deliberate iteration of a training element that already exists in digital games. The designer of 'serious games' turns the adaptive process of play into compulsion: the player is no longer invited to take the game more or less seriously, rather the game is to be taken seriously *from the start*. This is a powerful means of conveying a message, particularly if—like in *September 12th*, for example—the designers have considered delivering the message through the code of the game in the boundaries of the actions that may be taken in the game-space. But this approach, while harnessing play to an extent, does not capture everything about play. The significance of movements like serious games, and game art, is the acknowledgment that digital games as a medium can convey messages, challenge ideas, and change lives. Before 'serious games' existed, digital games were serious, just as they were artistic before game-art became a concept. This should be noted, not as an *a priori* trump—for both movements have their own important contributions to digital game design, development, and scholarship—but as a signal to what underlies the stakes of digital game play.

To understand these stakes involves re-examining the ambiguity between compulsion (training) and adaptation (practice). These concepts suggest a fundamental alignment inasmuch as they are relational; adaptation is a human activity that is a process of dealing with, and accommodating compulsions. These activities describe the individual's negotiations through a society character-ized by a bureaucracy that is maintained and cultivated by information technology. Bruno Latour's concepts of mediators and intermediaries provide a means of examining the stakes of tech-nological play in contemporary society. Latour argues that the various means that produce the social are individually conceived as either intermediaries or mediators. This distinction is crucial. He states: 'Mediators transform, translate, distort, and modify the meaning of the elements they are supposed to carry'.[2] While intermediaries merely act as a conduit, they: 'transport meaning or force without transformation'.[3] Using this distinction to locate the stakes of digital game play in the network society, or the global networks of the knowledge economy or information age reaf-firms digital games' ambiguous status. Do digital games change the potentiality of the networks in which they are imbricated or do they just convey, and reproduce, the logic of the network? Are they mediators or intermediaries?

This question is particularly important in relation to what Galloway calls the 'protocological soci-ety' and 'algorithmic culture'. Galloway's discussion of the 'control society' highlights how digital games encapsulate the undermining of the distinction between adaptation and compulsion. In this paradigm, the bottom line of digital game play is the configuration of a system; one that is designed with configuration in mind; all possibilities and potential outcomes are contained in the algorithm's code. Through this presupposition, by the deliberate design of the configurative or adaptive process of play, games establish a compulsive framework for adaptation.

Digital games suggest a new system of compulsion that both values adaptation and makes it necessary. But adaptation is limited to the context that the game presents: the configuration of variables, actions, strategies, objects and tactics. This involves consciously or unconsciously understanding the limits and flexibility of the games' underlying algorithm. For Galloway this is the field where gamic action takes place; counter-gaming operates from outside this field, seek-ing rather to transform the production of algorithms. This argument is a powerful presentation of the digital game as an intermediary. While Galloway does believe that digital games have the potential to be mediators—hence his theory of countergaming—this would require a fundamental rethinking of the business and design of digital games.

Underpinning the framing of digital games as intermediaries is the materiality of code. Together code and algorithm form the material basis for the experience of virtual worlds; they channel, constrain, and permit various configurations. Choices, movements, actions and configurations have little meaning outside of the context of individual incidents of game-play; because they are permitted, allowed, and enabled through code they cannot find a traction or critique on the smooth surface of algorithmic culture. This understanding of the game world is hermeneutic; the relation it describes is wholly contained in the code of the software. The game is a singularity, that may merely be unfolded in multiple ways designed in order to offer choice and interactivity, but because each choice is built into the game, it already exists as inert code that the player merely enacts. This perspective accounts for how digital games seek to discipline the users by acting as transporters or conduits of meaning. However, this observation focuses entirely on the interplay of, and feedback between, software and inputs. In short, the analysis of play remains deliberately in an entirely self-contained domain governed by code. Counterplay implies that to understand digital games we must move beyond the notion of the materiality of code—and a hermeneutic approach to digital game scholarship that conceptualizes digital games as clearly defined singular artifacts that may be examined and understand in isolation—in order to make visible the role of everyday life in shaping digital game play.

It is not my intention to suggest that digital game play is an experience that is not subject to regimes of discipline or compulsion. Rather that in relation to compulsions it is ambiguous and paradoxical; disciplinary and adaptive. It operates both as a mediator and an intermediary; consequently game play is in some contexts an impartial transferor of culture, but in others, a source of new culture and relations. This is not a binary relationship: adaptation and compulsion exist in an imbricated spectrum. Galloway's critique is most poignant: the adaptations, the practice found in digital game play is enacted through and contained in, code. It is a variable that designers account for, and seek to capture when they design new iterations of the game.

To move beyond the binary of compulsion and adaptation it is necessary to return to Latour's discussion of mediators and intermediaries. He argues that the distinction between these two roles that actors in networks are considered to have is largely immaterial. He states: 'there is no preferable type of social aggregates, there exist endless numbers of mediators, and when those are transformed into faithful intermediaries it is not the rule, but a rare exception that has to be accounted for by extra work – usually by the mobilization of even more mediators'.[4] For Latour, the role that an object, like a digital game, can play in a 'social aggregate' is not determined by anything 'essential' about its status, but rather by other elements to which it is perceived as being connected. By examining digital games as closed circuits of code that contain all possible actions and interactions, the network or social aggregate in which they are examined is reduced to a single loop of player and software. The goal of this work has been to underscore the necessity of bringing other elements into this network: bodies, hardware, spaces, the sociality of play, and how play is perceived culturally, which allows a balanced portrayal of digital game play as adaptive, as well as compulsive.

Counterplay Practices

This section focuses on two emergent elements of counterplay: resonance and exploits. They are emergent in the sense that they are fluid and evolving, taking on new iterations as new games and versions of games appear. The notion of resonance describes the outcomes of players' configurations that have a particular bearing on a local situation, or context. *Escape from Woomera,* for example, is not a meaningful media object just because of the design of the mod, but because of the particular resonance that it had in Australia at the time it was produced. The second element of counterplay that this section examines is that of the 'exploit', a term that is borrowed from gaming culture itself, and refers to the process of finding and exploiting small anomalies in the design of the digital game. The 'shot counting trick' from the classic *Space Invaders* is a simple example of an exploit. Players discovered that shooting the mystery or mother ship with the 22nd, and each subsequent 14th shot would net the maximum three hundred points, rather than a randomly allocated fifty to three hundred variation. As digital games have become more complex in the intervening years, so have the complexity of the exploits of players.

Configurative Resonance

By examining digital game play in the everyday lives of players, the configurable, contained, and virtual world of the game algorithm takes on a new significance. One example of counterplay that has particular relevance in the local occurs when a deliberate decision is made to configure a game in order to either establish a resonance or highlight a dissonance between the virtual and 'real' worlds. This occurs in numerous instances, players configuring avatars in order to reference other fictional or 'real' worlds,[5] or selecting a particular culture in *Civilization IV* in order to play out an alternative trajectory of world history.[6] In such cases, the rhythm of play not only accommodates or harmonizes with everyday life, but also establishes a contextual significance that speaks to the players' experience of everyday life.

There are many cases of resonances between digital game worlds and everyday life. The previous chapter discussed how local geopolitical concerns shaped how digital games with a strong—contemporary or even historical—geopolitical themes or settings are viewed. Particular themes and locations take on a significance based on 'fidelity of context'.[7] The resonance, or dissonance, between digital games and the specificity of their contexts of consumption is a great deal more significant when they are produced through the players' own process of configuration, rather than being based on an unalterable element of the game. For example, the use of Venezuela as a setting, and its President as the main villain, for *Tom Clancy's Rainbow Six 3*, establishes a potential for both dissonance and resonance between the game and players from Venezuela, but without involving any configuration of the game system, or active in-game choice on the players' part. This situation is the most common case: the games' resonating elements are coded into the game in a way that is unconfigurable without the deliberate intervention of a mod. But games also exist that permit configurations that can take on a context-dependent significance.

Configurative resonance, or dissonance, involves the player deliberately configuring, and/or performing actions in the game—out of all the possible potential configurations and performances—in order to create specific resonances. When Ajax started his first game of *The Sims 2* on one of the computers in Cybercafé Avila in June 2005, I observed with a certain degree of interest, as I was yet to play the game, or see it played. While Ajax was designing his characters, we joked about the resonances that some of the of the available features had with Venezuela, specifically the possibility of having characters wear red berets, which were an identifying symbol used by 'Chávistas', the staunch supporters of Chávez. Because of this feature, designed without this highly contextual political context, the game happened to resonate with the political climate in Venezuela. This meant that if Ajax had chosen to give his 'sims' the red berets, in order to establish a configurative resonance, the game would have taken on new stakes. Rather than the red beret merely being a digital object infinitely interchangeable with other pixilated headgear or hairstyles, the selection of the red beret became a political act, either of homage or satire. When I suggested that he should give some of his characters the item, his normally gregarious demeanor soured, and switching to English he said: 'are you crazy man? I don't need any shit from those guys', gesturing with his eyes towards a group of otherwise indistinguishable youths at the other end of the café.[8] In this case even being presented with such a choice had ramifications that extended outside of the virtual world of the game.

However, the resonance between the game and Ajax's experiences proved to be superficial. Over time it was apparent that rhythm of *The Sims 2* was strongly dissonant with Ajax's own experiences of everyday life. After he had been playing for several hours I noticed that the 'sims' he had designed were all caricatures of real people who were regulars of the café, including Ajax, Maxim and myself. When I asked Ajax about this, he began to complain: 'man, everyone who lives in the same house has to be related. That's annoying, that's why you are my father'. During the process of establishing resonance by configuring the characters appearances, he had run up against an inescapable coded limit of *The Sims 2* that meant all people living in one house had to be related (by blood or marriage). This was dissonant on two levels. First, Ajax wasn't able act as he pleased and create a space that simulated the internet café environment where people from different families, and family groups met. This is primarily because the designed aim of *The Sims 2* is to simulate domestic rather than public spaces.[9] The second level of dissonance follows from the first, as *The Sims 2* established procedural parameters for what could, and could not, constitute a family, Ajax was confronted with a particular paradigm of "family" that had little or no resonance in his own experiences. Like many of the children and young adults that frequented Cybercafé Avila his family life was not a simple nuclear family. While Ajax still had contact with his father, he lived with his mother, and spent a great deal of time with his aunts and cousins. The domestic arrangements that the game demanded did not resonate in the cultural context of family relations in Venezuela. Many families are affected by divorce and absentee fatherhood; combined with the high price of housing, this contributes to different family groups sharing accommodation.

Resonance between game and location takes on a special significance when the player has a significant role in establishing the connection. The connection is established and strengthened through configurations that adequately encapsulate an expression of their own predilections. Or alternately, in the case of dissonance, it is amplified when arrangements of configurations that appear 'natural' to the player are not available in the game. Juul's notion of 'expressive games' is illustrative of this point. He argues that the continuing success of open-ended games like *The Sims* and *Grand Theft Auto* series is based on those games' flexibility to a variety of playing styles, allowing players to express their individual preferences in a way that is meaningful to them. Their potential for expression may, if the players wish, also be enhanced and expanded by cheating.[10] It is because of this flexibility that expressive games have a greater capacity for resonance.

Even in games that do not fit Juul's category of expressive games, decisions are made based on how that particular choice resonates in a meaningful way in the context of local preferences. Chapter three described how some choices made about avatar items in *GunBound* were considered foolish because they were based on purely aesthetic purposes, in the case discussed this was 'cuteness'. However, this was not the only case of expression in *GunBound* that had no effect on the game's outcome. It was also very common for players to purchase flags for their avatars: among Venezuelan players the national flag was an extremely common avatar accessory, this phenomena was replicated in the international server, where symbols of national identity (like pandas) were common accessories for avatars.

This capacity that digital games have for expression has also become integrated into commercial developments by the digital game industry. Following the logic of the capture of counterplay games have been developed with expression in mind. Numerous examples exist, from games like *Second Life* and *PlayStation Home* that claim an almost limitless capacity for expression because all of the game's content is designed by the players, to the recently released *WarioWare D.I.Y.* that allows players to design, play, and share mini-games. The popular *Half-Life 2* mod *Garry's Mod*, and other games like *LittleBigPlanet* suggest an iteration of this trend, becoming games of near pure configuration. Both of these games involve live level design; the player designs the levels as they are being played, with the player moving fluidly between playing and configuration. This style of play is new for games with an emphasis on action; previous games that blended configuration with play—like *The Sims* and the *SimCity* series—were typically of the simulation genre. This new emphasis on configuration within games across the board suggests an expansion of possibilities for both resonant and dissonant configurations.

Distribution is the primary mode of industry capture or control of player configurations. The stakes of one player creating a particular object, level or character are greatly amplified by the ease of distributing digital materials across the internet. While some trading does take place in unofficial channels, new games that are focused on the configuration and creation of new content for the game by the players have official lines of exchange. This production and trading, or sharing of productions, takes place through clearly delineated in-game actions, which further blur the play of the game with configurative activities. For example, in *SimCity 4*, players can both upload their own cities and download other cities from a centralized site without leaving the game. Similar features exist in *The Sims 2* and *The Movies*. While official distribution enables the expressive possibilities of digital games to a certain extent by opening and sustaining channels of exchange between players, they also constrain the possibilities, by monitoring and regulating the exchanges according to official (policy and legal) guidelines. In addition, such forms of exchange often focus on ancillary materials, the paratexts rather than games *per se*. For example, the flourishing use of YouTube to communicate various aspects of gaming history and culture, does offer the possibility of player-to-player sharing of game-made productions, but the artifacts are visual only and the other players cannot reuse them again as games.

Expressive games reflect the ambiguity between intermediaries and mediators. Their wide range of potential configurations makes them difficult to understand in either of the binary categories of transmitters or transformers of culture. The expressive game suggests, rather, that there is a new focus on adaptive configurative actions in digital game play. In this type of digital game, the players' carve out a niche, within the digital gamespace based on their own predilections, thus establishing play through adaptation. But by celebrating and encouraging adaptation, expressive games function in a way that captures this element of play and turns it into a compulsion, a necessity, and a part of the typical experience of game play. Thus the adaptive and compulsive elements of the expressive game in particular become difficult to isolate. However, in this imbroglio, the notion that adaptation is the crucial process of the control society becomes salient; because while being neither fully adaptive nor fully compulsive digital games act as a conduit for this new status for adaptation. This amplifies the ambiguity between training and practices in digital game play by suggesting that digital games may be tools for training in adaptation. The important question then becomes: does this mean that practices cannot critique, or challenge the control society?

'Exploits'

The 'exploit' plays a key role in defining the limits of game play. One of the key points made by scholars of MMORPGs is that the games themselves cannot simply be measured and accounted for by examining their codified rules. It is in the interest of the games' corporate owners to conceptualize the genre in this way as rules, code, and ultimately intellectual property. However, numerous scholars have also argued the counterpoint; that these games are virtual worlds that are governed rather than owned outright.[11] Steinkuehler argues that it is through the negotiation of these positions that game culture emerges.[12] Game culture, she argues is 'interactively stabilized' through ongoing negotiation between a number of parties, prominently including the designers and owners of the game and the players themselves. Importantly though, Steinkuehler acknowledges the important role of a minority of players who are involved in innovative activities that have been discovered by the players through play, like 'gold farming' and 'griefing'. Counterplay actions by small groups players thus has a disproportionate role in defining the relations between gaming cultures and the codified rules of the game because they are concerned with challenging and exploiting the limits of the game.

'Exploits' have been previously defined in a number of ways. Galloway and Thacker describe the exploit as follows: *'Protocological struggles do not centre around changing existent technologies, but instead involve discovering holes in existent technologies and projecting potential change through those holes. Hackers call these holes "exploits"'.*[13] All the key definitions of exploits that specifically pertain to digital game play include factors that place them firmly in the realm of counterplay. Dibbell uses the term to describe the process of exploiting the algorithm of an MMORPG to create value.[14] To 'exploit' the game in this case is to maximize the economic benefit of play either in terms of time or in terms of profit (through real-world or virtual trading). Ludlow and Wallace use the term more generally to describe any action that is allowed by the game software, which was not intended by the games' designers.[15] These unintended actions open a space in games that cannot be entirely described by solely referring to the software or rules of the game, and often become regulated by the game players themselves, thus forming the nucleus for both virtual and situated gaming communities. Consalvo's definition of exploit reiterates that they are actions that are 'found' by the players, which are not a deliberately part of the original design of the game.[16] Her definition also states that 'exploits' do not involve changing the underlying code of the game. This suggests that digital game exploits are examples of counterplay as they involve locating and exploiting new modes of play, rather than of countergaming, or inventing new practices of game design.

Griefing is a form of counterplay in MMORPGs that exploits the community-forming aspect of that genre. While the specific activities of grief players vary from game to game, generally speaking the goal of the grief player is to play the game in a way that causes maximum annoyance to others. It is a highly contextual practice and whether an action is judged as 'griefing' depends entirely on the particular circumstances in which it takes, making it impossible to generalize even within a single game what exactly constitutes griefing.[17] Sivan outlines a number of general categories of grief-style play in *Second Life*: rude and aggressive behavior towards other play-ers; scammers that prey upon inexperienced players by proposing uneven business deals; and 'ideological griefers' who make overt political interventions in the gamespace.[18] From Sivan's categories, it is evident that a wide variety of activities are potentially grief play. Rude and ag-gressive demeanors are contrary to the sociality of game play, while scammers are deliberately predatory on new members of the community; such actives are often forbidden by the terms of service of the game, but continue to exist due to the difficulty of effectively policing them. Some activities also effectively fall into gray areas; one form of grief play that I encountered while playing *Runescape* was being lured unbeknown into PvP areas by experienced players under the guise of showing me the location of various minor but useful items (fishing rods, pickaxes, etc.), and subsequently being killed for their enjoyment, while being abused through the in-game chat.[19] While not against the rules per se, grief-style play as a form of counterplay, mobilizes the communicative functions between players within games, for purposes beyond the direct and im-mediate goals of play. This indicates that the algorithm of the digital game is not a conceptual horizon that defines the experience of play. This form of counterplay involves a re-conception of the goals of play, and subsequently the ways in which play is engaged, to better fit the players' or the play communities peculiar desires. While the term 'grief-play' is used to describe disrup-tive forms of play, the disruption is not necessarily of the smooth and harmonious rhythm of the game, but may also include interventions within the game that seek to politicize gamespace by establishing resonance between the virtual world of the game and real world events; of which Delappe's *dead-in-iraq* project inside *America's Army* is one example.

Gold farming is an important example of counterplay as, in addition to exploiting the algorithmic code of the digital game, it may also take advantage of the inequalities that exist between the locations connected by the global gaming networks. In Dibbel's expose of the virtual economies of digital games, he describes two distinct types of gold farming, one that is based on multiple computers running accounts managed by automated 'bots', and another that uses people.[20] Dur-ing the course of his investigation of *Ultima Online*, it became apparent that the gold farms run by 'bots' were not sustainable, as employees of Electronic Arts (the owner and publisher of *Ultima Online*), would locate avatars with bot-like behavior and test them for human responses. While various strategies were employed more or less successfully by the gold farmers to minimize the damage done to their business, ultimately they could do very little to prevent Electronic Arts from shutting them down as the use of bots was clearly against the terms of service of the game. Furthermore, by many of the players not involved in gold farming it was considered a nuisance, or inconvenience that defied what many players regarded as the community standard 'spirit' of the game.[21]

In December 2005, *The New York Times* broke the first major story of human-operated gold farms. Dibbell discussed similar farms—one allegedly operating in Mexico, and another in China—during the course of his investigation.[22] The farms described in *The New York Times* story were operating in China, and employed individuals to play various MMORPGs in 12 or 18 hour shifts.[23] By paying the player/workers in Chinese yuan, but exchanging the virtual currency that they ac-cumulated into higher valued currencies (primarily US dollars, but also the South Korean won and Japanese yen), the gold farming businesses were able to take advantage of the difference in standard wages and costs of living between China and other advanced economies. Needless to say, this development has been highly controversial for a number of reasons which range from concerns over the working conditions of the gold farming labor force, in-game racist backlashes against Asian players,[24] to the loss of institutional tax revenue as money is moved off-shore through real-money trading of virtual currencies.[25] Despite all this, it remains significant as a form of counterplay because the gold farming exploits demonstrate the global scope of the digital game ecology, and the connection between, and interdependence of, the global and virtual, and local situated conditions. Counterplay, does not necessarily only involve actions and configurations within games, but may also draw upon the global connectivity of digital games and the aggregation of spaces, humans and machines into the gaming network, to take advantage of the complexity, flux, uncertainty, and variety of the digital game ecology.

Counterplay consists of actions taken in games that are within the scope of the designed rules of the game but were not intended to exist or be a significant element of play. These actions are emergent forms of play. However, they often rely on intersections or overlaps with the game as it is intended to be played, and the disjuncture between the emergent practice of play and typical practices are key to the community's success. For example, gold farmers rely on other players to establish and sustain the economy that they then exploit. Counterplay may mobilize other resources, both human and machine (both software and hardware) to achieve its goals. It is in relation to the uneven development of global networks through which the digital game ecology is enacted that the crucial stakes of counterplay are established. In these situations, counterplay confronts the player with this unevenness, as it is through counterplay that the unevenness is negotiated, or overcome.

Playing the Margin

Game play as a segue into game design represents one extreme of the ambiguity between training and practice, while the idea that *Marc Ecko's Getting Up: Contents Under Pressure* is, or even potentially could be used as, a training simulation for criminal behavior is the other. However disparate, the logic of both positions relies on the core notion that games are about rules, and that mastery of digital games stems from learning and internalizing these rules. The rules, and the mastery of them, may be on either or both the configurative, and the narrative or 'diegetic' levels of digital games.[26] While digital games are forms of training or dressage, it is important to acknowledge that while containing disciplinary elements, they also rely on creative, innovative, and unruly practices. It is these latter attributes that when combined with the formal rules of the game provides a 'latitude' or 'margin' of action that 'is free within the limits set by the rules'.[27] The notion of a margin between training and practice has important consequences for arguments that position digital games as so thoroughly imbricated in the control society that they can neither provide "meaningful" choices, or are able to operate on the level of critique.[28] The following section will argue that the "margin" suggests a meaningful flexibility in action within tightly defined human-computer models of interaction such as Friedman's cybernetic feedback loop, and Galloway's operator/machine binary. While the margin is by no means a realm of pure potentiality it is also subject to exploits; that is human interventions which use the rules of the game and its material limits in manners that were previously unanticipated.

In order to expound this trajectory it is necessary to further unpack Caillois' notion of play. Caillois argues that all forms of play are governed by two opposing principles; the first is characterized by 'improvisation and joy', that he calls paidia,[29] while: 'At the opposite extreme, this frolicsome and impulsive exuberance is almost entirely absorbed or *disciplined* by a *complimentary*, and in some respects inverse, tendency to its anarchic and capricious nature'.[30] He calls this 'disciplinary' form of play ludus. This principle of play is characterized by the 'effort, patience, skill, or ingenuity' used by the players.[31] Caillois' concern is not to use these terms to formulate binary categories of games characterized by one or the other of these principles; rather he emphasizes the 'complimentary' operation of ludus and paidia.

The importance of paidia stems from how it compliments existing theories of play that focus on play as a culture building process. Lash and Lury argue that the notion of paidia constitutes Caillios' key intervention in Huizinga's argument regarding the role that play has in culture.[32] They suggest that Caillios' perceives Huizinga's conception of play as being entirely too indebted to ludus, order, and the impact that the ordering factors of game play have in nourishing various aspects of civilization. Paidia thus suggests a way of thinking about play that does not necessarily equate it to some extrinsic cultural or institutional value. By highlighting the interdependence of paidia and ludus in play, Caillois produces a model that acknowledges the entirety of play, rather just the utility.

Paidia and ludus are necessary in all situations where play takes place. While rules—exemplified by ludus—are integral to play, Caillois also maintains that play must allow for 'basic freedoms' that 'stimulate distraction and fantasy'.[33] While his argument does emphasize the important role that he believes ludus has in culture, Caillois never veers from the point that the two principles are complementary and imbricated. He states:

> [ludus] …is *complimentary* to and a *refinement of paidia*, which it disciplines and enriches. It provides an occasion for training and normally leads to the acquisition of a special skill, a particular mastery of the operation of one or another contraption…[34]

Caillois' positioning of ludus as a refinement of paidia does, however, suggest that he believes there is a hierarchical relation between the two principles. His emphasis on the importance of ludus is motivated by a concern for the role that play and games have in culture. Ludus disciplines paidia, play disciplines the mind and body. It is cast as a developmental process where the child-like, creative, naive, unruly, untamed, wild, elements of play are turned to tasks that register on grander scales than merely the playing field. However, in this context what is salient is the symbiotic relation that Caillois describes; where the value that society extracts from play comes from paidia as well as ludus.

This discussion of the 'margin' or 'latitude' of play highlights the contradictory and ambiguous attitudes that play fosters in relation to the rules. While the rules place limits on action, they are also what allows action and make it meaningful in the context of the game, and in the community of its players. In digital game play, the players are not free to take any action that they wish. The constraints of the rules establish a narrow margin where action is completely free so long as it is within the proscribed limits.

The operator/machine model of digital game play is inclined to understand the process of play as the mastery of an algorithm. Galloway states: 'To play the game means to play the code of the game. To win means to know the system. And thus to interpret a game means to interpret its algorithm'.[35] By focusing of the reciprocal feedback between operator and machine and the process of modulating responses according to that feedback, an impression of the narrowness and fragility of the creative margin of play is implicitly presented. As the feedback between operator and machine becomes increasingly faster, immediate and anticipated, the feedback loop tightens and closes, absorbing the creative margin of digital game play. Play instead becomes a series of scripted responses designed to modulate the anticipated processes of the algorithm of the game. As the margin of play retreats in the face of the closing feedback loop, so does the possibility of the player engaging in either meaningful action in, or critical reflection on, the game. This approach to understanding game play perceives play in this way because the central actions of game play—both configurative and diegetic—are conceptualized as forms of modulation of the game software's algorithm. Play is then contained completely in this pre-scripted algorithm, and any operator actions made during play are merely the selection of already existing courses or pathways through the game. Galloway goes so far as to compare the choices offered by games, the interventions that players make during play, to selecting options from menus.[36] While acknowledging that digital games' narrowing margin of play does restrict the player in ways that make digital games something considerably less than a realm of pure potential, the margin does allow for actions that should not necessarily be considered modulation.

By regarding all gamic action as being contained, a priori within the algorithmic code, counterplay is overlooked. Counterplay may be used in the game through 'exploits'; either by discovering or inventing new forms of actions, or by the possibilities established by the aggregation of people and/or machines in localized or global networks. In the first case, there are many discovered actions that are possible by the design of the game, but are either not anticipated by the designers, or are mistakes or 'glitches' in the programming. For example, in the original release of *Sid Meier's Civilization* a game-winning tactic was quickly developed that involved building large numbers of cities close to each other—so that their zones of influence overlapped—and then swamping the opposing civilizations with large numbers of low powered units. The correct use of this strategy meant that the game could easily be over, with the globe dominated by one culture by 400BC. Another example is the common glitch in games that allows players to see through walls. By turning rapidly when the avatar has a following camera, the player is able to briefly see what is on the other side of the wall before the camera adjusts its distance behind the avatar. Recent games containing such glitches include: *Lara Croft Tomb Raider: Anniversary*, *Mario Kart Wii*, and the PlayStation3 version of *Tom Clancy's Rainbow Six: Vegas*.[37] However, in the logic of digital games-as-algorithms, these discoveries are no different from anticipated and designed forms of modulation. While they fit perfectly with the notion of digital game play as modulation, they demonstrate something quite different about the notion of modulation in the society of control. Deleuze's own metaphors of a sieve that shifts its warp and weft to accommodate different sized objects and the branching of highway systems suggest a strongly controlling structure that filters and manages the flow within it. To a certain extent, Galloway is correct to point out that digital games embody this logic.[38] But, it is also important to acknowledge the adaptive dimensions of digital game play. Players of digital games are not simply operating on a meta-level configuring options on a series of menus. Some are also engaged in producing entirely new options through discovery and combination. This suggests that there is room for players to develop practices in digital game play. The software as code enacts all of the possibilities of the game, whether these possibilities are designed or not. But without the intervention of the operator the code is inert; a piece of game software that is not in play.

The code of the digital game, while material, is only potential until a player enacts it through, and in, the local. The complex aggregations of people and machines in the location opens digital game play to forms of counterplay that are clearly distanced from the algorithm of the game. These examples can be divided into two groups: counterplay that involves exploiting the aggregation of players in a localized space, and counterplay that exploits the aggregation of computers within and across locations through networks.

If digital game play is understood as taking place in a situated ecology, the instances of counter-play multiply. Take, for example, the communication between players that sharing the same space while playing cooperatively allows. Communication itself is disciplined or otherwise controlled in many multiplayer online games: either in terms of what languages may be spoken on open channels e.g. *Tibia*; or to whether a player may continue to communicate with other members of their team after the death of their avatar, e.g. *Counter-Strike*. In the case study internet cafés these regulations did not work. This is not to say communication is completely free; there were numerous times in Cybercafé Avila when Xavier raised his voice over the chatter, to announce that it was getting too noisy inside the cafe. But his problem was the volume; what had been spoken was not the issue. Communication about digital games being played in such spaces allows the players to coordinate their efforts in ways that the communication functions within digital games do not. Thus deliberately collaborative practices like 'ghosting' can emerge, as well as other forms of play that involve integrating information from sources beyond that immediately supplied to each individual player by the digital game: for example, the way that El Bebe cheated in Cybercafé Avila by looking at other players' screens while he was playing *Counter-Strike*. Broadly, this form of counterplay also extends to the playful communication between players involved in exploring the same gamespace, particularly the live exchange of paratextual information. This means that counterplay, like play, often involves people who may not necessarily be considered to be actually playing.

The other key manifestation of counterplay involves exploiting the machines, or the network of machines that enact the code of the game. A simple example that I saw at Cydus was the use of a coin to jam down a key in order to perform a power-up without having to either repeatedly press the same key, or even sit at the computer holding down that key. More complicated examples emerge if the scope considered is beyond an individual machine or location. Consider Mackenzie's description of playing *Avara* with a friend. He states:

> …something struck me as he quickly won a succession of games. He was not only anticipating most of my movements, and my gestures, he was also anticipating and manipulating in certain ways the delays introduced by the network we were playing on.[39]

Lag, caused by the uneven speed of data flows across the network, also becomes a site of play; a way of extending its margin. Other forms of lag cheating have been discussed, however, the exploitation of lag that Mackenzie describes does not rely on a built or designed cheat function, but rather on exploiting a logistical problem that effects all data transfers based on packet switching.[40] What makes this example significant is that it highlights how counterplay may be used to negotiate the limitations of the hardware on which the software is enacted. It also suggests that being globally networked multiplies the possibilities for counterplay; Mackenzie points out that the negative impact of lag on games is often experienced unevenly, because of the different distances between each location and where the game is being served.[41]

These are still forms of modulation or the control society, however the margin of play that these forms of counterplay produce, while constantly being encroached on and reabsorbed by capital, are at a certain point unassailable. Of course this is a problem for capital, but not necessarily for the control society. While not every aspect of digital game play can be captured by capital and commodified, in order to create situations where digital game play may take place, spaces, machines, objects and people must be modulated and configured in particular ways. Arrangements must be made for hardware, bandwidth, power, food supplies, waste disposal, to name but a few. Digital game play is reliant on these necessities, and is unavoidably tied to capital at this level at least. However, at while these material concerns demonstrate that digital game play is at the base level imbricated with capital, they indicate that digital games are not solely about the algorithm. The production of digital game play and counterplay, like any other form of capital, also involves the management of everyday life. It is at this point, where object, things, services, people, and networks start stacking up to produce gaming situations, that it might be useful to shift the metaphors of modulation and algorithmic culture from the play of games to the state of contemporary culture. This is the significance of Galloway's point about digital games as allegories of informatic control. However what counterplay suggests is that while the computers, and computer networks that are crucial to the contemporary control society often operate as instruments of compulsion, they also expand the scope of human adaptation to those compulsions.

Conclusion

Counterplay, as a form of creative and adaptive practices, establishes new forms of digital game play inside, and tangential to, the coded limits of the game space. At stake in these practices is a basic ambiguity about the role that play has in society: is it a form of discipline or training? Or does it establish new relations, connections, conceptions and modes of being? Turning to Caillois' notion of paidia suggests that play, and therefore digital game play, necessarily involves a creative margin. This space is established through the rules of the game, and the coded limits of the gamespace, but within these established boundaries it has no other limitations. But this does not mean that the actions of the players' are subsumed in the compulsive processes of algorithmic modulation. The margin of play is highly contextual, and can only be assed through a situated examination of digital game play that both takes into account the manner in which play is embedded and enacted in the local, and the way in which aggregations of people, technologies, and networks and formed and exploited in order to produce play. This provides considerable flexibility and scope within games, and gaming cultures for players' to leverage counterplay. However, as evident through the digital games industries' strategies for capturing counterplay, adaptation and the process of turning the necessities of play into practices and playful creations is being reterritorialized as a form of compulsion, or training.

However, the process of turning creation into necessity, of making playful innovation a key part of game play, still does not mean that capital is able to reabsorb all creations. Configurative resonance illustrates how in the process of configuration, even within a closed and limited system, player choice can produce outcomes that resonate with specific situations. The fact that the inputs and outputs are all contained in the games' algorithm is of limited relevance if the subsequent production is able to make a meaningful connection, or disjunction, with a players' own experience of everyday life. Some forms of exploits, in addition to setting that player against the rules of the game from within the game, also affirm and highlight the differences and inequalities between locations, by making those difference the subject of the exploit. Adaptation may become compulsive in the context of digital games, but the emphasis is on the adaptive process, which leaves room for individual creations, innovations, and practices.

Notes

1 Massumi, B. (2002). *Parables for the Virtual: Movement, Affect, Sensation.* Durham: Duke University Press: p. 77.

2 Latour, B. (2005). *Reassembling the Social: An Introduction to Actor-network Theory.* Oxford: Oxford University Press: p. 39.

3 Latour, *Reassembling the Social*: p. 39.

4 Latour, *Reassembling the Social*: p. 40.

5 In the case of fictional worlds, both Nintendo and Marvel have made lawsuits against MMOR-PGs that allow players to design characters that through selective configuration of a number of variables had appearances similar to trademarked characters. In the case of the real world configurations, games like *Tony Hawk Underground*, that allow the player to create the avatars' appearance from a digital photograph establish strong resonances with everyday life.

6 See Apperley (2007b); Everett (2005); Everett and Watkins (2008); and Squire (2008: p. 180-181).

7 Galloway, A. (2006). *Gaming: Essays on Algorithmic Culture.* Minneapolis: University of Minnesota Press: p. 78.

8 Ajax, like many other Venezuelans made it very clear to me where his political loyalties lay. He was an anti-Chávista. It remain unclear weather Ajax was concerned that the group he gestured towards were Chávista and would be offended by his portrayal, or if they were non-Chávista's who would misread his actions as a sign of respect and loyalty.

9 The numerous *The Sims* extension packs, like *The Sims 2: Nightlife* do deal with public space, however.

10 Juul, J. (2008). 'Without a Goal: On Open and Expressive Games'. In B. Atkins and T. Krzywinska (eds.). *Videogame, Player, Text.* Manchester: Manchester University Press: p. 199.

11 See the declaration of rights for avatars: Ludlow and Wallace (2007: pp. 268-273).

12 Steinkuehler, C. (2006). 'The Mangle of Play'. *Games and Culture* 1.3: p. 200.

13 Galloway, A. and Thacker, E. (2007). *The Exploit: A Theory of Networks.* Minneapolis: University of Minnesota Press: p. 81. Original Emphasis.

14 Dibbell, J. (2006). *Play Money, Or How I Quit my Day Job and Made Millions Trading Virtual Loot.* New York: Basic Books: p. 204.

15 Ludlow, P. and Wallace, M. (2007). *The Second Life Herald: The Virtual Tabloid that Witnessed the Dawn of the Metaverse.* Cambridge: MIT Press: p. 179.

16 Consalvo, M. (2007). *Cheating: Gaining Advantage in Videogames.* Cambridge: MIT Press:

p. 114.

17 See: Ludlow and Wallace, *The Second Life Herald*: p. 99; and Taylor, T. L. (2006a). *Play Between Worlds: Exploring Online Game Culture*. Cambridge: The MIT Press: p. 51.

18 Sivan, Y. Y. (2008). 'The 3D3C Metaverse: A New Medium in Born'. In T. Samuel-Azran and D. Caspi (eds.). *New Media and Innovative Technologies*. Beer-Shiva: Ben Gurion University Press/ Tzivonim Publishing: pp. 144-146.

19 e.g. PWNED NOOB!!!1

20 Dibbell, *Play Money*.

21 Research by Steinkuehler (2006) highlights the imbrication of gold farming with the typical community of players', many of whom rely of gold farmers to provide them with virtual currency in exchange for real currency.

22 Dibbell, *Play Money*: pp. 18-19 and 212-214.

23 Barboza, D. (2005). 'Ogre to Slay? Outsource it to China'. *The New York Times*.

24 See: Steinkuehler (2006); Taylor (2006b); and Thomas (2008).

25 See: Castronova (2003; 2005); and Dibbell (2006).

26 Galloway, *Gaming*: p. 7.

27 Caillois, R. (1961). Man, Play and Games. New York: Free Press of Glencoe: p. 8.

28 Galloway, *Gaming*: p. 102.

29 Caillois, *Man, Play and Games*: p. 27.

30 Caillois, *Man, Play and Games*: p. 13. Emphasis added.

31 Caillois, *Man, Play and Games*: p. 13.

32 Lash, S. and Lury, C. (2007). Global Culture Industry: The Mediation of Things. Cambridge: Polity: pp. 190-191.

33 Caillois, *Man, Play and Games*: p. 27.

34 Caillois, *Man, Play and Games*: p. 29. Emphasis added

35 Galloway, *Gaming*: pp. 90-91.

36 Galloway, *Gaming*: p. 102.

37 See Atkins's (2003), account of the *Tomb Raider* series for a description of some more glitches in that game.

38 Galloway, *Gaming*: p. 101.

39 Mackenzie, A. (2002). *Transductions: Bodies and Machines at Speed*. London: Continuum: p. 166.

40 Consalvo, M. (2007). *Cheating: Gaining Advantage in Videogames*. Cambridge: MIT Press: pp. 115-116.

41 Mackenzie, *Transductions*: p. 167. For example: the Australian *World of Warcraft* servers introduced in late 2005 where still served from the U.S.A., just set to Australian time. This did nothing to solve the lag problem that many players' had experienced, although at least everyone in the world now suffered from more or less the same degree of lag, thus removing the disadvantage many Australian players had previously felt.

CONCLUSION

Rhythmanalysis and everyday life are tools that bridge the situated and the global. Each instantiation of play, or culture of use is its own localized enactment, yet each is also situated not just in the local but in the global networks of communication in which gaming takes place. The situated ecology—an accumulation or assemblage of hardware, software, people, institutions—where the global and virtual is enacted in order to produce play, challenges abstract accounts of digital game play, to address digital games and players as they are, rather than as an ideal game played by an ideal player.

Situating digital game play in everyday life, the spaces and times of compulsion, highlights how digital game play is also characterized by individual and collective adaptive actions that mobilize both virtual in-game and offline resources. This process of adaptation takes players beyond the limits of the game as they must also adapt the digital game ecology to the local situation. The significance of counterplay as a concept is how it illustrates that digital game play draws on currents of training and practice. To return to the questions from the beginning of this book; the concern that digital games somehow 'do' something to players, the answer is: it is complicated. The concept of counterplay stresses that digital game play is an activity that is always a form of negotiation and adaptation. This is irrespective of how games might be designed in respect to particular ethics, ideologies, opinions, or viewpoints. While digital games are *always* forms of training, they also have scope for practice.

This latitude for practice is paradoxically both integral to digital games training role, and antithetical to it. Digital games are emblematic of the subordination of adaptation to compulsion. The fluidity and flexibility of the control society means that it is able to contain—but not completely constrain—the margin of play because of the centrality of adaptation. Counterplay is an important example of adaptation in the control society. Although digital games do suggest that adaptation has become a form of compulsion, this does not mean that adaptation is meaningless. Counterplay, is a practice that expands plays margins and—irrespective of whether these creative currents are harnessed to capital, or used to critique it—counterplay raises the stakes of play in locations marginalized by the uneven expansion and reach of global networks.

Of key importance to the concept of counterplay is its 'capture'. Counterplay is an important source of innovations for the digital games industry, as techniques are developed to encourage forms of play that may be easily re-integrated into the system of capital, or to eliminate forms of play that are more difficult to assimilate. This simultaneous absorption and disciplining of counterplay is symptomatic of modulation, and harkens a return to the general argument that digital games are the product par excellence of 'Empire', or the 'Control Society'. However, the centrality of the role of adaptation in counterplay in relation both to the digital game industry and the control society suggests that the ambiguous currents of counterplay could feed as easily into practices that politicize digital game play, as they do into practices that fuel innovation in the industry. This also points to the possibility of critique, creative practice, and meaningful action that are demonstrated by examining play in everyday life.

The oscillating rhythms between: training and practice; and counterplay and its capture, feed into forms of control as well as forms of practice and innovation. As practices of counterplay expand the margin of digital game play into new territories, and new corporate iterations of gaming seek to re-territorialize it, new forms of play and counterplay emerge.

WORKS CITED

Aarseth, E. (1997). *Cybertext: Perspectives on Ergodic Literature.* Baltimore: John Hopkins University Press.

Aarseth, E. (1999) 'Aporia and Epiphany in Doom and The Speaking Clock: The Temporality of Ergodic Art'. In M. Ryan (ed.). *Cyberspace Textuality: Computer Technology and Literary Theory* (pp. 31-41). Indiana University Press: Bloomington.

Abalieno (2005, January 29). 'These Screenshots Are Worth A "Ban"'. Retrieved 3 August, 2008. Message posted to http://www.cesspit.net/drupal/node/491

'Addicted: Suicide Over Everquest? Was he Obsessed?' (2002, 18 October). CBS News, retrieved 20 June 2007, from http://www.cbsnews.com/stories/2002/10/17/48hours/main525965. shtml

Adorno, T. (1991). *The Culture Industry: Selected Essays on Mass Culture.* Routledge: New York.

Amis, M. (1982). *Invasion of Space Invaders: An Addict's Guide to Battle Tactics, Big Scores and the Best Machines.* Hutchinson: London.

Amtrkblue (2008, February 13). Message posted to http://au.gamespot.com/news/6186009. html?action=convert&om_clk=latestnews&tag=latestnews%3Btitle%3B0&page=6

Anderson, J. (2005, September 13). 'Spot On: Korea Reacts to Increased Game Addiction'. *GameSpot.* Retrieved October 1, 2008, from http://au.gamespot.com/news/2005/09/12/ news_6132357.html

Androutsopoulos, J. (2006). 'Multilingualism, Diaspora and the Internet: Codes and Identities on German-based Diasporic Web-sites'. *The Journal of Sociolinguistics* 10.4: 520-547.

Anti-Defamation League (2002, February 19). 'Racist Group Using Gaming to Promote Violence Against Blacks, Latinos and Jews'. Retrieved 21 July, 2008, from http://www.adl.org/videogames/default.asp

Apperley, T. (2006). 'Genre and Game Studies: Towards a Critical Approach to Video Game Genres'. *Simulation & Gaming: An Interdisciplinary Journal of Theory, Practice and Research* 37(1), 6-23.

Apperley, T. (2007a). 'Games without borders: Globalization, gaming and mobility in Venezuela'. In G. Goggin and L. Hjorth (eds.). *Mobile Media 2007: Proceeding of an International Conference on Social and Cultural Aspects of Mobile Phones, Convergent Media, and Wireless Technologies* (pp. 171-178) Sydney: University of Sydney Press.

Apperley, T. (2007b). 'Virtual Unaustralia: Videogames and Australia's Colonial History'. In the refereed conference proceedings of CSAA 2006. Retrieved 16 April 2007, from http://www. unaustralia.com/electronicpdf/Unapperley.pdf

Apperley, T. (2008). 'Video games in Australia'. In M. J. P. Wolf (ed.). *The Video Game Explosion: A History from Pong to Playstation® and Beyond* (pp. 223-228). Westport: Greenwood Press.

'Army to Spend $50 Million on Video Games' (2008, 27 November). *kimatv.com.* Retrieved 13 July 2010, from http://www.kimatv.com/news/tech/35188284.html

Atkins, B. (2003). *More than a Game: The Computer Game as Fictional Form.* Manchester: University of Manchester Press.

Baer, R. (n.d.). 'Pong: Who did it First?'. *PONG-Story.* Retrieved October 2, 2008, from http:// www.pong-story.com/inventor.htm

Bahktin, M. (1984). *Rabelais and His World* (Trans. H. Iswolsky). Bloomington: Indiana University Press.

Banks, J. (2003). 'Gamers as Co-creators: Enlisting the Virtual Audience – a Report from the Netface'. In V. Nightengale and K. Ross (eds.). *Critical Readings: Media and Audiences (pp. 268-278).* Maidenhead: Open University Press.

Banks, J. (2009). 'Co-creative Expertise: Auran Games and Fury – A Case Study'. *Media International Australia* 130, 77-89.

Banks, J., and Humphreys, S. (2008). 'The Labour of User Co-creators: Emergent Social Markets?'. *Convergence: The International Journal of Research into New Media Technologies* 14.4: 401-418.

Barboza, D. (2005, December 12). 'Ogre to Slay? Outsource it to China'. *The New York Times.* Retrieved 25 June 2008, from http://www.nytimes.com/2005/12/09/technology/09gaming.ht ml?ex=1291784400&en=a723d0f8592dff2e&ei=5090&partner=rssuserland&emc=rss

Barr, T. (2000). *newmedia.com.au: The Changing Face of Australia's Media and Communications.* St. Leonards: Allen and Unwin.

Barrett, P. (2006). 'White Thumbs, Black Bodies: Race, Violence and Neo-liberal Fantasies in Grand Theft Auto: San Andreas'. *The Review of Education/Pedagogy/Cultural Studies* 28.1: 95-119.

Benjamin, W. (2003). *Selected Writings, vol. 4, 1938-1940* (Ed. H. Eiland and M. W. Jennings; Trans, E. Jephcott and others). Cambridge: Bellknap Press.

Benkler, Y. (2006). *The Wealth of Networks: How Social Production Transforms Markets and Freedoms.* New Haven: Yale University Press.

Bittanti, M. (2006). 'Intro – Game Art'. In M. Bittant and D. Quaranta (eds.). Gamescences: Art in the Age of Videogames (pp. 7-14). Milan: Johan Levi.

Boellstorff, T. (2006). 'A Ludicrous Discipline? Ethnography and Game Studies'. *Games and Culture* 1.1: 29-35.

Boellstorff, T. (2008). *Coming of Age in Second Life: An Anthropologist Explores the Virtually Human.* Princeton: Princeton University Press.

Boellstorff, T. (2009). 'Ethnography'. In B. Perron and M. J. P. Wolf (eds.). The Video Game Theory Reader 2 (pp. 348-349). New York: Routledge.

Bogost, I. (2006). *Unit Operations: An Approach to Videogame Criticism.* Cambridge: MIT Press.

Bogost, I. (2007). *Persuasive Games: The Expressive Power of Videogames.* Cambridge: MIT Press.

Bogost, I. and Klainbaum, D. (2006). 'Experiencing Place in Los Santos and Vice City'. In N. Garrelts (ed.). *The Meaning and Culture of Grand Theft Auto* (pp. 162-176), Jefferson: Macfarland.

Bolter, J. D. and Grusin, R. (1999). *Remediation: Understanding New Media.* Cambridge: MIT Press.

Bourdieu, P. (1984). *Distinction: A Social Critique of the Judgment of Taste* [trans. R. Nice]. Cambridge: Harvard University Press.

Brand, J. E. (2007). *Interactive Australia 2007: Facts about the Australian Computer and Video Game Industry.* Everleigh: Interactive Entertainment Association of Australia.

Brand, J. E., Majewski, J., and Knight, S. J. (2006). 'Representation of ALANA in computer and videogames'. In G. T. Meiss and A. A. Tait (eds.). *Ethnic Media in America: Building a System of Their Own* (pp. 105-124). Dubuque, Kendall/Hunt Publishing Company.

'Brazil Bans Popular Video Game Seen to Incite Violence' (2008, January 18). *MSN News.* Retrieved 24 August, 2008, from http://news.my.msn.com/sci-tech/article.aspx?cp-documentid=1197105

Brooke, J. (2005, December 7). 'South Koreans React to Video Games' Depiction of North Koreans'. The *New York Times*. Retrieved August 25, 2008, from http://www.nytimes.com/2005/12/07/arts/07game.html?pagewanted=print

Bruns, A. (2008). *Blogs, Wikipedia, Second Life and Beyond: From Production to Produsage.* New York: Peter Lang.

Bryce, J. and Rutter, J. (2005). 'Gendered Gaming in Gendered Space'. In J. Raessens and J. Goldstein (eds.). *Handbook of Computer Game Studies* (pp. 301-310). Cambridge: MIT Press.

Burnham, V. (2001). *Supercade: A Visual History of the Videogame Age 1971-1984.* Cambridge: MIT Press.

Burrill, D. A. (2008). *Die Tryin': Videogames, Masculinity, Culture.* New York: Peter Lang.

Caillois, R. (1961). *Man, Play and Games* (Trans. M. Barash). New York: Free Press of Glencoe.

Caldwell, J. T. (2003). 'Second Shift Media Aesthetics: Programming, Interactivity, and User Flows'. In A. Everett and J. T. Caldwell (eds.). *New Media: Theories and Practices of Digitextuality* (pp. 127-144). New York: Routledge.

Caldwell, N. (1998). 'Games R Us – and Most of the Western World as Well: The Hegemony of the Strategic Computer Game'. In *M/C Journal: A Journal of Media and Culture* 1.5. Retrieved April 16, 2007, from http://journal.media-culture.org.au/9812/strat.php

Caldwell, N. (2000). 'Settler Stories: Representational Ideologies in Computer Strategy Gaming'. In *M/C Journal: A Journal of Media and Culture* 3.5. Retrieved April 16, 2007, from http://journal.media-culture.org.au/0010/settlers.php

Cannon, R. (2007). 'Meltdown'. In A. Clarke and G. Mitchell (eds.). *Videogames and Art* (pp. 38-53). Bristol: Intellect.

Cap, T. (2004). 'Interview with Joakim Berggwist'. GamersHell. Retrieved 24 August, 2008, from http://news.my.msn.com/sci-tech/article.aspx?cp-documentid=1197105

Carr, D. (2002). 'Playing with Lara'. In G. King and T. Krzywinska (eds.). *ScreenPlay: Cinema/videogames/interfaces* (pp. 171-180). London: Wallflower.

Cassell, J. and Jenkins, H. (eds.) (1998). *From Barbie to Mortal Kombat: Gender and Computer games.* Cambridge: MIT Press.

Castells, M. (1995). *The Rise of the Networked Society,* [Second Edition]. Oxford: Blackwell.

Castells, M. (2000). *End of Millennium.* Malden: Blackwell.

Castronova, E. (2003). 'On Virtual Economies'. In *Game Studies: the International Journal of Computer Game Research* 3.2. Retrieved January 9 2007, from http://www.gamestudies.org/0302/castronova/

Castronova, E. (2005). *Synthetic Worlds: The Business and Culture of Online Games.* Chicago: University of Chicago Press.

Cesarini, P. (2004). '"Opening" the Xbox: Linux, Microsoft and Control'. In *M/C: A Journal of Media and Culture* 7.3. Retrieved 4 February, 2009, from http://www.media-culture.org.au/0406/08_Cesarini.php

Chan, D. (2005). 'Playing with Race: The Ethics of Racialized Representations in e-Games'. *International Review of Information Ethics* 4: 25-30.

Chan, D. (2009). 'Beyond the "Great Fire-Wall": The Case of In-Game Protests in China'. In L. Hjorth and D. Chan (eds.) *Gaming Cultures and Place in the Asia-Pacific* (pp. 141-157). London: Routledge.

'Chávez to Shut Down Opposition TV'. (2006, December 29). *BBC News.* Retrieved February 8, 2007, from http://news.bbc.co.uk/2/6215815.stm

'Chávez la emprende de nuevo contra la muñeca "Barbie" y la "Play Station"'. (2010, 17 January). *Noticias 24.* Retrieved 10 July, 2010, from http://www.noticias24.com/actualidad/noticia/139787/chavez-la-emprende-de-nuevo-contra-la-muneca-barbie-y-la-play-station/

Chesher, C. (2004). 'Neither a Gaze Nor a Glance, but a Glaze: Relating to Console Game Screens'. *Scan: A Journal of Media Arts Culture* 1.1. Retrieved April 17 2007, from http://scan.net.au/scan/journal/display.php?journal_id=19

'China Imposes Online Gaming Curbs' (2005, August 25). *BBC News.* Retrieved October 1, 2008, from http://news.bbc.co.uk/2/hi/technology/4183340.stm

City of Melbourne. Retrieved 11 June, 2008, from http://www.melbourne.vic.gov.au/info.cfm?top=66&pa=779&pg=782

Coalli, E. (2008, August 5). 'Auran shutting down FURY MMO'. *Worlds in Motion.* Retrieved 1 February 2009, from http://www.worldsinmotion.biz/2008/08/auran_shutting_down_fury_mmo.php

Consalvo, M. (2003a). 'Hot Dates and Fairy-tale Romances: Studying Sexuality in Videogames. In M. J. P. Wolf and B. Perron (eds.). *The Video Game Theory Reader* (pp. 171-194). New York: Routledge.

Consalvo, M. (2003b). Zelda 64 and Videogame Fans: A Walkthrough of Games, Intertextuality, and Narrative. *Television and New Media* 4.3: 321-334.

Consalvo, M. (2006). Console Video Games and Global Corporations: Creating a Hybrid Culture. *New Media and Society* 8.1: 117-137.

Consalvo, M. (2007). *Cheating: Gaining Advantage in Videogames.* Cambridge: MIT Press.

Consalvo, M. and Dutton, N. (2006). 'Game Analysis: Developing a Methodological Toolkit for the Qualitative Study of Games'. Game Studies: the International Journal of Computer Game Research 6.1. Retrieved 15 August, 2007, from http://gamestudies.org/0601/articles/consalvo_dutton

Coughlan, S. (2006, June 1). 'Just One More'. *BBC News Magazine.* Retrieved 21 June, 2007, from http://news.bbc.co.uk/1/hi/magazine/5034756.stm

Crogan, P. (2004a). 'Games, Simulation and Serious Fun: An Interview with Espen Aarseth'. *Scan: Journal of Media Arts Culture* 1.1. Retrieved June 3, 2007, from http://scan.net.au/scan/journal/display.php?journal_id=20

Crogan, P. (2004b). 'The Game Thing: Ludology and Other Theory Games'. *Media International Australia* 110: 10-18.

Cunningham, H. (2000). 'Moral Kombat and Computer Game Girls'. In J. T. Caldwell (ed.). *Theories of the New Media: A Historical Perspective* (pp. 213-226). London: Athlone.

Darley, A. (2000). *Visual Digital Culture: Surface Play and Spectacle in New Media Genres.* London: Routledge.

de Certeau, M. (1984). *The Practice of Everyday Life* (Trans. S. F. Rendall). Berkeley: University of California Press.

de Peuter, G. and Dyer-Witheford, N. (2005). 'A Playful Multitude? Mobilising and Counter-mobilising Immaterial Game Labour'. In *The Fibreculture Journal* 5. Retrieved January 9, 2007, from http://journal.fibreculture.org/issue5/depeuter_dyerwitheford.html

Deleuze, G. (1995). *Negotiations* 1972-1990 (Trans. M. Joughin). New York: Columbia University Press.

Deleuze, G (2006). *Two Regimes of Madness: Texts and Interviews 1975-1995* (Trans. A. Hodges and M. Taorimina). Los Angeles: Semiotexte.

Dibbell, J. (2006). *Play Money, Or How I Quit my Day Job and Made Millions Trading Virtual Loot.* New York: Basic Books.

DiSalvo, B., Crowley, K., and Norwood, R. (2008). 'Learning in Context: Digital Games and Young Black Men'. *Games and Culture* 3.2: 131-141.

Douglas, C. (2002). '"You Have Unleashed a Horde of Barbarians": Fighting Indians, Playing Games, Forming Disciplines'. *Postmodern Culture* 13.1. Retrieved September 28, 2006, from http://muse.jhu.edu/journals/postmodern_culture/toc/pmc13.1.html

drsvss (2008, February 15). 'Make Leeching Impossible (msg 1)'. Message posted to http://forums.legendro.net/index.php?showtopic=137485

Elkington, T. (2009). 'Too Many Cooks: Media Convergence and Self-defeating Adaptations'. In B. Perron and M. J. P. Wolf (eds.). *The Video Game Theory Reader 2* (pp. 213-236). New York: Routledge.

Escape from Woomera Project Team (n.d.). Escape From Woomera Design Preview. Retrieved 2 August, 2008, from http://www.selectparks.net/archive/escapefromwoomera/design.htm

Eskelinen, M. (2001). 'The Gaming Situation'. In *Game Studies: the International Journal of Computer Game Research* 1.1. Retrieved 16 April 2007, from http://www.gamestudies.org/0101/

Everett, A (2005). 'Serious Play: Playing with Race in Contemporary Gaming Culture'. In J. Raessens and J. Goldstein (eds.). *The Handbook of Computer Game Studies* (pp. 311-326). Cambridge: MIT Press.

Everett, A. and Watkins, S. C. (2008). 'The Power of Play: The Portrayal and Performance of Race in Videogames'. In K. Salen (ed.). *The Ecology of Games: Connecting Youth, Games and Learning* (pp, 141-164). Cambridge: MIT Press.

Failkova, L. and Yelenevskaya, M. N. (2005). 'Incipient Soviet Diaspora: Encounters in Cyberspace'. *Narodna Umjetnost: the Croatian Journal of Ethnography and Folklore* 42(1), 83-99.

Fitzgerald, B., Humphreys, S., Banks, J., Done, K., and Suzor, N. (2007). 'Games and the Law: History, Content, Practice and Law'. Conference paper at Open content licensing: Cultivating the creative commons. Brisbane 2005. Retrieved 1 February, 2009, from http://ses.library.usyd.edu.au/bitstream/2123/1586/1/C14_Fitzgerald.pdf

Flew, T. (2008). *New Media: An Introduction*, [3rd Edition]. Oxford: Oxford University Press.

Flew, T. and Humphreys, S. (2008). 'Games: Technology, Industry, Culture'. In *New Media: An Introduction*, [3rd Edition] (pp. 126-142). Oxford: Oxford University Press.

Flynn, B. (2003). 'Geographies of the Digital Hearth'. Information, Communication and Society 6.4: 551-576.

Foucault, M. (1995). *Discipline and Punish: The Birth of the Prison* [2nd Edition]. New York: Vintage Books.

Frasca, G. (2003). 'Simulation Versus Narrative: Introduction to Ludology'. In M. J. P. Wolf and B. Perron (eds.). *The Video Game Theory Reader* (pp. 221-236). New York: Routledge.

Friedman, T. (1995). 'Making Sense of Software: Computer Games and Interactive Textuality'. In S. Jones (ed.). *Cybersociety: Computer Mediated Communication and Community* (pp. 73-89). London: Sage.

Friedman, T. (1999). 'Civilization and its Discontents: Simulation, Subjectivity, and Space'. In G. M. Smith (ed.). *On a Silver Platter: CD-ROMs and the Promise of a New Technology* (pp. 132-150). New York: New York University Press.

Fuller, M. (2005). *Media Ecologies: Materialist Energies in Art and Technoculture.* Cambridge: MIT Press.

Galloway, A. (2004). *Protocol: How Control Exists After Decentralization.* Cambridge: MIT Press.

Galloway, A. (2006). *Gaming: Essays on Algorithmic Culture.* Minneapolis: University of Minnesota Press.

Galloway, A. (2007). 'StarCraft, or, Balance'. *Grey Room* 28: 86-107.

Galloway, A. and Thacker, E. (2007). *The Exploit: A Theory of Networks.* Minneapolis: University of Minnesota Press.

García Canclini, N. (2001). *Consumers and Citizens: Globalization and Multicultural Conflicts.* Minneapolis: University of Minnesota Press.

Ghamari-Tabrizi, S. (2004). 'The Convergence of the Pentagon and Hollywood: The Next Generation of Military Training Simulators'. In L. Rabinovitz and A. Geil (eds.). *Memory Bytes: History, Technology, and Digital Culture* (pp. 150- 173). Durham: Duke University Press.

Giddings, S. (2007). 'Dionysiac Machines: Videogames and the Triumph of the Simulacra'. *Convergence: The International Journal of Research into New Media Technologies* 13(4), 417-431.

Gillespie, T. (2007). *Wired Shut: Copyright and the Shape of Digital Culture.* Cambridge: MIT Press.

Gott, R. (2005). *Hugo Chávez and the Bolivarian Revolution. London*; New York: Verso.

Graetz, J. M. (2001). 'The Origin of Spacewar!'. In V. Burnham (Ed.). *Supercade: A visual history of the videogame age 1971-1984* (pp. 42-48). Cambridge: The MIT Press.

Grimes, S. M. (2006). 'Online Multiplayer Games: A Virtual Space for Intellectual Property Debates?'. *New Media and Society* 8.6: 969-990.

Grimes, S. M. (2007). 'Terms and Service and Terms of Play in Children's Online Gaming'. In J. P. Williams and J. H. Smith (eds.). *The Players' Realm: Studies on the Culture of Video Games and Gaming* (pp. 33-55). Jefferson: McFarland.

Guattari, F. (2000). *The Three Ecologies* (Trans. I. Pindar and P. Sutton). London: Athlone Press.

Hall, S. (1980). *Culture, Media, Language: Working Papers in Cultural Studies, 1972-1979.* London: Hutchinson.

Halter, E. (2006). *From Sun-Tzu to Xbox: War and Video Games.* New York: Thunder Mouth Press.

Hardt, M. and Negri, A. (2000). *Empire.* Cambridge: Harvard University Press.

Harlow, J. and Baxter, S. (2005, March 2007). 'Hilary Opens Up Morality War on Violent Video Games'. *Times Online.* Retrieved 4 February, 2009, from http://www.timesonline.co.uk/tol/news/world/article438332.ece

Hartley, J. (2005). 'Creative Industries'. In J. Hartley (ed.). *Creative Industries: A Reader* (pp. 1-40). Malden: Blackwell.

Harvey, D. (1990). *The Condition of Postmodernity: An Enquiry into the Origins of Cultural Change.* Oxford: Blackwell.

Herz, J. C. (1997). Joystick Nation: How Videogames Ate Our Quarters, Won Our Hearts, and Rewired Our Minds. London: Abacus.

Herz, J. C. (2005). 'Harnessing the Hive'. In J. Hartley (ed.). *Creative Industries: A Reader* (pp. 327-342). Malden: Blackwell.

Hill, J. (2006, September 7). 'Game Industry at the Crossroads'. *The Age.* Retrieved 12 June, 2008, from http://www.theage.com.au/news/games/game-industry-at-the-crossroads/2006/09/06/1157222139337.html?page=fullpage

Holguin, J. (2005, February 8). 'Uncle Sam Want Video Gamers: Playing Games Could Help Build Careers in The U.S. Military'. *CBS Evening News* Retrieved 7 February, 2009, from http://www.cbsnews.com/stories/2005/02/08/eveningnews/main672455.shtml

Howkins, J. (2005). 'The Mayor's Commission on the Creative industries'. In J. Hartley (ed.). *Creative Industries: A Reader* (pp. 117-125). Malden: Blackwell.

Huhtamo, E. (1999). 'Game Patch – the Son of Scratch: Plug-ins and Patches as Hacker Art'. *Switch* 12. Retrieved 19 July, 2007 from http://switch.sjsu.edu/nextswitch/switch_engine/front/front.php?artc=119

Huizinga, J. (1970/1938). *Homo Ludens: A Study of the Play Element in Culture.* London: Paladin.

Humphreys, S. (2003). 'Online Multi-user Games: Playing for Real'. *The Australian Journal of Communication* 30.1: 79-91.

Humphreys, S. (2005). 'Productive Players: Online Computer Games' Challenge to Traditional Media Forms'. *Communication and Critical/Cultural Studies* 2.1: 37-51.

Humphreys, S (2007). 'You're In Our World Now: Ownership and Access in the Proprietary Community of an MMOG'. In V. Sugumaran (ed.). *Intelligent Information Technologies: Concepts, Methodologies, Tools, and Applications* (pp. 2058-2072). Information Science Reference (IGI Global).

Humphreys, S., Fitzgerald, B., Banks, J., and Suzor, N. (2005). 'Fan-based Production for Computer Games: User-led Innovation, the "Drift of Value" and Intellectual Property Rights'. *Media International Australia* 114: 16-29.

Hunger, F. (2007). 'Perspective Engines: An Interview with JODI'. In A. Clarke and G. Mitchell (eds.). *Videogames and Art* (pp. 152-160). Bristol: Intellect.

Indymedia Argentina (2003). 'Chronology of the April Coup'. In G. Wilpert (ed.). *Coup Against Chavez in Venezuela: The Best International Reports of What Actually Happened in April 2002* (pp. 209-216). Caracas: Fundación Venezolana para la Justicia Global.

Jameson, F. (1991). *Postmodernism or, the Cultural Logic of Late Capitalism.* Durham: Duke University Press.

Jansz, J. and Martens, L. (2005). 'Gaming at a LAN Event: The Social Context of Playing Videogames'. *New Media and Society* 7.3: 333-355.

Jappe, A. (1993). *Guy Debord* (Trans. D. Nicholson-Smith). Berkeley, University of California Press.

Jenkins, H. (1992). *Textual Poachers: Television Fans and Participatory Cultures.* London: Routledge.

Jenkins, H. (2003). 'From Barbie to Mortal Kombat: Further Reflections'. In J. T. Caldwell and A. Everett (eds.). *New Media: Theories and Practices of Digitextuality* (pp. 249-253). New York: Routledge.

Jenkins, H. (2006). *Convergence Culture: Where Old and New Media Collide.* New York: New York University Press.

Jones, C. (2006, July 8). 'Terror on the Strip'. *Las Vegas Review-Journal.* Retrieved 24 August, 2008, from http://www.reviewjournal.com/lvrj_home/2006/Jul-08-Sat-2006/news/8367726.html

Juul, J. (2005). *Half-Real: Video Games Between Real Rules and Fictional Worlds.* Cambridge: MIT Press.

Juul, J. (2008). 'Without a Goal: On Open and Expressive Games'. In B. Atkins and T. Krzywinska (eds.). *Videogame, Player, Text* (pp. 191-203). Manchester: Manchester University Press.

Keisler, J. (2007, August 26). 'The Top 100 PC Games of the 21st Century'. *Next-Generation: Interactive Entertainment Today*. Retrieved July 2, 2007, from http://www.next-gen.biz/index.php?option=com_content&task=view&id=3695&Itemid=2&limit=1&limitstart=7

Kent, S. L. (2000). *The First Quarter: A 25 year History of Video Games*. Bothell: BWD Press.

Kerr, A. (2006). *The Business and Culture of Digital Games: Gamework/Gameplay*. London: Sage.

Kerr, A., Kücklich, J., and Brereton, P. (2006). 'New Media – New Pleasures?'. *International Journal of Cultural Studies* 9.1: 63-82.

Kinder, M. (1991). *Playing with Power In Television and Videogames: From Teenage Mutant Ninja Turtles to Muppet Babies*. Berkeley: University of California Press.

King, G. (2008). 'Play, Modality, and Claims of Realism in Full Spectrum Warrior'. In B. Atkins and T. Krzywinska (eds.). *Videogame, Player, Text* (pp. 52-65). Manchester: University of Manchester Press.

King, G. and Krzywinska, T. (2002). 'Introduction'. In G. King and T. Krzywinska (eds.). *ScreenPlay: Cinema/videogames/interfaces* (pp. 1-32). London: Wallflower Press.

King, G. and Krzywinksa, T. (2006). *Tomb Raiders & Space Invaders: Videogames Forms and Contexts*. London: I. B. Tauris.

Klang, M. (2004). 'Avatar: From Deity to Corporate Property: A Philosophical Inquiry into Digital Property in Online Games'. Information, Communication, and Society 7.3: 389-402.

Kline, S., Dyer-Witheford, N., and de Peuter, G. (2003). Digital|Play: The Intersection of Culture, Technology, and Marketing. Montreal and Kingston: McGill-Queen's University Press.

Kohler, C. (2006). 'Cheer Squad: Why iNiS Want to Make You Happier'. *1Up.com*. Retrieved 13 July, 2010, from http://www.1up.com/do/feature?pager.offset=0&cId=3153670

Kraul, C. (2006, December 4). 'Venezuela's Chavez Reelected'. *Los Angeles Times*. Retrieved January 15, 2007, from http://www.latimes.com/nationworld/world/la-fgvenezuela4dec04,0,1803165.story?coll=la-home-world

Krzywinska, T. (2002). 'Hands on horror'. In G. King and T. Krzywinska (eds.). *ScreenPlay: Cinema/videogames/interfaces* (pp. 206-223). London: Wallflower.

Kücklich, J. (2005). 'Precarious Playbour: Modders and the Digital Games Industry'. *The Fibreculture Journal* 5. Retrieved January 9, 2007, from http://journal.fibreculture.org/issue5/kucklich.html

Lahti, M. (2003). 'As We Become Machines: Corporealized Pleasures in Video Games'. In M. J. P. Wolf and B. Perron (eds.). *The Video Game Theory Reader* (pp. 157-170). New York: Routledge.

Lange, A. (2002). 'Report from the PAL Zone: European Games Culture'. In L. King (ed.). *Game On: The History and Culture of Videogames* (pp. 46-55). London: Lawrence King Publishing Ltd.

Lash, S. (2002). *Critique of Information*. London: Sage.

Lash, S. and Lury, C. (2007). *Global Culture Industry: The Mediation of Things*. Cambridge: Polity.

Laso, P. W. (2007). 'Games of Pain: Pain as Haptic Stimulation in Computer-game-based Media Art'. *LEONARDO* 40.3: 238-242.

Lastokwa, G. (2006). 'Law and Game Studies'. *Games and Culture* 1.1: 25-28.

Latour, B. (2005). *Reassembling the Social: An Introduction to Actor-network Theory*. Oxford: Oxford University Press.

Leadbeater, C (1999). *Living on Thin Air: The New Economy*. London: Viking.

Lefebvre, H. (1984). *Everyday Life in the Modern World* (Trans. S. Rabinovitch). New Brunswick: Transaction Books.

Lefebvre, H. (1991). *Critique of Everyday Life: Volume 2* (Trans. J. Moore). London: Verso.

Lefebvre, H. (2004). Rhythmanalysis: Space, Time and Everyday Life (Trans. S. Elden and G. Moore). London: Continuum.

Lefebvre, H. and Régulier, C. (1996). 'Rhythmanalysis of Mediterranean Cities'. In E. Kofman and E. Lebas (eds. and Trans.) *Writings on Cities* (pp. 228-240). Oxford: Blackwell.

Lemoine, M. (2003). 'How Hate Media Incited the Coup Against the President' [Trans. J. Stoker]. In G. Wilpert (ed.). *Coup Against Chavez in Venezuela: The Best International Reports of What Actually Happened in April 2002* (pp. 151-160). Caracas: Fundación Venezolana para la Justicia Global.

Lemon, S. (2006, November 7). 'Worldbeat – Chinese take Ani-Japanese Protest On-line'. *Networked World*. Retrieved 2 August, 2008, from http://www.networkworld.com/news/2006/071106-worldbeat-chinese-take-anti-japan-protest.html?page=1

Leonard, D. (2006a). 'Not a Hater, Just Keeping It Real: The Importance of Race – and Gender – Based Games'. Games and Culture 1.1: 83-88.

Leonard, D. (2006b). 'Virtual Gangstas, Coming to a Suburban House Near You: Demonization, Commodification, and Policing Blackness'. In N. Garrelts (ed.). *The Meaning and Culture of Grand Theft Auto* (pp. 49-69). Jefferson: Macfarland.

Leung, R. (2005, June 19). 'Can a Video game Lead to Murder? Did "Grand Theft Auto" Cause One Teenager to Kill?'. *CBS News*. Retrieved 4 February, 2009, from http://www.cbsnews.com/stories/2005/06/17/60minutes/main702599.shtml

Lin, H. (2008). 'Body, Space, and Gendered Gaming Experiences: A Cultural Geography of Homes, Cybercafés and Dormitories'. In Y. B. Kafai, C. Heeter, J. Denner and J. Y. Sun (eds.). *Beyond Barbie and Mortal Kombat: New Perspectives on Gender and Gaming* (pp. 67-82). Cambridge: MIT Press.

Loftus, G. R. and Loftus, E. F. (1983). *Mind at Play: The Psychology of Video Games*. New York: Basic Books.

Lovink, G. and Rossiter, N. (2007). *MyCreativity Reader: A Critique of Creative Industries*. Amsterdam: Institute of Network Cultures.

Ludlow, P. and Wallace, M. (2007). *The Second Life Herald: The Virtual Tabloid that Witnessed the Dawn of the Metaverse*. Cambridge: MIT Press.

Lugo, J., Sampson, T., and Lossada, M. (2002). Latin America's New Cultural Industries Still Play Old Games: From Donkey Kong to Banana Republic. *Game Studies: the International Journal of Computer Game Research* 2.2. Retrieved December 12, 2006, from http://www.gamestudies.org/0202/lugo/

Lyon, D. (1994). *The Electronic Eye: The Rise of the Surveillance Society*. Cambridge: Polity Press.

Mackenzie, A. (2002). *Transductions: Bodies and Machines at Speed*. London: Continuum.

Manovich, L. (1996). 'The Labour of Perception'. In L. Hershman-Leeson (ed.). *Clicking In: Hot Links to a Digital Culture* (pp. 183-193). Seattle: Bay Press.

Manovich, L. (2000). *The Language of New Media*. Cambridge: MIT Press.

Marks, R. B. (2003). *EverQuest Companion: The Inside Lore of the Game World*. New York, McGraw-Hill/Osborne.

Márquez, P. C. (1999). *The Street is My Home: Youth and Violence in Caracas*. Stanford: Stanford University Press.

Marshall, P. D. (2004). New Media Cultures. London: Arnold.

Marx, K. (1977). *Capital, vol. 1* (trans. B. Fowkes). New York: Vintage.

Massumi, B. (2002). *Parables for the Virtual: Movement, Affect, Sensation.* Durham: Duke University Press.

Matthews, A. (2001, August 20). 'Computer Games Make Children Anti-social'. *Telegraph.co.uk.* Retrieved 4 February, 2009, from http://www.telegraph.co.uk/news/uknews/1337971/Computer-games-make-children-anti-social.html

Mäyrä, F. (2008). *An Introduction to Game Studies.* Los Angeles: Sage.

McChesney, R. (1999). *Rich Media, Poor Democracy: Communication Politics in Dubious Times.* New York: New Press.

McLuhan, M. (1964). *Understanding Media: The Extensions of Man.* New York: McGraw-Hill.

Moore, C. (2005). 'Commonizing the Enclosure: Online Games and Reforming Intellectual Property Regimes'. *Australian Journal of Emerging Technology and Society* 3.2: 100-114. Retrieved 14 August, 2007, from http://www.swinburne.edu.au/sbs/ajets/journal/V3N2/pdf/V3N2-4-Moore.pdf

Morris, S. (2002). 'First-person Shooters – A Game Apparatus'. In G. King and T. Krzywinska (eds.). *ScreenPlay: Cinema/videogames/interfaces* (pp. 81-97). London: Wallflower.

Morris, S. (2004). 'Co-creative Media: Online Multiplayer Computer Game Culture'. *Scan: Journal of Media Arts Culture* 1.1. Retrieved December 22, 2005, from http://scan.net.au/scan/journal/display.php?journal_id=16

Mosco, V. (1997). 'Citizenship and the Technopoles'. *Javnost (The Public)* 4.4: 35-46.

Moses, A. (2008, July 15). 'Fallout Continues from Ban on Game'. *The Age.* Retrieved August 26, 2008, from http://www.theage.com.au/news/articles/fallout-continues-from-ban-on-game/2008/07/15/1215887586091.html

Murphie, A. (2004). 'Vertiginous Mediations: Sketches for a Dynamic Pluralism in the Study of Computer Games'. *Media International Australia* 110: 73-95.

Myers, D. (2003). *The Nature of Computer Games: Play as Semiosis.* New York: Peter Lang.

Nakumara, L. (2001). 'Race in/for Cyberspace: Identity Tourism and Racial Passing on the Internet'. In D. Trent (ed.). *Reading Digital Culture* (pp. 226-235). Malden: Blackwell.

Naughton, P. (2005, August 10). 'Korean Drops Dead After 50-hour Gaming Marathon'. *Times Online.* Retrieved 20 June, 2007, from http://www.timesonline.co.uk/tol/news/world/article553840.ece

Navarro, A. (2005, December 7). 'Animal Crossing: Review'. *Gamespot.* Retrieved April 17, 2007, from http://au.gamespot.com/ds/rpg/animalcrossingds/review.html?om_act=convert&om_clk=gssummary&tag=summary;review

Ndalianis, A. (2004). *Neo-Baroque Aesthetics and Contemporary Entertainment.* Cambridge: MIT Press.

Newman, J. (2002). 'The Myth of the Ergodic Videogame: Some Thoughts on Player-character Relationships in Videogames'. *Game Studies: the International Journal of Computer Game Research* 2.1. Retrieved April 17, 2007, from http://www.gamestudies.org/0102/newman/

Newman, J. (2004). *Videogames.* London: Routledge.

Nicholls, S. (2003, April 30). 'Ruddock Fury Over Woomera Computer Game'. *The Age.* Retrieved September 6, 2008, from http://www.theage.com.au/articles/2003/04/29/1051381948773.html

Nietzsche, F. (2003). *Beyond Good and Evil: Prelude to the Philosophy of the Future* (Trans. R. J. Hollingdale). London: Penguin.

Ow, J. (2000). 'The Revenge of the Yellowfaced Cyborg: The Rape of Digital Geishas and the Colonization of Cyber-coolies in 3D Realms' Shadow Warrior'. In B. Kolko, L. Nakamura and G. Rodman (eds.). *Race in Cyberspace* (pp. 51-68). New York: Routledge.

Padovani, C. and Nordenstreng, K. (2005). From NWICO to WSIS: another world information and communication order?: Introduction. *Global Media and Communication* 1.3: 264-272.

Pearce, C. (2002). 'Emergent Authorship: The Next Interactive Revolution'. *Computers and Graphics* 26.1: 21-29.

Pearce, C. (2006). 'Productive Play: Game Culture from the Bottom Up'. *Games and Culture* 1.1: 17-24.

Pelletier, C. and Oliver, M. (2006). 'Learning to Play in Digital Games'. *Learning, Media, and Technology* 31.4: 329-342.

Perron, B. (2003). 'From Gamers to Players and Game Players: The Example of Interactive Movies'. In M. J. P. Wolf and B. Perron (eds.). *The Video Game Theory Reader* (pp. 237-258). New York: Routledge.

Pindar, I. and Sutton, P. (2000). Translators' Introduction. In Guattari, F. *The Three Ecologies* (Trans. I. Pindar and P. Sutton). London: Athlone Press.

Postigo, H. (2003). 'From Pong to Planet Quake: Post-industrial Transitions from Leisure to Work'. *Information, Communication, and Society* 6.4: 593-607.

Prensky, M. (2001). *Digital Game-based Learning*. New York: McGraw-Hill.

Qvortrup, L. (2003). *Hypercomplex Society*. New York: Peter Lang.

Ray, S. G. (2003). *Gender Inclusive Game Design: Expanding the Market*. Boston: Charles River Media.

Reach Out Central (2007) 'Reach Out Central'. Retrieved 2 August, 2008, from http://www.reachoutcentral.com.au/

Redmond, D. (2006). 'Grand Theft Video: Running and Gunning for the U.S. Empire'. In N. Garrelts (ed.). *The Meaning and Culture of Grand Theft Auto* (pp. 104-114). Jefferson: Macfarland.

Rodriguez, H. (2006). 'The Playful and the Serious: An Approximation to Huizinga's Homo Ludens'. *Game Studies: the International Journal of Computer Game Research* 6.1. Retrieved 24 August, 2007, from http://gamestudies.org/0601/articles/rodriges

Rosenberg, S. (2007). *Dreaming in Code: Two Dozen Programmers, Three Years, 4,732 Bugs and One Quest for Transcendent Software*. New York: Crown.

Rosenberg, T. (2005, December 30). 'What Lara Croft Would Look Like if She Carried Rice Bags'. *The New York Times*. Retrieved 2 August, 2008, from http://query.nytimes.com/gst/fullpage.html?res=9F06EED81330F933A05751C1A9639C8B63

Rossiter, N. (2006). *Organized Networks: Media Theory, Creative Labor, New Institutions*. Amsterdam: Institute of Networked Cultures

Ruggill, J. E., McAllister, K., and Menchaca, D. (2004). 'The Gamework'. *Communication and Critical/Cultural Studies* 1.4: 297-312.

Salen, K. (2008). 'Toward an Ecology of Gaming'. In K. Salen (ed.). The Ecology of Games: *Connecting Youth, Games and Learning* (pp. 1-17). Cambridge: MIT Press.

Santamaria, F. and Guillen, C. (2007, May 27). 'Chavez Closes Opposition TV Station; Thousands Protest'. *CNN International*. Retrieved 11 June, 2008, from http://edition.cnn.com/2007/WORLD/americas/05/27/venezuela.protest/index.html

Sassen, S, (2006). *Territory, Authority, Rights: Global Assemblages*. Princeton: Princeton University Press.

Satre, J-P. (1965). *Situations*. Greenwich: Fawcett Publications.

Schiller, D. (2000). *Digital Capitalism: Networking the Global Market System*. Cambridge: MIT Press.

Schleiner, A. (1999). 'Editorial Notes from Switch Art and Games Issue'. *Switch* 12. Retrieved 28 September, 2008, from http://switch.sjsu.edu/nextswitch/switch_engine/front/front.php?artc=49

Schiesel, S. (2007, April 30). 'P.E. Classes Turn to Video Game that Works Legs'. *The New York Times*. Retrieved 4 February, 2009, from http://www.nytimes.com/2007/04/30/health/30exer.html

Sivan, Y. Y. (2008). 'The 3D3C Metaverse: A New Medium Is Born'. In T. Samuel-Azran and D. Caspi (eds.). *New Media and Innovative Technologies* (pp. 132-159), Beer-Shiva: Ben Gurion University Press/Tzivonim Publishing.

Smith, J. H. (2007). 'Who Governs the Gamers?'. In J. P. Williams and J. H. Smith (eds.). *The Players' Realm: Studies on the Culture of Video Games and Gaming* (pp. 17-32). Jefferson: McFarland.

Squire, K. (2008). 'Open-ended Videogames: A Model for Developing Learning for the Interactive Age'. In K. Salen (ed.). *The Ecology of Games: Connecting Youth, Games, and Learning* (pp. 167-198). Cambridge: MIT Press.

Stallabrass, J. (1996). *Gargantua: Manufactured Mass Culture*. London: Verso.

Steinkuehler, C. (2006). 'The Mangle of Play'. *Games and Culture* 1(3), 199-213.

Stevens, R., Satwicz, T., and McCarthy, L. (2008). 'In-Game, In-Room, In-World: Recconecting Videogames to the Rest of Kids' Lives'. In K. Salen (ed.). *The Ecology of Games: Connecting Youth, Games and Learning* (pp. 41-66). Cambridge: MIT Press.

Stockburger, A. (2007). 'From Appropriation to Approximation'. In A. Clarke and G. Mitchell (eds.). Videogames and Art (pp. 25-37). Bristol: Intellect.

streak000 (2008, February 13). Message posted http://au.gamespot.com/news/6186009.html?action=convert&om_clk=latestnews&tag=latestnews%3Btitle%3B0&page=6

Swallwell, M. (2003). 'The Meme Game: Escape from Woomera'. *RealTime* 55. Retrieved August 26, 2008, from http://rt.airstrip.com.au/article/55/7103

'Swedish Videogame Banned for Damaging China's Sovereignty' (2004, May 29). *China Daily*. Retrieved 30 July, 2007, from http://www.chinadaily.com.cn/english/doc/2004-05/29/content_334845.htm

Sze-Fai Shiu, A. (2006). 'What Yellowface Hides: Video Games, Whiteness, and the American Racial Other'. *The Journal of Popular Culture* 39.1: 109-125.

Takahashi, D. (2002). Opening the Xbox: Inside Microsoft's Plan to Release an Entertainment Revolution. Roseville: Prima Publishing.

Taylor, T. L. (2002). 'Whose Game is this Anyway?: Negotiating Corporate Ownership in a Virtual World'. In F. Mäyrä (ed.). *Computer Games and Digital Cultures* (pp. 227-242). Tampere: Tampere Univeristy Press.

Taylor, T. L. (2006a). *Play Between Worlds: Exploring Online Game Culture*. Cambridge: The MIT Press.

Taylor, T. L. (2006b). 'Does WoW Change Everything? How a PvP Server, Multinational Player Base, and Surveillance Mod Scene Caused Me Pause'. *Games and Culture* 1.4: 318-337.

'teleSUR and Al-Jazeera Sign Deal' (2006, February 1). *BBC News*. Retrieved 11 June, 2008, from http://news.bbc.co.uk/2/hi/americas/4669268.stm

Thomas, D. (2008). 'KPK, Inc.: Race, Nation, and Emergent Culture in Online Games'. In A. Everett (ed.). *Learning Race and Ethnicity: Youth and Digital Media* (pp. 155-174). Cambridge: MIT Press.

Thomas, D. and Brown, J. S. (2007). 'The Play of Imagination: Extending the Literary Mind'. *Games and Culture* 2.2:149-172.

Tierney, J. (2004, January 4). 'The 2004 Campaign: Political Points'. *The New York Times*. Retrieved 2 August, 2008, from http://query.nytimes.com/gst/fullpage.html?res=9F03E0DB1431 F937A35752C0A9629C8B63

Toothaker, C. (2006, June 3). 'Video Game Simulating Invasion of Venezuela Raise Ire of Chavez's Allies'. *USA Today*. Retrieved 24 August, 2008, from http://www.usatoday.com/tech/ gaming/2006-05-24-venezuela-game_x.htm

Touraine, A. (1971). *The Post-Industrial Society: Tomorrow's Social History: Class, Conflicts and Culture in the Programmed Society* (Trans. L. F. X. Mayhew). New York: Random House.

Turkle, S. (1995). *Life on the Screen: Identity in the Age of the Internet*. New York: Simon and Schuster.

van Dijk, J. and Hacker, K. (2003). 'The Digital Divide as a Complex Dynamic Phenomenon'. *The Information Society* 19: 315-326.

VanOrd, K. (2007). 'Fury Review'. *Gamespot Australia*. Retrieved 13 July, 2010, from http:// au.gamespot.com/pc/rpg/fury/review.html

'Venezuelan Anger at Computer Game' (2006, May 25). *BBC News*. Retrieved 24 August, 2008, from http://www.usatoday.com/tech/gaming/2006-05-24-venezuela-game_x.htm

Venezuelan Solidarity Network (2007, October 2). 'Grassroots Group Celebrates Delay of Game Attacking Venezuela'. Venezuelanalysis.com. Retrieved 24 August, 2008, from http://www.venezuelanalysis.com/news/2672

Wander, P. (1984). 'Introduction'. In Lefebvre, H. *Everyday Life in the Modern World,* (Trans. S. Rabinovitch). New Brunswick: Transaction Books.

Ward, M. (2006, February 13). 'Gay Rights Win in Warcraft World'. *BBC*. Retrieved 19 July, 2010, from http://news.bbc.co.uk/2/hi/technology/4700754.stm

Wark, M. (1994). 'The Video Game as an Emergent Media Form'. *Media International Australia* 71: 21-30.

Wark, M. (2007). Gamer Theory. Cambridge: Harvard University Press.

Warren, J. (2006, November 25) 'A Wii Workout: When Videogames Hurt'. The Wall Street Journal. Retrieved 24 August 2007, from http://online.wsj.com/public/article/SB116441076273232312- IHR8Xf3YEG61QlW0e7hA_kHAA8w_20061224.html

Warschauer, M. (2000). 'Language, identity and the Internet'. In B. Kolko, L. Nakamura and G. Rodman (eds.). *Race in Cyberspace* (pp. 151-170). New York: Routledge.

Williams, D. (2005). 'Bridging the Methodological Divide in Games Research'. *Simulation & Gaming: An Interdisciplinary Journal of Theory, Practice and Research* 36.4: 447-463.

Williams, D., Ducheneaunt, N., Yuanyuan Zhang, L., Yee, N., and Nickell, E. (2006). 'From Tree House to Barracks: The Social Life of Guilds in the World of Warcraft'. *Games and Culture* 1.4: 338-361.

Winet, J. (2007). 'In Conversation Fall 2003: An Interview with Joseph DeLappe'. In A. Clarke and G. Mitchell (eds.). *Videogames and Art* (pp. 94-106). Bristol: Intellect.

Wood, J. (2001). 'Images in Paediatric Medicine: The "Howl" sign – a Central Palmar Blister'. *Archives of Disease in Childhood* 84.4: 288.

Yar, M. (2005). 'The Global "Epidemic" of Movie "Piracy": Crime-wave or Social Construction?'. *Media, Culture, and Society* 27.5: 677-696.

Yar, M. (2008). 'The Rhetorics and Myths of Anti-piracy Campaigns: Criminalization, Moral Pedagogy, and Capitalist Property Relations in the Classroom'. *New Media and Society* 10.4: 605-623.

Yates, S. J. and Littleton, K. (2001). 'Understanding Computer Game Cultures: A Situated Approach'. In E. Green and A. Adam (eds.). *Virtual gender: Technology, Consumption and Identity* (pp. 103-123). London: Routledge.

Yee, N. (2006). 'The Labour of Fun: How Computer Games Blur the Boundaries of Work and Play'. *Games and Culture* 1.1: 68-71.

Yudice, G. (2003). *The Expediency of Culture: Uses of Culture in the Global Era*. Durham: Duke University Press.

Zimmerman, E. (2009). 'Gaming Literacy: Game Design as a Model for Literacy in the 21st Century'. In B. Perron and M. J. P. Wolf (eds.). *The Video Game Theory Reader* 2 (pp. 23-32). New York: Routledge.

ART WORKS CITED

Black Square (Kazimir Malevich, 1913).
crtl-space (JODI, 2006).
dead-in-iraq (Joseph Delappe, 2006-).
Escape from Woomera (Andrea Blundell, Justin Halliday, Matt Harrigan, Stephen Honegger, Ian Malcolm, Chris Markwart, Julian Oliver, Darren Taylor, and Kate Wild, 2003).
Legshocker (Tilman Reiff and Volker Morawe, 2002).
Pain Station (Tilman Reiff and Volker Morawe, 2001-2003).
SOD (JODI, 2000).
Super Mario Clouds (Cory Arcangel, 2002).
untitled game (JODI, 1996).
The Velvet Strike (Anne-Marie Schleiner, Joan Leandre, and Brody Condon, 2002).
War Poets Online (Joseph Delappe, 2002-).

DIGITAL GAMES CITED

ADVENT. (1975). Will Crowther (and Dan Woods).
Age of Empires II: The Age of Kings (1999). Ensemble Studios, Microsoft Game Studios (Windows).
Age of Empires II: The Conquerors (2000). Ensemble Studios, Microsoft Game Studios (Windows).
Ages of Empires III (2005). Ensemble Studios, Microsoft Game Studios (Windows).
Age of Mythology: The Titans (2003). Ensemble Studios, Microsoft Game Studios (Windows).
America's Army (2004). US Army, US Army (Windows).
*Animal Crossing (*2002). Nintendo EAD, Nintendo (Nintendo GameCube).
*Animal Crossing: Wild World (*2005). Nintendo EAD, Nintendo (Nintendo DS).
Animal Forest (2001). Nintendo EAD, Nintendo (Nintendo GameCube).
Avara (1996). Ambrosia Software, Ambrosia Software (Macintosh).
Bejeweled 2 (2004). PopCap Games, PopCap Games (Windows).
Beyond Good and Evil (2003). Ubisoft Montpellier, Ubisoft (PlayStation2).
Blade and Sword (2003). Pixel Multimedia, Whiptail Interactive (Windows).
Blitz: The League (2005). Midway Games, Midway Games (Xbox).
Blue Dragon (2007). Artoon/Mistwalker, Microsoft Game Studios (Xbox 360).
Brian Lara International Cricket 2005 (2005). Swordfish Studios, Codemasters (PlayStation2).
City of Heroes (2004). Cryptic Studios, NCsoft (Windows).
Computer Space (1971). Nutting Associates, Nutting Associates (Arcade).
Cooking Mama (2005). Office Create, Taito (Nintendo DS).
Counter-Strike (2000). Valve Software, Vivendi Universal, (Windows).
Darfur is Dying (2006). Take Action Games, mtvU (Web browser).
Dark Sector (2008). Digital Extremes, D3 Publisher (Xbox 360).
Delta Force: Black Hawk Down (2003). NovaLogic, NovaLogic (Windows).
Demon's Souls (2009). From Software, Sony Computer Entertainment (PS3).
Diablo II (2000). Blizzard North, Blizzard Entertainment (Windows).
Doom (1993). id Software, id software (Windows).
Driv3r (2004). Reflections Interactive, Atari (Xbox).
Dungeon Siege (2002). Gas Powered Games, Microsoft Game Studios (Windows).
Elite Beat Agents (2006). iNiS, Nintendo (Nintendo DS).
EverQuest (1999). Sony Online Entertainment, Sony Online Entertainment (Windows).
FIFA 2000 (1999). EA Sports, Electronic Arts (Windows).
FIFA 2002 (2001). EA Sports, Electronic Arts (PlayStation2).
FIFA 2004 (2003). EA Canada, Electronic Arts (Nintendo GameCube).
FIFA 2005 (2004). EA Canada, Electronic Arts (Nintendo GameCube).
FIFA 2005 (2004). EA Canada, Electronic Arts (Windows).
Fable (2004). Lionhead Studios, Microsoft Game Studios (Xbox).
Fallout 3 (2008). Bethesda Game Studios, Bethesda Softworks (Windows).
Fantasy Westward Journey (2004). Netease, Netease (Windows).
Flight Control (2009). Firemint, Firemint (iPhone).

Flyff (2004). Aeonsoft, Gpotato Game Portal (Windows).

Food Force (2005). Deepend/Playerthree, United Nations World Food Programme (Windows).

Full Spectrum Warrior (2004). Pandemic Studios, THQ (Windows/Xbox).

FURY (2007). Auran, Gamecock Media Group (Windows).

Garry's Mod (2007). Team Garry, Valve Corporation (Windows).

Grand Theft Auto: San Andreas (2005). Rockstar North, Rockstar Games (Windows).

Grand Theft Auto: Vice City (2003). Rockstar North, Rockstar Games (Windows).

Guild Wars (2005). ArenaNet, NCsoft (Windows).

GunBound World Championship (2005). Softnyx, Softnyx (Windows).

Half-Life (1998). Valve Software, Sierra Studios (Windows).

Half-Life 2 (2004). Valve Software, Valve Corporation (Windows).

Hamurabi (1969). Richard Merrill.

Harry Potter and the Chamber of Secrets (2002). Amaze Entertainment, EA Games/Warner Brothers Interactive (Windows).

Hero Online (2006). Netgame, Mgame USA (Windows).

Heroes Over Europe (2009). Transmission Games, Ubisoft (PS3).

Habbo (2000). Sulake Corporation, Sulake Corporation (Windows).

Hearts of Iron (2002). Paradox Interactive, Strategy First (Windows).

Howard Dean for Iowa (2003). Persuasive Games (Windows).

Ico (2001). Team Ico, Sony Computer Entertainment (PlayStation2).

Jet Set Radio Future (2002). Smilebit, Sega (Xbox).

Lara Croft Tomb Raider: Anniversary (2007). Crystal Dynamics/Buzz Monkey, Software Eidos Interactive (Windows).

Left 4 Dead 2 (2009). Valve Corporation, Valve (Windows).

Lego Star Wars: The Video Game (2005). Traveller's Tales, Eidos Interactive/LucasArts (Windows).

Lineage II: The Chaotic Chronicle (2003). NCsoft, NCsoft (Windows).

LittleBigPlanet (2008). Media Molecule, Sony Computer Entertainment Europe (PlayStation3).

Lord of the Rings: Battle for Middle Earth (2004). EA Los Angles, EA Games (Windows).

MU Online (2001). Webzen, K2 Network Inc. (Windows).

MVP Baseball 2005 (2005). EA Canada, Electronic Arts (Windows).

Marc Ecko's Getting Up: Contents Under Pressure (2006). The Collective, Atari (PlayStation2).

MarioKart Wii (2008). Nintendo EAD, Nintendo (Wii).

Mario Party (1996). Hudson Soft, Nintendo (Nintendo 64).

Max Payne 2: The Fall of Max Payne (2003). Remedy Entertainment, Rockstar Games (Windows).

Mazinger Z Salvo a Venezuela (2002). Mediatech, Mediatech (Windows).

Medal of Honor: Allied Assault (2002). 2015 Inc, Electronic Arts (Windows).

Medieval: Total War (2002). Creative Assembly, Activision (Windows).

Mercenaries: Playground of Destruction (2005). Pandemic Studios, LucasArts (Xbox).

Mercenaries 2: World in Flames (2008). Pandemic Studios, Electronic Arts (PS3).

Myst (1993). Cyan Worlds, Brøderbund (Windows).

Need For Speed: Underground (2003). EA Black Box, EA Games (Windows).

Nexus: Kingdom of the Winds (1998). Nexon, Kru Interactive (Windows).

Osu! Tatakei! Ouendan (2005). iNiS, Nintendo (Nintendo DS).

Pac-Man (1979). Namco, Midway (Arcade).

Playboy: The Mansion (2005). Cyberlore Studios, ARUSH Entertainment/Groove Games (Windows).

PlayStation Home (2008). Sony Computer Entertainment, Sony Computer Entertainment (PS3).

PONG (1972). Atari Inc., Atari Inc. (Arcade).

Project Gotham Racing 2 (2003). Bizarre Creations, Microsoft Game Studios (Xbox).

PuzzleQuest: Galactrix (2009). Infinite Interactive, D3 Publisher (Nintendo DS).

Quake (1996). id Software, GT Interactive (Windows).

ROSE Online (2005). Triggersoft, Gravity Interactive (Windows).

Ragnarok Online (2003) Gravity Co. Ltd., Gravity Co. Ltd. (Windows).

Reach Out! Central (2007) The Inspire Foundation (Windows).

Red Dead Redemption (2010). Rockstar San Diego, Rockstar Games (All).

Ricky Ponting Cricket 2005 (2005). Swordfish Studios, Codemasters (PlayStation2).

Rome: Total War. (2004) Creative Assembly, Sega (Windows).

RuneScape (2001). Jagex Ltd, Jagex Ltd (Windows).

SOCOM: US Navy Seals (2002). Zipper Intercative, Sony Computer

SWAT 3: Close Quarters Battle (1999). Sierra Northwest, Sierra Entertainment (Windows).

Second Life (2003). Linden Research Inc., Free Dowload (Windows).

September 12th (2003). Newsgaming (Web Browser).

Shadow of the Colossus (2005). Team Ico, Sony Computer Entertainment (PlayStation2).

Shenmue (2000). Sega-AM2, Sega (Dreamcast).

Sid Meier's Civilization (1991). MicroProse, MicroProse (Windows).

Sid Meier's Civilization II (1996). MicroProse, MicroProse (Windows).

Sid Meier's Civilization IV (2005). Firaxis Games, 2K Games (Windows).

SimCity (1989). Maxis, Brøderbund (Windows).

SimCity 4 (2003). Maxis, Electronic Arts (Windows).

Soldier of Fortune: Payback (2008). Cauldron HQ, Activision Value (Windows).

Solitaire (1990). Microsoft, Microsoft (Windows).

Space Invaders (1978). Taito, Midway (Arcade).

Spacewar! (1962). Steve Russell, Martin Graetz and Wayne Witaenem.

Spore (2008). Maxis, Electronic Arts (Windows).

Star Wars Galaxies (2003). Sony Online Entertainment, LucasArts (Windows).

Star Wars: Knights of the Old Republic II: The Sith Lords (2004). Obsidian Entertainment, LucasArts (Windows).

StarCraft (1998). Blizzard Entertainment, Blizzard Entertainment (Windows).

Steamboy (2005). Bandai, Namco (PlayStation2).

Super Mario Bros. (1985). Nintendo EAD, Nintendo (Nintendo Entertainment System).

Super Mario Sunshine (2002). Nintendo EAD, Nintendo (Nintendo GameCube).

Tennis (1972). Magnavox, Magnavox (Magnavox Odyssey)

Tennis for Two (1958). William Higinbotham

The Movies (2005). Lionhead Studios, Activision (Windows).

The Sims (2000). Maxis, Electronic Arts (Windows).

The Sims 2 (2004). Maxis, Electronic Arts (Windows).

The Sims 2: Nightlife (2005). Maxis, Electronic Arts (Windows).

Tibia (1997). CipSoft GmbH, CipSoft GmbH (Windows).

Tomb Raider: Angel of Darkness (2003). Core Design, Eidos Interactive (PlayStation2).

Tom Clancy's Ghost Recon 2 (2004). Red Storm Entertainment, Ubisoft (PlayStation2).

Tom Clancy's Rainbow Six 3 (2003). Ubisoft Montreal, Ubisoft (Xbox).

Tom Clancy's Rainbow Six 3: Raven Shield (2003). Ubisoft Montreal/Red Storm, Entertainment Ubisoft (Windows).

Tom Clancy's Rainbow Six: Rogue Spear (1999). Red Storm Entertainment, Red Storm Entertainment (Windows).

Tom Clancy's Rainbow Six: Vegas (2006). Ubisoft, Montreal Ubisoft (Windows).

Tom Clancy's Rainbow Six: Vegas (2007). Ubisoft, Montreal Ubisoft (PlayStation3).

Trainz (2001-). Auran, Auran (Windows).

Ultima Online (1997). Origin Systems, Electronic Arts (Windows).

Vietcong (2003). Pterodon/Illusion Softworks, Gathering Of Developers (Windows).

Warcraft III: Reign of Chaos (2002). Blizzard Entertainment ,Blizzard Entertainment (Windows).

Warcraft III: The Frozen Throne (2003). Blizzard Entertainment, Blizzard Entertainment (Windows).

WarioWare D.I.Y. (2010). Nintendo SPD/Intelligent Systems, Nintendo (Nintendo DS).

World of Warcraft (2004). Blizzard Entertainment, Vivendi Universal (Windows).

Media Cited

MEDIA CITED

Bergman, M. (Producer) and De Palma, B. (Director). (1983). *Scarface* [Motion Picture]. USA: Universal Pictures.

Binder, J. and Rotenberg, M. (Producers) and Binder, M. (Director). *Reign Over Me* [Motion Picture]. USA: Columbia Pictures.

Burge, C. M., Kern, B., Spelling, A., and Vincent, E. D. (Producers). (1998-2006) *Charmed* [Televisions Series]. Los Angeles: Paramount Pictures.

Covert, A. and Sandler, A. (Producers) and Goossen, N. (Director). (2006). *Grandma's Boy* [Motion Picture]. USA: 20th Century Fox.

Finestra, C., MacFadzean, D., and Williams, M. (Producers). (1991-1999). *Home Improvement* [Television Series]. Burbank: Touchstone Television.

Hanson, C., Grazer, B., and Iovine, J. (Producers) and Hanson, C. (Director). (2002). *8 Mile* [Motion Picture]. USA: Imagine Entertainment.

Mann, M. (Producer). (1984-1990). *Miami Vice* [Television Series]. Miami: Universal Television.

Parker, T., and Stone, M. (Producers). (1997-). *South Park* [Television Series]. Culver City: Comedy Central.

Schiff, P. (Producer) and Bochner, H. (Director). (1994). *PCU* [Motion Picture]. USA: 20th Century Fox.

Sugar, J. B. and Sugar, L. (Producers). (2008). *jPod* [Television Series]. Vancouver: I'm Feeling Lucky Productions.